D1233276

Coming of Age in Arabia

COMING OF AGE
IN ARABIA

a memoir of Aden before the terror

Tom Henighan

PENUMBRA PRESS

LIBRARY AND ARCHIVES CANADA CATALOGUING IN PUBLICATION

Henighan, Tom
Coming of age in Arabia : a memoir of Aden before
the terror / Tom Henighan.
Includes bibliographical references.
ISBN 1-894131-64-9
1. Henighan, Tom. 2. Aden (Protectorate)--History--
Description and travel. 3. Protectorate of South Arabia--
Description and travel. 4. Consuls--Yemen--Biography.
I. Title.
DS247.A28H45 2004   953.35'04'092   C2004-906763-X

Penumbra Press gratefully acknowledges the Canada Council for the Arts and
the Ontario Arts Council for supporting its publishing programme. The
publisher further acknowledges the financial support of the Government of
Canada through the Book Publishing Industry Development Program
(BPIDP) for our publishing activities. We also acknowledge the Government
of Ontario through the Ontario Media Development Corporation's Ontario
Book Initiative.

To Coco and Michael Sterner

Solitudinem faciunt, pacem apellant
[They make a desert, and call it peace]
Tacitus, Agricola (98 C.E.)

I have been a stranger in a strange land
Exodus, 22

Contents

A Note on Orthography & Measurements

The spelling of Arabic words offers a special problem in a text such as this. The accepted transliteration of Arabic names has changed since my time in Aden, and I have generally adopted the new style (e.g. Bayhan over Baihan or Beihan, Muhammad over Mohammed, etc.). However, I find it most disconcerting to change the spelling of the names of people and places I knew well in the old orthography, for example, Ali Esmail, Ta'iz, or Socotra. I have therefore retained the old spellings where they seem to jar with the images I have of the people and places referred to. I have also used the imperial (or u.s.) system of measurements as more consonant with the era and locale described.

Acknowledgements

This book could not have appeared in its present form without the inspiration, encouragement, and practical help of a number of people, both in the past and present. I would like to thank the following, and apologize if I have overlooked anyone.

Diana MacDonald, for being there, and for passing on some useful Aden material to me.

Tom Lucey, for putting up with my stories about Aden for so many years, for collaborating with me on an abortive Aden literary project, and for staying in touch.

Stephen Henighan, for his criticism of an earlier Aden manuscript, and his general encouragement of my writing.

Marilyn Carson Henighan, for her always strong and intelligent criticism, and her unstinting support of what I write, even when she thinks I should be writing something else.

Michael Henighan, for much practical advice and emotional support, and Phoebe Henighan for her sustained interest in Aden and what happened there.

Michael and Coco Sterner, for their unfailing intelligence, humour, and personal warmth, and especially for putting up with me for so long, first at close quarters, and in recent decades from a distance. Thanks also to Michael for allowing me to use a couple of his excellent photographs. (Other well-remembered and memorable Aden friends are mentioned in the text.)

Rick Taylor, whose wonderful *House Inside the Waves* reminded me of the autobiography I wanted to write, and Andy Little, whose equally wonderful and also terrifying *Before Whispers Become Silence* did likewise. Thanks also to Andy for advice concerning the photographs.

John Flood, my publisher, for seeing the point of this book and taking it on.

Patricia Marsden-Dole, for general encouragement, highly intelligent textual criticism, and her sense of what the book might offer readers.

Julian Paxton of the British-Yemeni Society for some helpful advice at a critical moment.

My colleague Douglas Campbell, whose learning, painstaking attention to detail, and sensitivity to the written word were applied unstintingly to this text, much to the benefit of the author.

Preface

I served as an American vice consul in Aden, South Arabia, from 1957 to 1959. Aden has changed much since then and is now a part of the Republic of Yemen, but I remember the old British colony very well. It was a shabby mercantile world, set in a moon landscape, with a busy harbour city rising like a mirage among the bleak cliffs and rocky inlets bordering on the Indian Ocean. Yemeni Arabs, Somalis, tribesmen from the Aden Protectorates; British officials, entrepreneurs, and military personnel; French, British, Indian, and Italian merchants; adventurers, diplomats, and spies from many countries — all could be found in this unlikely place, an outpost at the edge of a Biblical wilderness, partially enclosed by an extinct volcano.

For despite its unpromising ambience and its questionable political underpinnings, colonial Aden was a great fuelling port and one of the important commercial way stations of the Empire. The British had clung to it with some tenacity for over a century, while also exercising control over the 115,000 square miles of the surrounding area of the south Arabian peninsula. Although Britain's rule in South Arabia brought with it some economic and social benefits, her colonial record was not a good one. Aden Colony was racist, paternalistic, and in most ways stifling for the majority of the population — the native Adenis, Yemen Arabs, and the Somalis who lived and worked there — while the Protectorate areas remained largely poor and undeveloped.

After the Second World War, British control in the area was strengthened, but with the emergence of pan-Arab nationalism, following the rise of Gamel Abdul Nasser in Egypt in the 1950s, a nervousness set in. North of the British territory lay the kingdom of Yemen, at that time ruled as a medieval autocracy by an ailing king, or Imam. Yemenis of nearly all political persuasions bitterly resented the British presence and plausibly argued that the southlands had more than once been part of a unified Arabian state, and should be again. Their view was supported by all of the Arab nations, the Soviet bloc, and China, as well as by many of the unaligned countries of the world.

My own story begins at the very end of the colonial period, some years before the British departed in 1967. It is first of all an account of my coming of age as a young American in a colonial society that was moving very rapidly from stability to chaos. In truth, I was an American innocent abroad, at first isolated and not quite sure what to make of my surroundings. Only later did I realize that my own growth from naïveté and unawareness to a more direct confrontation with reality subtly paralleled the changing character of the world around me. During my time in the colony I met an array of colourful characters, and played a small part in some unforgettable scenes, both comical and noir. Not only did my duties as a political and economic reporter allow me to visit the British Protectorates and Yemen, but my work as a vice consul drew me to investigate and help solve a sensational murder that took place on an American ship near Aden.

The real excitement in the colony, however — as I slowly realized — concerned the historical changes occurring right under my nose.

During my residence in Aden, Islamic insurgents had already begun their struggle for independence from British rule. Soon after, peaceful resistance turned into terrorism, and before long the slide from order into confusion and chaos became precipitous. When the British finally departed "under the gun," South Arabia became a Marxist republic and a haven for Carlos the Terrorist, the Baader-Meinhof gang, and other predecessors of Osama bin Laden (whose family originated in the Hadhramaut region in the old British Protectorate). Thousands of people were to die in the violence that afflicted the area from the early 1960s until the first — only temporary — union between north and south Yemen in 1990. Through the 1990s — even after the Yemen civil war of 1994 and the final unification of north and south — new violence broke out, taking the form of terrorism against Americans and other westerners, who were denounced as "unbelievers" and enemies of Islam. The blowing up of the *U.S.S. Cole* in Aden harbour in October 2000 is only one of the more horrific acts perpetrated by Islamic radicals within the new Yemen, which — despite such incidents and the country's enduring "tribalism" — has so far proved to be one of the more stable and politically flexible Islamic nations in the Middle East.

While my book deals with many political issues touching both past and present, it does so in a very personal way. Emerson reminds us that most of what we call history is really biography, and although this is no doubt an exaggeration, it is at least a fruitful one. My book, in short, is a kind of Bildungsroman (although it is not fiction), describing my first, rather tentative, sometimes comical, stepping into life. One aspect of this involves my waking up to the realities of colonialism and my growing sense of the suspicion and hatred with which much of the Arab world regards the West. Another strand describes my initiation as an American foreign service officer, one who began with a far too naive attitude to the possibilities of class and career bias and bureaucratic one-upmanship. A third involves my role as a spectator and witness during some of the last hectic days of the old British colonial rule.

In writing this account I sometimes resort to the techniques of fiction, but these, I would argue, may occasionally serve to reveal truths that elude more distanced and "objective" historical narratives. A smile, the gesture of a hand, the wording of an invitation, the brand of a cigarette, the style of a dress — these may tell us much more about "the way it was" than judicious political summaries and earnest social analyses.

I have, however, invented nothing (although in a few cases I have substituted fictional names for the real ones). I have sought to recover the drama, the comedy, and indeed the unexpected epiphanies I sometimes experienced in Aden. For the facts, I have relied mostly on my own diaries, letters, and photographs, as well as on old reports, newspaper stories, and State Department records. I have also consulted a great many books, articles, and web stories covering not only the period I write about and the early years of independence, but also the past history and archaeology of southern Arabia.

If, in James Joyce's memorable phrase, history is a nightmare from which we are trying to awake, my experience in Aden, comical in part but also dream-burdened and nightmarish, forced me to wake up to history. In the pages that follow, I tell the story of that awakening.

Tom Henighan
Ottawa, 2004

ONE

Genius Loci

I lived once between the desert and the sea, next to an extinct volcano, in a cool and spacious apartment, with two servants to look after all my needs. I had money enough for food and rent, and the servants were a bargain.

Every morning one of them, the boy Ali, would wake me up. He would shake me gently, his dark eyes confident, not at all tentative, and carefully set my coffee on the bedside table. I would yawn, roll over, blink, and reach blindly for the hot drink. Hizam, the other servant, a much older man, would be making breakfast in the kitchen.

The table was set at the far end of the big living room, behind a tall bamboo screen. Soon I would sit down to scrambled eggs with bacon, or sausages and chips — the usual English fare. Ali would carry the food out, fill up my coffee cup, then discreetly disappear. Sometimes I would hear him in the kitchen, piping up in the middle of one of Hizam's interminable monologues. I would eat quickly, and clap my hands to summon the boy when it was time to clear away the dishes, or when something wasn't to my liking. In fact I seldom complained — I was too busy observing things around me. This morning ritual seemed to me a charade, one among many, and like the others it referred to a whole set of subjects I had decided to ignore. Mostly I just kept my mouth shut and waited for the necessary cues.

I was young and my interests were not very political. As an American vice consul posted to Aden I could afford to keep my distance from the events that unfolded in the Colony — or so I thought. I saw myself as a spectator and was fortunate to be in a place where there was much to see. Or so I imagined.

One night, for example, I surfaced from some complex dream to hear, not the usual drone of the air conditioner, but silence. The bedclothes, normally cool and crisp, had grown heavy; I found myself sweating in my thin pajamas. I groped for a light, but the electricity was out. Power failure ....

I staggered into the living room, throwing off my pajamas as I went. In the hall I found a flashlight. It didn't work. I stood wondering what I might do. Already the air had grown suffocating; I could hardly breathe. Sleep was out of the question; ventilation impossible: the windows of the apartment had never been opened.

Then, from below, from under the floor tiles, came a wailing and chanting, a sustained clamour, a broken, throaty song. This was followed by outbursts of giggles, raucous female laughter, a few shrieks. "Animal noises" the small British woman who occupied the next flat had called them. Was she frightened, or envious? The sounds were very human. Somali whores who occupied the basement were having their nightly rout, only now, with the power out and my ears alert, I couldn't help but hear them. Unlike the British woman, I hadn't been prepared to label them — I found other ways to keep my distance, to insulate myself from their racket. When the air conditioners and the hum of the ceiling fans failed to drown them out, my stereo system would usually serve.

But now my barriers were down and the noise assaulted me. I was getting more uncomfortable by the minute. I stood in uncertainty, then found a candle in a drawer and managed to light it. In those days, when I smoked, there were always plenty of matches around, and a Ronson lighter too. I sat in my living room, Buddha-style, the lighted candle between my legs, and smoked a couple of Black Sobranies.

The room looked eerie in this light, cavernous and menacing; deep shadows seemed to engulf the place. The racket continued from below, interrupted by nervous moments of silence.

I was uncomfortable, sweating a little, but not unhappy. The lighting was seductive. I was content with my expensive cigarettes, with my own naked body, with being alone and untouched. The black women in the basement — I thought of their trade with a slight revulsion — were of no concern to me. Everything looked pleasant and familiar: the big brass lamps, though unlighted, were reassuring, the heavy cane furniture was solid, the rows of books seemed like known faces. I had brought my whole library from New York and as I sat there I could make out some familiar volumes: *The Good Soldier* by Ford Madox Ford, Ivan Bunin's short stories in the fine Knopf editions, *The Voices of Silence* by André Malraux. I had no expensive art, but my familiar old posters and prints were quite satisfactory: a Picasso grotesque of a woman, *Don Quixote* by Daumier, and Rousseau's *The Sleeping Gypsy*.

It was all just like home, and yet, thank God, I wasn't home. Who, at age twenty-two, in good health and full of curiosity about the world, would want to be at home? There was nothing at home. Here there was emptiness — and possibility. The isolation was wonderful. All this, remember, happened long ago. Electronics were primitive, hardly anybody phoned out of the Colony, and letters to and from the States took at least seven days. One might as well have been light years away. *That world*, the world of "home," was like those distant stars whose light we see yet that may already have ceased to exist. Seven days is a long time. Why was I in Aden? Sheer chance, it seemed. I had no training in Arabic culture or language, and I was not the sort of recruit that the American Foreign Service had traditionally encouraged. I was no child of the eastern aristocracy, far from it. Yet during the late 1950s the State Department had decided to try to bring its officer corps more into line with the wider American demographics. An elite origin was no longer a *sine qua non*, and young officers came from remote areas of the country and from all kinds of educational backgrounds. A wonderful idea, yet, as I learned to my sorrow, the old prejudices and barriers could not easily be legislated out of existence.

That dark night in my Khormaksar apartment, however, I was still an innocent. Even the power failure seemed to me an opportunity for some grand adventure. I got up and used the candle to find some clothes. I was going for a walk, but I wanted a drink first.

I hesitated to enter the kitchen. I knew what would happen when I did. Still, I was very thirsty. I carried the candle into the hall. In the kitchen, I stopped. The walls had moved slightly. I saw this without looking. I fetched a beer from the fridge, opened it, and retreated at once.

The beer was perfect. Even my half-sight of the cockroaches didn't spoil it. They were very large cockroaches, larger even than the ones in New York City. When you switched the light on in the kitchen the walls seemed to freeze, to go into stop motion. Only when you looked closely would the dark blood spots become visible. If you brushed at them they'd move. Such were the Aden cockroaches. But at least there were no rats. The Rodmans, members of the consulate who had moved from this building to a new apartment in Steamer Point, had rats. A harbour setting, even with nice views, could have its drawbacks.

I locked my apartment door and got myself outside. The air was heavy, stifling. Shrill female voices, the sound of clapping hands … dancing shadows at the bottom of the basement stairs. There were smells of cooked meat, and maybe of hashish, or *qat*, the favoured local narcotic. But *qat*, I remembered, had no smell. Probably Hizam and little Ali were down there, enjoying the party. Well, what did it matter? They would be up in the morning to serve me as usual, that was certain.

I stumbled forward into the rocky field that surrounded the flats; the sky bent over me, crowded with unfamiliar stars. Right above my head the large Magellanic Cloud blazed like an annunciation. I gaped at it, amazed as always. I might as well have been on some satellite of Altair. Quickly, I walked toward the beach. The sea, wrinkled with starlight, stretched out and met the sky, and its low sultry murmur reassured me. A beautiful sea when you came to know it, but remote and untouchable, the Arabian Sea, the Indian Ocean.

It would have been just fine if I could have flung my clothes off and plunged into the water. Only a few months ago, however, on the other side of the Colony, a woman had been killed by a sand shark. She had been wading with her young child in a placid bay at noon when the shark attacked her. An Arab boatman ran to rescue her and beat off the shark with an oar, saving the child, but the woman bled to death before they got her to the hospital. That was in broad daylight. Sharks were much more common at night.

In Aden we swam behind shark nets, protected from the dangerous beauty of the sea. My life had its boundaries, rigid ones, not all of my own making.

Now, looking back toward Crater, the old Aden, I could see ramparts of beetling rock, beacons of radio towers, and square blocks of flats along the beach. Nearby, I knew, was a hospital, a school, and an army barracks, yet such man-made objects were insignificant in comparison with the sky, the ocean, or the endless barren land.

I turned and walked up the beach, away from the city and the crater. Low cresting whitecaps spent themselves on the flat shore. The damp air shivered with light. Suddenly, for no particular reason, I wanted to shout, or sing — the *Ode to Joy*, perhaps, or some tremendous Schubert song. Great and ancient names floated through my mind: Shiva, Kali, Prometheus, Gaia.

If I walked far enough I would pass the little inland agricultural settlement of Abyan and, by skirting the towering black cliffs of the Western Protectorate, reach Mukalla. That city, with its ancient gates, its dazzling white spires, its streets full of merchants, craftsmen, camel drivers, and beggars, haunted me. So far I had only read about it, but I was eager for a visit. Sometimes the Colony seemed a prison, its routines a festival of absurdities: it became a matter of sanity to escape them. Mukalla offered something different; much more than British Aden, it must be a gateway to the real Arabia.

I drifted along, cherishing my dream of escape. After a while I noticed that I had made my way past the army barracks, the hospital, and even the airport. I followed the beach, where a few parked cars were the only signs of human intrusion, yet ahead of me, on the edge of the running waves, a light flashed, then disappeared. I heard voices, laughter. Shadowy forms seemed to float above the sand.

I saw a hut, a jerry-built shack like an outhouse. A small fire blazed on the sand beside it, and tongues of light flashed on its rough boards. What was this? I had walked this beach many times and had never seen such a thing.

I strode on toward the place, approaching to within a few yards. A young Arab stepped out of the darkness. He was naked, his muscular body clothed only in shadows. In his right hand he held a large fish. Two boys, much younger, and wearing shabby loincloths, materialized beside him. They pointed at him, grinned at me, and pointed again. The young man didn't move. He swung the fish back and forth, slapping it mechanically against his bare thighs. I retreated a step, my eyes fixed on his face, which was one of the ugliest I had ever seen and which contrasted sharply with his beautiful body. A dull, drugged face, the brow very low, the lips thick and swollen. His nose was squashed and flat, and his small glassy eyes stared at me with something like contempt or hatred.

I took a deep breath. The young man reached down and with one hand touched his genitals, while with the other he raised the raw fish to his mouth and began, slowly and deliberately, to lick at it with his fat pink tongue.

I turned on my heels and stumbled down the beach, moving quickly between the dark land and the ocean. The scene disgusted me but I didn't want to run; running would have been undignified. Only when I had scrambled some distance away did I finally turn back. The tiny shack and the flickering fire were visible, but the human figures had vanished, swallowed up, it seemed, by the night, the ocean, and the sand.

Breathing hard, I stumbled along, veering close to the waves. I moved in a kind of hectic stupor, with no idea of what I had really seen. The night had opened up to show me something — a mystery, or an obscenity? I couldn't tell. The beach post might have been some night fisherman's shack, or an improvised booth to peddle sex to soldiers from the British camp. A few servant-class Arabs might have been having a party. I would probably never know; yet this odd encounter was disturbing. Another boundary.

Minutes passed. The beach seemed an endless track. Yet when I saw the lights of my block of flats blazing up ahead I knew the electricity was back on. Now I could settle in and wait for the place to cool down again. I could shut out the sky and the dangerous night, play some Mozart, and perhaps — after another cold beer and a couple of Sobranies — get some sleep.

TWO

One Size Fits All

One of the first official things I did in Aden was to bury a man. It wasn't as easy as you might think.

The phone rang one morning before I left my flat. It was Esmail, my Somali assistant, calling from the consulate, and in a few rasping sentences he told me about the accident. Had I by any chance met Charles Porter, an American businessman, at Gold Mohur Beach? No, I hadn't — but he had been pointed out to me. A tall, dark-haired man who sunned himself on the terrace, chatted with some British officers, drank beer, and swam. He had only been in the Colony for a few days — the representative of a midwestern food company, on his way to India.

Now, suddenly, he was dead. He had dived into the shallow water near the Gold Mohur shark net, gagged on his lunch, and choked to death. They had taken him to the Queen Elizabeth Hospital, not far from my flat, and Esmail suggested that I might want to see the body before I made the necessary arrangements.

"Why should I want to see the body?"

"To verify the death certificate," Esmail explained, "and also to get his measurements."

"His measurements?"

"For the coffin."

I climbed into my Volkswagen and drove slowly toward the hospital along the isthmus road. It was September, the season of the monsoon, yet the air was stagnant, windless, and heavy with moisture. A fat pink sky lowered over the barren dunes.

Very soon I reached the Seedaseer army encampment, whose rows of tents and dingy buildings were apparently deserted. The men must already be at their various chores, or perhaps on desert manoeuvres. Another routine day — but soldiers lived by routine. Their lives were placid then. Very few of them would see any action; most of them would never hear a shot fired. Some would suffer from diarrhea or heat exhaustion before they shipped out, but they would not be shot at or bombed.

Their wives might be glad to leave — shoddy housing and nothing much to do with the kids — but the men probably counted it a pretty good post. I thought of how many times in my letters I had reassured my mother that life in Aden was not dangerous. One might die of boredom here, as Rimbaud, in his days as a clerk, feared he would, but sudden death from violence or accident seemed unlikely. The local flying was good; there were only seventy-six miles of roads, most of them easy. The Colony had no crime to speak of, and the British, who ruled with a certain low-key ruthlessness, suffered no political challenges. There were good hospitals, shark nets on the beaches, no fever worth mentioning. A clean place, Aden, an unlikely place to die.

Yet Porter had managed it. How must he have felt, gasping for breath, struggling in the water, choking on his own vomit before anyone could help him? Nothing exotic in his last moments, nothing redeeming. The same thing could have happened at Key West, or Coney Island. He didn't have to fly to Aden to do it.

The hospital, an irregular low-lying T-shaped building, seemed to float out of the dingy Khormaksar sands like a white mirage. Relatively new, the place was air-conditioned throughout, but it already wore that air of indefinable shabbiness that enveloped everything in Aden after a few months.

I got inside as quickly as possible, explained at the desk who I was, and got directions to the morgue section. The halls had a cool fluorescent sheen; no one paid me any attention.

The British had carefully divided the hospital into "European" and "Asian" wards, pointing out in their brochures that this was necessary because of "differences in diet." There was some separation, too, of the paying and the non-paying customers. The morgue, however, did duty for all races and all conditions of pocketbook.

It was an unforgettable place, not hushed, tidy, and discreet as I somehow expected, but noisy and bustling, like the kitchen of a large, friendly restaurant. The smell, however, was not the homey one of fried chicken or fresh-baked apple pie, but a sour astringent odour, the reek of an unpleasant, superficial cleanliness.

This large freezer room, as they called it, was crowded with tables, most of them bearing naked, dark-skinned bodies. Arabs in loincloths, their arms and shoulders glistening with sweat despite the air conditioning, struggled across the tiled floor, shifting corpses here and there, while a short, burly British nursing sister directed them.

This woman, a savage-eyed apparition in white, roared orders at her helpers, her voice blurred and magnified by the room's hard surfaces. She was a little too emphatic, I thought, and I took her rage to be existential — which was how I regarded everything in those days — whereas it might have been merely therapeutic, a way of coping with her awful job.

I stopped in my tracks, unwilling to go very far into that place. The Arab orderlies grunted and continued to move the bodies. They might have been playing some absurd game with them. The sister approached me, hard-eyed and impersonal. I explained why I was there; she looked at me skeptically. For her, I could see, living visitors were divided into two categories, those who were obviously uncomfortable in her domain and those who pretended not to be.

As the nursing sister spoke, I caught a glimpse of the corner table where they had laid out Porter. I moved a bit closer and saw that he was a large man, perhaps thirty years old, strong and muscular. Although rigid in death, he looked in good enough shape to get up and walk, to eat a hearty meal, to play a round of golf, to bed some vigorous woman, and I found it absurd that he should just lie there and let this happen to him. If he could have seen where he was he would have moved soon enough, I knew.

"What do you want with him?" the sister asked, breaking in on my thoughts. She saw that I was nonplussed and was no doubt struck by the usual question: why had they sent this young man to do such a job? Most of the British were surprised by how young I looked. The consul was only twenty-nine and there were jokes going around the Colony that I was his illegitimate son.

"That's Mr. Porter, I take it," I mumbled at her, keeping a discreet distance from the table. "I need to know how tall he is."

"How tall?"

"For the coffin."

"Oh, yes. Just a minute."

She shouted some instructions at one of her helpers. We stood there awkwardly, waiting, then she asked, "Are you going to fly him back to the States?"

"I don't know. I guess so. It depends on the family."

"No one would want to be buried here," she said.

The assistant returned with a tape and she started to measure the body. "Hold that end," she said, "if you don't mind."

I held the tape measure next to his turned-up feet, gazing up the length of the body: legs, thighs, sexual organs, chest, arms, neck, head — all the basic human machinery, but unfixable.

"Six feet two inches," the nurse declared. "Do you need his weight?"

"That's all I need."

I thanked her, picked up the bag containing Porter's possessions, and escaped the room. It was a relief to get out of there. The unrelenting heat outside seemed almost pleasant. I mopped my brow, took a deep breath, and drove back toward Steamer Point, where the consulate was.

I drove through the area they called Ma'alla. The British were building a new home trade quay there. Respectable residences, spiffy, whitewashed buildings, stood out in the jumble of slum or makeshift housing, shabby warehouses, and desolate lots piled up with oil drums, lumber, and rusted-out machinery. The shore was crowded with small boats, barges, and old sailing vessels that had seen better times. Arabs lounged around gabbing, or struggled in and out of warehouses under impossible burdens.

I leaned on my horn in a vain effort to speed the traffic and scatter the browsing goats. My VW had no air conditioning — which meant that I had to drive with the window open and deal with the sickening smell of the place. It was a relief to come to the outskirts of Steamer Point, where there were many offices and flats, and where they had put up what they called "Class C" housing for the lesser civil servants and the British ranks. Insubstantial and grim as these were in their cardboard box monotony, they were at least laid out in a kind of order — a change from the chaos of Ma'alla. This was a grim place in its own way, but along my route there were no squatting Arabs, no goats, and somebody was picking up the garbage.

I was now almost in the heart of the Colony, which comprised a treeless volcanic landscape of seventy-five square miles — "the barren rocks of Aden," in Kipling's phrase. Aden was relentlessly claustrophobic but the layout was complex and interesting. Imagine two enormous claws jutting south into the Arabian Sea, or Indian Ocean, from the south Arabian coast. The main part of the easternmost or right-hand claw was called Crater, the old Arabic city set inside a dead volcano and topped by the towering mass of Jebel Shamsan. Khormaksar, where my flat was, was the ligament that bound this claw to the mainland. Ma'alla was located between the two claws, and from there you could either go up through the steep pass and into Crater, or take the road to Steamer Point, also called Tawahi, where the P&O ships disembarked their day tourists, and where most of the British Administration had settled in.

The other, or left-hand claw, was Little Aden, and on that desolate rock British Petroleum had built a huge refinery. Aden was a great fuelling port, handling some four or five thousand ships a year. It was also a free port for transshipping manufactured goods, sugar, cotton, and the like, and so had become the centre of the British strategic military occupation of South Arabia. Stretching far to the east and west were the Protectorates, where the British had made treaties with the various tribes, and which they patrolled with their own and native troops, with an occasional RAF squadron to help out.

I was there because the Americans were just getting into the game and Washington had increased the number of personnel at the consulate. We were supposed to keep in touch with the British, and to keep an eye on the Russians and Chinese, who were in the process of extending their influence into the independent kingdom of Yemen in the northwest.

This is the bare bones of it, in fact it's the kind of summary Porter might have heard or recited to himself when he was sipping his beer, sunning himself at the beach, and waiting to keep his appointment in Samarra.

I, whose appointment was a little further down the road, drove on along what they ambitiously called the Queensway, past Ras Hedjuff, with its offices and warehouses, past Flint Island, and straight into Steamer Point. I didn't stop at the nearby American Consulate. I had to pick up Porter's things at the hotel.

He was staying at the Crescent, in those days the best and still the most famous hotel in the Colony. The building overlooked the main "downtown" parade ground, the place where the British troops performed ceremonial manoeuvres on the high holidays of empire. The Crescent was a pleasing rectangular shape, mustard yellow, whose facade was a grid of reticulated squares like an oriental screen, four panels on either side of the central tower. It had a private, inward-looking exterior, quite appropriate in view of the strange things that must have taken place there over the decades. Many famous people had stayed at the hotel, and Evelyn Waugh had written wittily about it. On a good evening its bar — if you were there with the right people — could seem like the most interesting hangout in the universe.

I picked up the room key from the European manager, a tight-lipped but usually helpful tough guy whose car — a Kharman-Ghia — always intrigued me. He didn't ask any questions, although he looked a little stunned; the death of a guest, especially an American guest, was not an everyday event.

Porter's room, one of the hotel's best, was neat and tidy. I sat down with a cigarette and began making a list of his possessions. There wasn't much: a couple of suits, shirts and ties, underwear, shoes and socks, and a bag of toiletries that included toothbrush, shaving gear, deodorant, and a box of condoms. There was also a folder full of business papers, a couple of magazines, and a map of the Near East. I noted everything down and then packed it all away in his suitcase. I hauled the suitcase down to my car, picked up the hotel bill, and drove over to the consulate.

In my office I wrote a dispatch to the State Department. I suggested that we arrange for a local funeral with the idea of transferring the remains later — anything else would be tricky. The Department, I knew, would get in touch with Porter's next of kin, pass along the information, and get back to us. It all happened just like that and instructions arrived the next day. Yes, we could go ahead with the funeral, but Porter was married, his wife was flying out right away, and we should expect her in a day or so; we were to delay the ceremonies until her arrival.

Ali Esmail was a master of consular procedures. A former mayor of Aden, he knew everyone in the Colony and had a line on nearly every activity, especially the illegal ones. He was a Somali, tall and rail thin, with a rasping British-accented voice and a hugely animated presence. He loved any kind of sensation; Porter's death aroused his sense of drama and provoked his irony.

"I see no reference to his religion, sir," Esmail noted, having glanced over my memo. "I presume he was a Protestant, wouldn't you say?"

"It's probable, I guess."

"I have a suspicion, sir, that the Anglican Church will not bury him. They will offer condolences and make some excuse, then explain that since he was not a member of the congregation …"

"That's just great. What do we do then?"

"There are other denominations represented here."

"Start looking them up then — as soon as possible. But first let's visit the coffin-maker."

We found a carpenter in a back street of nearby Tawahi and gave him the instructions and measurements. Then came the hard part — finding someone to read a service over Porter and a place to bury him. Aden was blessed with quite a few priests and ministers, and with several cemeteries. But most of the population was Muslim and none of the resident Christian clergy seemed to want to do the honours. Then there were the usual problems about finding burial space on short notice.

Two days later Mrs. Porter arrived. A young woman, attractive and soft-spoken, she carried herself with a kind of sombre dignity. Understandably, she had been dazed by events. I took her to the Crescent Hotel, explained our plans, and told her to get some rest.

All the same, I was beginning to wonder if the burial would take place on schedule. I had located an available plot in one of the Ma'alla cemeteries. The place had almost nothing to recommend it, but it was a solution and, given Mrs. Porter's tolerance, I thought she might accept it. As for a clergyman, my last hope seemed to be a Danish pastor attached to a local missionary group. I went to see him and begged him to do this for us. To my relief this kindly old man agreed to perform a graveside service in English.

Mrs. Porter visited the Queen Elizabeth Hospital to see her husband. She decided to have him buried in his favourite suit, which she had brought with her from the States. She left the suit with me. I took her back to the hotel, then drove over to meet the carpenter. They got the coffin into a van hired for the occasion. I drove out with the carpenter and his assistant to the Queen Elizabeth Hospital, but decided to wait outside the freezer room and let the experts do the packing job.

I paced up and down the corridor smoking cigarette after cigarette, as nervous as if I were anticipating the birth of a child.

After a while, the burly, grim-faced nursing sister I had met before came out and told me the coffin wouldn't work. The carpenter hadn't made it long enough.

"Not long enough? But we took measurements!"

"I'm sorry. It's several inches too short. We're also having trouble getting the suit on. It's been a few days, you know …"

I collapsed in a chair. My thoughts were not pleasant. I felt a tantrum coming on. I would have gladly bought a coffin for the carpenter. Mrs. Porter would be waiting to hear from me. She had wanted to see her husband one more time. There was only one thing to do now.

"Just squeeze him into the box," I told the sister. "Fold up the suit and put it in with him. You know what the Bible says: *Naked came I from my mother's womb.*"

She gaped at me. "We may have to break his legs," she said.

"All right — but have that idiotic carpenter seal up the coffin right away. Maybe he can get that part right!"

She shrugged her shoulders and departed. I had no real authority to close the coffin without Mrs. Porter's permission, but I wasn't going to expose her to this fiasco. I intended to salvage some dignity out of this, for her sake as much as for Porter's.

I worked up my courage and called Mrs. Porter at the hotel. "Everything's fine," I told her, "but there's a detail I have to check out … I'd like to have your husband's coffin closed right here. I'd appreciate it if you would allow me to do this."

"I'd like to see him one more time," she said. "At the service."

I swallowed hard, picturing what she would see. "I wouldn't advise that, Mrs. Porter," I said. "I think it's better that we go ahead with a closed coffin burial. It's been a few days now … I hope you understand."

A long silence at the other end. "All right," she acquiesced, "if you think so."

I bowed my head in gratitude. By some miracle I had sounded the right note — and no doubt, whatever her sense of duty, one part of Mrs. Porter's mind hated the idea of seeing the dead body of her husband again.

I told her we would pick her up in about an hour, then called the parson to make sure he was ready.

They brought the coffin out. The carpenter was not at all apologetic. He claimed we had given him the wrong measurements, which was a lie. He had probably bought the coffin from someone, or foisted a spare one on us, or perhaps he disbelieved our figures for Porter's height. I tried to think of a way to dock his wages, though I knew he would probably sue us if we did that.

We drove back to the consulate, where I discarded my white cotton shirt and working shorts and changed into a blue seersucker (I didn't have anything darker — nobody in Washington had told me I might have to do funeral duty). The coffin was transferred to a hired limo and Cathy, the consulate secretary, came along to the hotel. With her usual ingenuity she had found a dark suit for the occasion.

We picked up Mrs. Porter and followed the black Lincoln through the streets of Steamer Point.

The weather had just turned, and the day was gloomily overcast, the sky shot through with the pink glare of a half-concealed sunlight. Dust blew up from the roadside; the jerry-built housing looked desolate. On the Ma'alla Wharf Road, work was going on as usual, men hauling sacks in and out of the warehouses, trucks groaning up from the docks. Masts swayed in the wind, the barges ran through white-tipped waves. A few men huddled around a smoking brazier, drinking coffee and pointing to something in a newspaper. The black ramparts of the high cliffs flashed with sullen light.

I sat beside Mrs. Porter, badly wanting to console her, to apologize for what had gone amiss — even for her husband's death. Not for the first time in Aden I found myself struggling with my sense of reality. All this was happening, I knew, and yet it was absurd: the ridiculous accidental death, the botched coffin, the impromptu nature of these last rites.

We made our way up the hillside, past a mosque and the Christian mission, and stopped beside a desolate field marked by rows of tombstones, a rusted iron gate, and a single, badly weathered stone cross. A couple of men with shovels were standing some way up the hillside, beside the freshly dug grave.

Our four hired attendants lifted the coffin out of the limousine, balanced it precariously for a moment, then shouldered it slowly to where the gravediggers waited.

The wind blew harder, dust swirled everywhere, and Mrs. Porter and Cathy, standing together, shrouded in dark clothes, drew their kerchiefs tighter around their heads.

The parson put on his glasses and began to read from the Bible. He read in a clear, strong, and unaffected voice:

> The Lord bless thee and keep thee:
> The Lord make his face shine upon thee, and be gracious unto thee:
> The Lord lift up his countenance upon thee, and give thee peace.

The Lord's Prayer followed, and one or two other brief selections. With subdued voices, we joined in where we could. The coffin was lowered into the grave and the parson gave his blessing, sprinkling some earth over it as he did so.

We stood for a few minutes on those desolate heights, beneath the ramparts of the rock, looking down on the roofs of the ramshackle buildings, on the warehouses, the docks, and the ruffled harbour waters. The wind blew around us and we huddled together. Gently, the parson comforted Mrs. Porter; then he took her arm and led her toward the car.

I exchanged a glance with Cathy. There was no need to speak, no need to articulate anything. We knew what we had accomplished, and what the grim ambience of Aden — despite its surrealism and absurdity — had sanctioned for us.

We drove away from the cemetery, the resting place of an American businessman I had never even met. Mrs. Porter wrote a note to the consulate, praising my work. Years later, the grave was opened and the body flown back to the States. I wasn't around to see it off.

THREE

The Kiss

Freud's desolating twins, Eros and Thanatos, both reigned supreme in Aden Colony. Death was certainly present, and touched many of us, while — possibly as a compensation — we were all hugely vulnerable to the temptations of erotic escapism.

The raw crude generated by British Petroleum had its counterpart in the sexual libido that stirred most of us benighted Aden residents and carried us through the daily tedium of our working and social lives. Bound to our desks, caught up in an endless round of parties and receptions — beach gatherings, curry lunches, camel races — we bore the double burden of work and dutiful socializing. Despite the Colony's exotic aspects, daily life (and night life) in Aden was often tedious, and many sought relief in travel or in new relationships. While a trip "out" was always welcome, and a casual flirtation might serve to liven things up, a full-fledged affair promised bliss enough to revivify the life of even the most jaded colonist.

In Aden, almost everyone was "on the make." A subterranean energy fed our dreams and disturbed our nights with reflections that, however calculating, threatened always to turn into an obscene caterwauling. Was it isolation that caused this? The confining space of the Colony? Did this hunger connect, subtly or directly, with the degradation, the ultimate anarchy engendered by colonial rule?

The natives of Aden were, in a real sense, our prisoners. But we were often the captives of our own paltry lusts. Our daily comedy of the senses, one resembling nothing so much as Schnitzler's *La Ronde*, with occasionally a touch of Chaplin or the Keystone Cops, was oddly situated in our bleak, sandy wasteland.

Or was it? Why did the erotic element become such a complex ingredient in what the explorer Richard Burton called this "devil's punch-bowl" of a colony?

There are several good reasons. First, the relatively rigid British code of social behaviour invited violation. Perfection always conjures up challenge; the shadow side flourishes best where the social rules are strait-jacketing. British women had definite and openly declared "standards," which made it all the more exciting to overcome them, both for them and for us. Of course many of the "rules" had to do with racism. I pick up an old Aden newspaper and find a story about a young RAF man who is charged with strangling a Somali servant girl in a building adjoining the residence where he lived with his respectable middle-class parents. What caused the tragedy? Rejection? Frustration? One may never know. But what is clear is the contrast of expectations. The Somali women in Aden, although Muslim, were less socially restricted than their Arab sisters, not to mention far more sexually attractive. A seventeen-year-old British male tries to exercise power over a black woman — and is frustrated. Perhaps he had failed to connect with the available British girls; now he has failed with a Somali woman (or succeeded, and became frightened by the consequences). Violence ensues.

Racism destroys the possibility of human relations. In a French colony, where colour was never a barrier to sexual connection, the situation would have been different. I am not blaming the individual British colonists. My own case was no better than that of most "respectable" British males. It would have been impossible for me to find a "respectable" native woman; even so, it would have done me a lot of good to have spent some time with the Somali whores — as quite a few of the ordinary British soldiers did. But I had come from a puritanical background in the American racist society of the 1950s, and I was a vice consul. My conduct was scrutinized, not least by myself; I had high standards. So, instead of sensibly enlisting Esmail's help as a go-between in solving my frustrations and getting on to more important life-business, I sat on the beach at Gold Mohur and pined after the lily-white daughters of empire.

Not only race but class played a part in Aden's sexual games. Middle-class British women — nurses, secretaries, the daughters of the merchant class, of the officers or administrators — hardly any of them would even look at an ordinary soldier, a mechanic, or a refinery worker, never mind start a relationship with him. I once invited the Aden nurses to come to a beach party to meet the boys from one of the American destroyers. Even though most of these women spent a good deal of their time complaining about the absence of male company, not a single one turned up to meet the sailors. If I had advertised it as an officers' party, the results would have been completely different.

In fact, one of the things that raised the erotic temperature in Aden was the relative scarcity of women. Any available, reasonably attractive white female was under constant siege. Because of the reigning taboos, she would have her pick and could change partners often — even on a whim.

A few months before I arrived in Aden a Norwegian passenger ship caught fire in the Indian Ocean several hundred miles east of the Colony. It was carrying nearly 2,000 souls, or, more to the point, bodies, most of them young women destined for the far distant lonely beds of a great number of long-suffering Australian sheep ranchers. In a brilliant rescue operation, every single one of the passengers was transferred to a luxury liner heading west. For a few days the ladies were wined and wooed, and otherwise allowed to enjoy the privileges and exemptions of those who have had a close bout with death. By the time they got to Aden most of the women were in a state of ecstasy bordering on the trances of the tantric Buddhists, who are reputed to sustain their sexual bliss to such a pitch that eventually every atom of the body seethes with it.

As a euphemistic notice in the *Port of Aden Annual* later suggested, these women were given a "wonderful reception" in the Colony. For days, in fact, while they waited for another ship, Aden was transformed into a veritable Venusberg of the desert. A hum of excitement enlivened the bachelor flats and clubs and spilled over into the dusty streets and onto the beaches. Tall blondes and striking brunettes wandered everywhere, accepting food and drink. They swarmed by night down to the netless sand coves, where they would fling off their bathing suits and run prancing and splashing just beyond the reach of the lazier sharks and subalterns.

All this in the buttoned-up 1950s, before X-rated films or porno shops on Main Street, and prior to anyone's "coming out." But of course we were in Aden.

The Norse beauties, alas, moved on. But the Colony clung to its share of freelance sirens. There was a Valkyrie named Brunnhilde, a dynamic freebooting type, a large but shapely blonde, articulate and full of confidence. Her status was a little unclear, but she hung out with various powerful men. Our consul, Bill Crawford, much to his wife's disgust, once paid her fare from Aden to Ta'iz. I could understand why; she was magnetic, but at one level unthreatening.

Several of the British officials acquired live-in mistresses, although this was not quite respectable — it was much more common to keep separate accommodations. There was a Romanian "count" whose *amie*, incredibly enough, was a woman from Brooklyn named Maisie. She was petite and perky, no beauty, but a real ingenue, with amazing energy and a shameless gift of conversation. And she spoke with an accent that left most of the British dumbfounded with admiration and disbelief.

There were two lovely Aden Airways hostesses. One was an attractive blonde woman named Herta, a German, while the other, Rosanna, was a raven-haired Italian beauty. They spent a great deal of time at the beach (presumably to torture the unlucky), and were under the special protection of the Italian chargé from Ta'iz, Amadeo Guillet, a notorious and — to some — amusing midnight rambler. "*La favorita*," he declared to me once, pointing to his wife, a sad, worn-out woman with a martyr's face — after which he promptly decamped to join Herta and Rosanna. The air hostess metaphor is in fact a good one. Single young women constantly flew in and out of Aden, visiting relatives, vacationing, or on their way to another destination. They would lounge around the beach, attracting swarms of males, then enter the mad whirl of the party or club scene. They would be seen for a while with this or that young man, then vanish. In Aden, Eros was often in transit.

I experienced this myself in a striking way. In Aden there were parties nearly every night, but they were mostly routine and unsatisfying. Yet once, early in my tour, I attended a duty barbecue on the roof patio of the consulate, a little gathering designed to entertain some American naval officers from a visiting ship. Bill and Ginger Crawford, the reigning American consular couple, presided, displaying their usual fine-tuned if rather businesslike charm. The sailors appeared, and behaved with predictable jollity. There was, however, a surprise visitor, a young woman I had not seen before in the Colony.

She was from South Africa and her name was Jill Harvey. Charming, vivacious, and decidedly beautiful, she had a way of putting herself in motion that was hypnotizing. In Aden I had met many quick-witted people, but this blue-eyed blonde, slender, shapely, and full of life, was their equal. To my astonishment, after some preliminary scouting she pounced on me. I was instantly snared, and followed her around like an acolyte, managing at least to hold my own in the verbal fireworks and allowing myself to be manoeuvred into corners where a touch of the hand or a cheek-to-cheek conversation seemed not amiss.

Thus began an evening's flirtation, one that was carried on by both of us with witty aplomb, and with outrageous indifference to everyone else in attendance. The boredom of Aden was forgotten; the night took on a special glow. The dried flowers on the table came alive; the harbour lights glittered like tinsel stars. The wine, for once, became a magic potion. I was transported to F. Scott Fitzgerald's Riviera — I knew I had found my Nicole or my Rosemary, and that life would never be the same.

Inevitably, the night waned. I remember feeling it leak away with a sense of utter hopelessness — after such an evening, I knew I would land very hard on the ordinary earth. How could I see this charming woman again? How could I make it last? Unfortunately, she was being picked up after the party by her uncle, a British colonel. Well, I would call her in the morning!

Then, just when everything seemed about to end, the unexpected happened, an occurrence that capped the adventure of the evening and turned my fleeting, perhaps temporary bedazzlement into something memorable, something almost mythical.

Ad astra per aspera. The consulate suite adjoining the balcony held the make-up room and toilet. She wandered in there and I followed, rummaging around the corridor, looking for a cigarette lighter or a box of matches, or perhaps just because all the light in my life had suddenly left the terrace.

Everything was subdued, private. I was alone, out of the party, but in a daze of happiness.

She appeared then, out of nowhere, said not a word, but came forward and put her arms around me. Locked together, we exchanged a long and passionate kiss. These were ancient times: I was twenty-three and had never been kissed like that.

A door opened beside us and the consul walked out. His expression was not approving; did I read some envy there? "Time to rejoin the party," he said. The party was in our bodies, our hearts, but we unclenched, reluctantly, and followed him, hand in hand, back to reality.

"We'll meet again," she whispered.

We never did. The next day I consulted our inimitable secretary Cathy O'Hara about getting in touch with Jill. "No point in bothering," she told me. "She's leaving in a few days."

I was torn, tormented, but finally didn't bother. Later, I remembered Chekhov's story "The Kiss," in which the pathetic hero, after a similarly ecstatic but accidental and one-sided encounter, never sees the woman again. His life is ruined as a consequence. But of course my case wasn't like that — not even in my deepest wallow of self-pity did it seem so. Still, there was something to think about, some inner message, in the way that my balloon of exquisite pleasure had been punctured by the consul and the secretary, the two evil angels of my Aden life.

FOUR

Enter Sally Bowles

Cathy O'Hara was twenty-seven years old, a brunette with a generous mouth and the intense, occasionally skewering gaze of someone who is both highly extroverted and desperately nearsighted. She was strong-boned but almost fleshless, so nervously quick in her movements that she often gave the impression of being frantically possessed when in fact she was doing some quite simple thing such as pouring tea or answering the telephone.

When I first arrived in Aden, Cathy was one of the consulate group who greeted me at the airport. I was replacing a young vice consul named Steve, who was unduly peeved because I had left Washington without receiving his request to bring over several LP recordings of *My Fair Lady*, just then a hot musical item among the British. He was hoping to use the albums as farewell gifts to his various ladies, including Cathy.

His cinematic airport parting with her took place the next day; she seemed genuinely affected, yet within a few weeks was stringing along a goodly number of new flames. Among these were Tony Ramus, the routinely suave aide-de-camp to the governor, Terry Caitliff, a bitterly sardonic Oxford Irishman, and a madcap RAF pilot of the old school named Chidley. To these were added later a few officers from the Cameron and Buff regiments, among them a lugubrious youth named Angus, a jovial, bumptious one named Alistair, and assorted others.

Cathy was one of two single women at the post; the other was Carmela Natale, a pleasant, plain Italian girl from Boston. Each of the two represented one aspect of the erotic problem: Carmela, a wounded and long-suffering monogamy, Cathy, manic promiscuity.

Cathy was no beauty, but she was slender, good-looking, vivacious, and above all, in the game. Carmela was short, chubby, bespectacled, and kind. She soon found a friend in Malcolm, an Englishman who worked for a local importer. Carmela's ideals were domestic: she cooked spaghetti for her lover in a tiny flat that formed part of the consulate building in Steamer Point. Occasionally Malcolm went away, or they fought about something. At such times Carmela was desolate. Her sad, self-mocking little laugh was pathetic to hear; but she was a good soul. And her relationship was typical of one kind of "love arrangement" in Aden.

Except in one important respect, I had little to do with Carmela, but my relationship with Cathy became complex, disturbing, and often downright comical. We carried on a running flirtation, one that was cynical on both sides and had more to do with the rather mindless momentum that social life in Aden often acquired than with any mutual attraction. At the same time she took on the role of a somewhat scornful big sister, selecting me as a companion who could keep her amused when she had nothing else to do, treating me as a confidant in the matter of her amours, while offering me advice (mostly bad) about mine.

One of the things that drew us together is that we had similar backgrounds. We were both from New York (her brother had attended my high school) and we knew what it meant to grow up in the city, to migrate to the suburbs in Westchester, to shop at Bloomingdale's, to go to ball games at Yankee Stadium, to spend Sundays at the Museum of Natural History.

Because of this familiarity, and because of my age and youthful appearance, Cathy was inclined to treat me with condescension. I was not, like my colleagues, one of the Harvard elect, but just a boy from back home. As a result, she consistently referred to me as "the second vice consul" when I was actually of the same rank as my colleague Michael Sterner. In the consulate listing in the Aden phone book my name was misspelled, and I was not given my title at all, implying that I was a staff employee and not a regular foreign service officer. Irritatingly, she refused to allow me to enter the inner sanctum of the code room, on the grounds that I had no top secret security clearance, an absurd formality at a tiny consulate like Aden.

Far from softening the bias that Bill Crawford, our consul, had immediately formed against me, Cathy conspired to promote it — not consciously perhaps, but by playing up the madcap nature of our adventures together, while at the same time presenting me as a brooding Byronic hero, quite unsuitable for the brisk social side of my vice consular duties.

Despite such tensions, we spent a good deal of time together. Before I acquired a loan of some 4,000 East African shillings from Ali Esmail and the Bank of India to enable me to buy my own car, Cathy drove me everywhere.

The consulate day ended at 2:00 p.m., and since most of the interesting destinations were closer to Steamer Point than to my flat at Khormaksar, I would wait in the office for her to change. We would pile

into her Morris Minor and go to Gold Mohur Beach, to the Crescent or
Crater for shopping, to the Sirah Tennis club, or on special days to Little
Aden or to the camel races in Khormaksar. Later, possibly, we would stop
for a meal at the Rex Restaurant, where there was wonderful fresh crab,
homemade pasta, veal cutlets, espresso, and spumoni. We would end up
in a drinking bout with some of her "boys" at the Crescent Hotel bar or
the Officers' Club, or else head for some tedious duty party at the
Refinery or Government House.

Quite often I was dragged along against my will, but after all, there
was little else to do, and Cathy would seldom take no for an answer. I
could not spend all my time reading Robert Graves and the *Tao Te
Ching*, listening to my Heinrich Schlusnus recordings, or writing
lugubrious entries in my diary. As part of the devil's bargain for all these
rides, however, I would sometimes have to run interference for Cathy in
one of the dreadful social games she delighted in playing. A single example should serve to illustrate the nature of my service and suggest some
of the everyday craziness all of us in Aden took for granted.

As a siren Cathy had surprisingly few rivals, but among them was a
British woman named Glynis, who turned up faithfully wherever she
could hobnob with what the Colony offered of the handsome, the rich,
or the influential. Glynis had a sly and persistent manner, and some
social standing, so that she had power, despite her rather heavy horse-
faced charm, her shapeless figure, and her addiction to large flower-print
dresses. She was also a devoted reader of Nancy Mitford, on whose categories of "U" (upper-crust) and "non-U" (the despicable others) she
based her system of acquaintances. Cathy was more than a little afraid of
her.

One evening Cathy and I were invited to a party in Little Aden.
While I waited in her flat for her to change, the phone rang. Cathy
explained that it was probably Glynis: could I please get rid of her and,
above all, not let her know where we were headed?

Cathy's intuition was in good order. It *was* Glynis, and I attempted,
not very artfully, to put her off. Cathy, I told her, was out for the rest of
the day.

"Oh, and you're there by yourself? Well, I'm quite close by. I'll just
drop in and wait for her."

I overreacted and tried a little too hard to dissuade her, giving away
the game as a consequence. When the phone clicked dead at the other
end, I knew Glynis was on her way over.

Cathy, furious, took a large swig of the gin and tonic I had made for
her and decided to hide in the kitchen.

"Just get rid of her, or I'll be stuck with her all night!" she commanded. Her gambit seemed to me a weak one. Cathy's flat was on the second floor of the consulate building — a tiny, one-bedroom affair with a kitchen the size of a telephone booth, separated from the rest by a swinging door. Glynis's car arrived and she climbed out, sniffed the air like a bloodhound, and marched imperiously past the vigorous but perfunctory bows of the consulate's Arab guardian.

Cathy, still in her bra and panties, dove for the bar and squashed out her cigarette. She crawled on her hands and knees underneath the swinging door and into the kitchen. Seconds later, Glynis peered in through the balcony door and I came face to face with her arched eyebrows, her buck teeth, and her gimlet-like social judgment.

I was really not up to this challenge, but I did my best.

"Well, as you see, Cathy's not here," I explained. Glynis had come into the room and her glance took in everything. Luckily, it was not a murder investigation. "Can I get you a drink, maybe?" I offered.

This was another blunder. It drew Glynis's eyes to the bar, where Cathy's half-swigged drink sat in plain sight.

"In fact I just made you one," I went on, growing more inspired as the charade continued. I handed her Cathy's drink. She gave it a scornful glance. My deceit was too transparent, not worthy of her talents for exposure.

"I understand that the Hulls are having a party in Little Aden … Tony Ramus is going to be there."

Aha! She hadn't been invited and the idea was just to tag along. The prospect of a twenty-mile drive with Glynis, however, steeled my determination. Was there some way I could lock her in the bedroom?

"I understand that Terry Caitliff is going to be there too," she continued, her gaze freezing me on the sofa. (Of course he was another point of rivalry between the two women.)

"I don't know," I mumbled.

"You're not very well informed."

"I have to go, Glynis. Perhaps we should break this up?"

"Why are you in such a hurry?"

She put down the glass, sniffed the air again, and took a step toward the kitchen.

"Actually, you're in grave danger here," I said. "I've been sleeping with Somali women and may be infected. The very glass you're touching is probably a deadly carrier."

Glynis barely tittered. "Really? Sleeping with Somalis? Was it fun?"

I shrugged my shoulders. There was no beating this woman.

"You're sure Cathy's not here?" she persisted.

Then I had a genuine inspiration. "Of course she is," I said. "She's hiding in the kitchen."

Glynis looked at me searchingly, then she laughed, showing her big white teeth. "Oh, what a naughty person you are!"

Nonetheless, she tiptoed over and pushed open the kitchen door. I waited for the revelation. But the kitchen appeared empty.

Glynis had had enough. "Pity I missed her, then," she said, and clumped out, wearing a somewhat puzzled expression, her final glance once again fixed on the drink tray.

The front door clanged shut behind her. I watched her clip-clop down the stairs. A clatter from the kitchen pulled me out of my trance.

Cathy stood in the doorway, clinging tight to a broomstick.

"I was hiding in the goddamned closet," she said. "It was like a furnace in there."

"I think the proper uppercrust word is cupboard," I suggested. "We don't want Glynis coming back to correct us, now, do we?"

We had a few drinks and headed for Little Aden, but I found the party a bit of an anticlimax.

Later I wondered why the madcap Cathy, far better-looking and more sexually desirable than Glynis, allowed herself to be intimidated by the Englishwoman. It occurred to me that although Glynis could be as dotty as her rival, she had a superior social confidence, based on the fanaticism of her class. Cathy was promiscuous, not out of passion, but out of boredom, and as part of a carelessness that encompassed first of all her own body. If a man were at all presentable, it was easier to go to bed with him than to explain why you didn't want to. But Cathy had also accepted Glynis's definition of what was presentable, one that was based strongly on class and race. The rivalry that ensued was not only a personal battle, but the struggle of two women who, like most of us, had learned to play by the Colony's insane rules.

FIVE

An Outpost of Progress

William Rex Crawford Jr., the American Consul in Aden during most of my time there, was an excellent foreign service officer, one who was later awarded the State Department's Meritorious Service Award for his work in the Colony and Yemen. In 1972, he was appointed American ambassador to Yemen. Not quite thirty years old when he served in Aden, Crawford seemed to be quite popular with the British. In fact, apart from our Arab employees (whose exact opinions were hard to fathom), I knew of only two people in the whole of South Arabia who disliked him. One was Bruce de Bourbon Condé, an eccentric American expatriate who lived in Ta'iz, and whom few took seriously, and the other was Chuck Ferguson, the officer who ran our Ta'iz post for some months before deserting diplomacy for the oil business.

Handsome, compactly built, with an efficient manner and a cool steady gaze, Bill Crawford at first glance seemed the ideal diplomat. He had a long, finely moulded face, and his low-pitched voice was mellifluous. In company he laughed quite readily, although his sense of humour was unexpansive. Quite often he seemed detached and rather cold, and his conversation occasionally resembled a low-key lecture, although he was seldom boring. He would gaze past his audience, measuring out words for a certain effect, smiling now and then as if he had privately noted some irony in an otherwise commonplace situation.

As principal officer, Crawford was sharply intelligent and very demanding. He listened to the ideas of others and read reports with great seriousness, as if he were judging them against some abstract standard to which he had privileged access. Yet he would pounce very quickly on a questionable assumption, or an inexact (or too colourful) phrase. Sometimes this was to your benefit, even though you sensed he was merely confirming his suspicions about your deficiencies. At other times he simply seemed to be enjoying his power.

As I learned, his boyish and almost Boy Scout conception of duty (so typically American) lacked depth and shading, while his efficiency was the bloodless brother of a calculating ruthlessness. Of course, it was precisely these things that guaranteed his success in the American diplomatic corps.

Bill Crawford's wife Ginger, clever, petite, attractive, and smoothly turned out, at first sight appeared to be a mere twin of her husband. So much so that one might have rashly concluded that they were a 1950s diplomatic version of Barbie and Ken. That, however, would have been slightly inaccurate, since Ginger, true to her name, was far more earthy and spicy, far more directly combative and humanly engaging, and much less "diplomatic" than her husband. It was Ginger who pointed out vividly that one of the suavest and most *lézard* of our Arab friends "smelled like a French whore." And when one of my fledgling attempts to cook for the Crawfords ended in a disaster of blandness, it was Ginger who delivered the deadly aside, "Some little thing you whipped up yourself, Tom?"

The Crawfords were young and childless, but they kept as pets two ferocious Alsatian dogs, quite dangerous animals that were given the run of the consulate storage rooms, right beside the main residence flat. Once when the Crawfords went away and left the feeding of the dogs to an obliging CIA communications man, he ended up with a torn, bloody hand for his trouble. Marine Guards were not assigned to consulates, but in our case they would have been unnecessary; the Crawford dogs kept all enemies at bay.

I myself always thought of these pets as symbolic, that they represented in some way the vicious animal underside of the smooth Crawford facade. Occasionally, at one of the consul's parties, as the dinner service glittered in the candlelight and a polite murmur of conversation sounded around the table, one would hear, through the walls, muffled growls and scratching, as if some dangerous beast were about to break in upon the civilized ambience of the dining room.

When I first arrived in Aden, starry-eyed and naive, I could see nothing but good in my colleagues. I wrote enthusiastically to my mother, "I couldn't have been posted anywhere in the world and found two better officers to serve with." Afflicted by the American love virus, I wanted to embrace everyone and see everyone happy. But I was beginning to be wary. My dismay at the acceptance by many of my young friends of Senator McCarthy's demagoguery, my dislike of the Dulles brinkmanship, and my timely reading of Reinhold Niebuhr's monitory book *The Irony of American History* had begun to awaken me. I was fast losing the certainty that American policy was always morally right, that "evil" was something to be found "out there." I had arrived in the Colony still too naive and uncritical of things American, but persons and events in Aden would soon change my perspective.

My initial enthusiasm was not at all quenched, however, by my encounter with the "first" vice consul, Michael Sterner, and his wife Coco. Michael, I assumed, was a rich boy from New York City. He was tall, large-boned, but thin and graceful, with a handsome, high-browed oval face. The son of an architect, he had been shunted off to some New England prep school, where he had acquired the insouciant self-confidence that could only belong — or so I thought — to a well-heeled society brat.

Michael Sterner had a pleasantly detached manner, and from some-one of his intelligence one might have expected irony. Instead, there was curiosity, shrewd insight, and an infectious humour. He was a kindly man, but never wore his heart on his sleeve. He could go suddenly into a rage (although not a very terrifying one) and then dissolve in laughter at his own vehemence. He had a slow, precise manner of speech, won-derfully cultivated, and he used some curious old-fashioned expressions. "My word!" he would say, without sounding at all like a phony anglophile. His taste was very sophisticated and smacked of New York. We often talked about art and the current books, and loaned each other LPs. I remember borrowing a recording of the Shostakovich First Symphony from him — one of his favourite pieces.

One got the impression that although he had been carefully brought up, Michael had been something of an underloved child. His mother used to send him meticulously packaged clippings from *The New York Times*, and once in my presence he rummaged through such a bundle, then threw it down suddenly with the comment, "All this information and not one personal word from her!"

Who knows how Michael Sterner would have fared in Aden without his wife Coco? He would have been more at sea, more edgy, but no doubt just as inimitable. But Coco made a difference; she would have made a difference to anyone.

Courtenay Sterner, born in Georgia, was a lovely soft blonde woman, with refined looks and unselfconscious charm. She was dignified and high-minded, and at the same time capable of great warmth. Her voice was mellifluous, and her soft Georgia accent ran deep with teasing humour. In intimate dialogue especially she was a pleasure to talk to, and she was also a receptive listener. Her ideas were always intelligent, and often full of poetry. And she took great pains to understand people.

In Coco, it seemed to me, the mythical hypersensitivity of the south-ern belle was attenuated, so that in all but one's most raucous moments one felt completely at ease in her company. Did she use her "sensitivity" as a weapon, as a facade to distance or shut out other people? Occasionally, perhaps. And although, like her husband, she was capable of sudden flashes of anger when some matter of frustration surfaced, for the most part she was restrained, tolerant, perfect in demeanour.

It is clear to me now, many years later, that my view of the Sterners was enlivened by a few mythical projections. Although certainly born in Georgia, Coco was not really a descendent of antebellum plantation owners. And Michael was not in fact a New York society boy, nor quite as rich as I had been led to believe. But I was hungry for heroes, and this charming and sophisticated couple, who were so kind to me, stirred my youthful imagination.

I connected with the Sterners on many memorable occasions in Aden, and later saw them a few times in other parts of the world, but one or two incidents that took place in the Colony stick in my mind.

Right at the beginning of my time in Aden I was given the job of pursuing an American swindler who had visited the shops in Steamer Point and helped himself to a variety of goods, ranging from cameras to expensive clothing. When asked for payment he had loftily commanded the merchants to send the bill along to the American Consulate. Soon our office phone began ringing and I headed out to find him in order to put a stop to the nonsense. After some days, I tracked him to a room in the Rock Hotel, a functional but somewhat dreary edifice not far from the consulate itself. Michael Sterner, who was acting consul, came along with me and we found ourselves quickly infected by the Raymond Chandler aspects of the caper.

We got a key at the desk and burst into the room. A stocky, dark-haired young man sprang from the bed and made a dash for the door. We grabbed him and forced him back and into a chair. He sat there sweating and glowering at us while, with our tough guy personae firmly in place, we grilled him.

It turned out that he was a junior officer from one of the American ships that periodically docked in Aden. I had visited the ship and heard about the desertion, but I didn't immediately make the connection. Our captive and another sailor had jumped off the vessel and tried to swim to shore. His companion had turned back, and when our man crawled ashore he had no money and needed food, clothing, and a place to stay.

"The harbour's full of sharks," I told him. "You were damned lucky to make it." He shrugged his shoulders. "I won't go back to the ship," he said.

He and his friend, it seems, had been lovers, and when they were threatened by their shipmates they decided to escape. Their plan was to swim to shore and hitchhike up through Yemen and Saudi Arabia to the Mediterranean! (The naval briefings on local geography and transportation obviously left something to be desired.)

Our captive, who turned out to be the son of an admiral, was glib, verbally aggressive, and unrepentant, a thoroughly dislikable character. For every kind of reason it was impossible for him to return to the ship, so I telegraphed his father and got funds to fly him home.

I had been working on this case for some forty-eight hours, with very little sleep. We delivered the sailor to custody early in the morning, upon which Michael Sterner suggested that I go home and go to bed. It was a simple gesture but a considerate one, and typical of him.

While Michael was shrewd, kindly, and practical, Coco could be something of a sibyl, and she had the knack of briskly summing up both experiences and people without diminishing them. Here is part of a letter she wrote me later in which she describes an odd Aden character, whom she had observed on the diplomatic cocktail rounds in Cairo:

> In a society very much afraid of boring others, A. dives in headfirst, grasps people, and either bores or entertains them profoundly. He is not insensitive to the fact that he is doing either the one or the other, but doesn't overestimate the importance of either side. In this regard he is a good deal saner than most of us. [He is] a deep wrought pessimist, because an idealist without sufficient intellectual brawn....

Of all the people I knew in Aden, Coco Sterner struck me as the one with the most "literary" take on people and events.

Once I climbed Shamsan, Aden's highest peak, with the Sterners and a couple of others. Near the top I picked up a pair of spectacles carefully placed on a rock. Later I found the owner and returned them, but with my sense of the meaningfulness of even insignificant events — more developed in those days than now — I took this to be a sign that I should look closely around me and remember.

It was Coco, however, who made us all pay attention. She sat on the peak and expounded to us the wonders of the landscape that spread out before us at high noon that dazzling day. "There can't be many views like this in the world," she concluded. And she was right.

We were perched on the bleak heights of the volcano, some 2,100 feet above sea level. Below us, on one side, lay Crater, with its dusty roofs, stunted minarets, and dark slits of shadowy alleyways. Traffic crawled in and out of the pass; a few street radios sent up mournful messages. High on the rocky cliffs, yet far below us, the white circle of the Parsee Tower of Silence sat like a geometric emblem of eternity.

As we gazed in each direction in turn, we saw the chaos of the Ma'alla wharfs and warehouses, the expansive harbour of Steamer Point, and the ragged cliffs and beaches of Gold Mohur, to which we would shortly descend.

Stretching away to the northeast we could see the great curving line of Khormaksar beach. Our privileged view showed those dreary acres as a breathtaking arc, with the sultry harbour on one side, the glittering white-capped sea on the other.

Flying into Aden for the first time I had looked down on a moon landscape, marred by the haphazard sprawl of one of those "outposts of progress" that Joseph Conrad had scathingly portrayed in his fiction: a dreary labyrinth in which economic man had trapped himself without redemption.

But on Shamsan, in touch with the heat and the rocks, the sand and the air, and looking down through those shimmering spaces from one's own achieved perch, one could feel the breadth and the majesty of the natural scene, and ignore, for a moment, the human mistakes that had turned promise into petrifaction.

In such moments the Sterners were alert allies and inspiring inter-preters, but they, too, for all their sophistication and detachment, could get bogged down in Aden's social absurdities.

Early in their tour of duty and mine, they gave an intimate dinner party for some British officials and also invited a couple who would loom large in my own Aden landscape, the Mukalla Fisheries Officer Mark Veevers-Carter and his wife Wendy Day.

Drinks and anecdotes, gossip and jokes preceded dinner. Coco Sterner seemed unusually harassed that evening, I noticed, and her equa-nimity was not improved when a mouse ran out of the kitchen and pre-cipitated a Charlie Chaplin slapstick of pursuit by her guests. At last the consulate cat solved the problem by catching the intrusive rodent and making a dignified exit with the prey held firmly between whiskered jaws.

Possibly playing off this initial farce, Mark Veevers-Carter, an amaz-ing character who will be described later in this account, proceeded to tell a story out of the *Arabian Nights*. Mark had a wonderful social tact when he wanted to, but when the mood seized him he could also play the *enfant terrible*. Quite often he seemed to delight in his own outra-geousness, and that night at the Sterners' party he was in good form.

He immediately began to recount for us a genuine *Arabian Nights* tale, although not one of the more poetic or imaginative ones. It was the story of how Abu Hassan farted. Interestingly, that tale is set in Yemen, and as a matter of fact Richard Burton, the Victorian explorer, had first conceived the idea of translating the *Arabian Nights* stories in Steamer

Point, probably not far from the spot where Mark sat that night and played the role of an improbable Scheherazade.

The tale in question tells of a colossal but ill-timed and highly public breaking of wind by the unfortunate Abu Hassan, who in humiliation and shame flees from his town in "al-Yaman." Years later he returns, certain that his heinous act will have been long forgotten. As he stealthily creeps back, however, he overhears a conversation between a mother and daughter in which the daughter asks what year she was born and the mother replies, "the year Abu Hassan farted." Whereupon our hero flies his native place forever.

Mark told his tale with great relish, seemingly oblivious to the effect it was having on Coco Sterner, who suddenly assumed the tragic air of one of Tennessee Williams's complexly strung-out southern belles. (This was not Coco's idea of the kind of narrative a guest should recite before mixed company at a civilized Aden dinner party!) While Mark's dark beard waggled and his white teeth flashed, she pressed her lips together, turned slightly pale, and played hostess in the manner of a frustrated Borgia. The story ended at last and the evening continued smoothly, although the debriefing following the departure of the Veevers-Carters and the other non-consulate guests was ferocious.

Perhaps my best times with the Sterners, however, were those occasions on which I had them to myself. On New Year's Eve, 1957, I went with them to see *Saratoga Trunk* at the Astra (outdoor) Cinema. Later, my friends hauled out the consulate's ancient record player and we sat on the terrace overlooking the harbour, drinking champagne and listening to Bach's B Minor Mass. At midnight, the ships anchored out in the darkness marked the occasion with a few feeble signals. Horns blew, one or two lights blinked, then a deeper silence fell and we heard the slap of waves against the nearby piers. After a while Michael drifted off to bed and I sat for some hours talking to Coco. In my innocent way, I was — as the Burton of the *Arabian Nights* would have pedantically put it — *ensorcelled* by her. She was wise and good, patient and attentive, unflirtatious and utterly sincere. I had no idea then how rare such moments are, how seldom a young man and a woman barely older could sustain such a dialogue. I took everything for granted, but the stars moved, the wind stirred, and when silence fell suddenly on our conversation, I felt the first slight chill of winter descend on the Colony.

I drove home through the silent streets. Although I had some serious doubts about the way my life was unfolding, the year ahead seemed promising enough. In fact it would be a memorable one, if not quite the triumph my youthful dreams envisaged.

SIX

Off Limits

Although it looked out on Aden's spectacular harbour and on Flint Island (the old quarantine station), the American Consulate had a very poor view. Its meagre lawn was enclosed by an ugly iron fence, and the street that abutted the compound was most often dusty and desolate. Sitting on the spacious terrace on the second floor one could enjoy the harbour sights, especially at night, but the first floor offices had little to recommend them.

You entered the building from the shore side and found yourself in a large air-conditioned room, sectioned off by a low wooden railing that enclosed the actual working space. On the left was an old-fashioned telephone switchboard. An Arab operator, Fuad Ihnsanullah, sat there, his back to visitors as they entered. On the right, beyond the railing and facing it, was the desk of Ali Esmail, the visa and consular clerk. Directly opposite the entrance sat Ali Muhammad, the political adviser, while Mr. Bamatraf, a jack of all trades in the office, occupied the desk beside him.

My own windowless office was in the far right recesses of the consulate, behind Esmail, and here I spent every weekday and part of Saturday from 7:30 a.m. to 2:00 p.m. during my two-year tour of duty in the Colony.

As a rule, the consulate's local staff were not invited to official functions, and fraternization between Americans and locals was limited. The Sterners, however, became good friends with Ali Muhammad, while I got to know both Ali Esmail and Fuad beyond the confines of office routine. The nature of my work naturally brought me closest to Esmail, the remarkable Somali, to whom I have already referred. While remaining in so many ways a complete stranger, Esmail soon became a friend and confidant.

The man was tall and spidery thin, but strong-boned and agile, in build a typical Somali, with chocolate brown skin, mobile features, and a thoroughly energized manner. His face was long, narrow, and strikingly handsome, with high cheekbones, an impressive brow, and a prominent nose. He had been well educated in British schools and spoke in a sharp rasping voice that could convey a wide range of emotions, although irony was one of his favourite modes, and his laugh was delightfully wicked and quite unforgettable. Esmail was extremely intelligent, very well informed, and no doubt thoroughly corrupt, although in a relatively harmless and traditionally Eastern way. He would certainly have been worthy of a place at some *Arabian Nights* court — as a scheming Grand Vizier in Harun al-Rashid's Baghdad he would have shone.

Esmail worked for me and reported directly to me, but I arrived in Aden in a state of some vulnerability (I was ignorant of colonial life, of course, and rather short of cash) and I soon grew quite dependent on his skills, his experience, and his bankroll. For those who assume that I should have done quite well enough on my State Department salary, some explanation is necessary.

In fact, the Department had sent me to Aden without making proper arrangements for my housing. I had to cover the rent of my first flat out of pocket (about $130 a month, very high in 1957 terms). I also had to pay the $45 monthly salary of my servant/cook (and a bit more later when his "assistant" came on board). In addition, I had to dole out weekly household money to him, and was no doubt taken advantage of in the usual manner. It was impossible to function in Aden without a car, so another unexpected expense materialized. All of this, plus the necessary outlays of a busy social life, soon drained away my by-no-means princely salary of some $4,750 per annum.

Luckily for me, Ali Esmail, who earned "officially" only about $2,000 a year, and claimed to have six children to support, stepped into the breach with a $300 car loan. Not only that, he drove me around the Colony to look for a vehicle, bargained with the dealer, got me through a great deal of red tape, and in general made the car purchase possible.

His assistance was all the more valuable because Bill Crawford had reacted with tight-lipped disbelief when he learned that I couldn't drive, and had given only half-scornful approval to my suggestion that I acquire a motorbike — just about the only vehicle I could afford. A motorbike was clearly not Bill's idea of proper transportation, and as consul he himself had no car expenses, since he had access to our official sedan and Jeep.

The local office staff had, however, quickly pitched in to help me. Ali Ahmad, our chief driver, gave me excellent driving lessons, and Esmail saw to the car purchase. Later, he also managed another loan, this time for a Grundig open-reel tape recorder. In exchange for this, I ordered for him (as previous vice consuls had done) some suits from Schwartz of Baltimore, a firm much patronized in those days by foreign service officers.

Esmail and I went to movies together, and on a few occasions he came over to my Khormaksar apartment. I fed him, gave him a drink (privately, he was quite fond of a drink), and played some favourite recordings for him. I put on some flamenco (which he had never heard), and we were both struck by its similarities to Arabic music, this no doubt connected with the long period of Islamic rule in parts of Spain. He grew enthusiastic at hearing an old Szigeti recording that featured Mozart and Prokofiev violin concertos, and confessed that he played the instrument a little. Back he came one evening, carrying his violin, and gave me some examples of his skill. He was quite good, and I taped some of his efforts on my open-reel recorder.

In the course of these visits we exchanged ideas about the political situation and the arts, and I learned something of the history of the consulate, in so far as Esmail knew it. He told me a great deal about the Wendell Phillips expedition, for example.

Phillips, an enterprising young man from California, had led a famous archaeological expedition to South Arabia during 1950–1951. In his excellent book, *Qataban and Sheba*, which I had read before arriving in Aden, Phillips recounts the adventures of the "American Expedition for the Study of Man," as he called it, in Bayhan and Ma'rib (both now part of the Republic of Yemen). Phillips was a pretty good organizer, as well as an excellent promoter and publicist. (When I met him in Aden, he was actually wearing the pearl-handled revolvers that at first caused much amusement and some alarm in the Colony.) Phillips used his southern Arabian contacts later to get seriously ensconced in the business of oil exploration — although, to be fair, some State Department officials did the same.

The Phillips expedition suffered several major catastrophes, lost much equipment, and eventually had to flee Yemen. It was criticized as more of a show than a scientific enterprise, but it did do valuable archaeological work, thanks to the presence of W.F. Albright and other highly respected scholars. In some hilarious consular dispatches written in the form of short playscripts, John McGrath, then the American vice consul in Aden, dramatized the confrontations between Phillips and the exasperated Sir Tom Hickinbotham, British governor of Aden at the time. I doubt if these wonderfully satirical reports served to enhance Wendell Phillips's credibility with the State Department!

Esmail had been a witness to some of the Phillips disasters and recounted local gossip about the expedition, which he claimed should have been called "The American Expedition for the Study of Woman." He also had many stories to tell about John McGrath himself, and everything I heard about the man caused me to regret that I had not served with him in Aden.

After a few visits Esmail began to relax, and so did I. His ironical defences dissolved a little and he spoke more directly. He revealed to me the secret nicknames the local staff had coined for the Americans they worked with, giving me the Arabic and then an English translation, which is all I recorded at the time.

Bill Crawford, it seems, was called "the snooper," a mocking tribute to his close attention to all aspects of the consulate's business. Michael Sterner, for obvious reasons, was "the kind one." Cathy O'Hara was "the bitch" (I suspect that was an expurgated translation). Carmela Natale, as accountant and bookkeeper, was "the money-bag," George Rodman "the bellows" (full of hot air?), while I was merely "baby-face." Esmail informed me about the latter nickname only with some reluctance, but if true, it was certainly fair enough.

I was genuinely shocked at Esmail's hardly concealed dislike for Bill Crawford, for there were still many days on which Bill stood out for me as a kind of foreign service ideal, an officer whose style I felt I could do nothing better than to emulate. But Esmail, without saying it in so many words, delivered a warning that I should not trust in my chief's apparently benign and tolerant attitude to me.

I can still see my old Somali friend leaning forward in one of those big green-cushioned cane chairs that sat beneath my print of *The Sleeping Gypsy*, his eyes widening perceptibly as he cautioned me, "I don't want to alarm you, sir. It's really none of my business, but if I were you …"

Here occurred a dramatic pause. Esmail stretched his long neck and cast a glance at the tape recorder, perhaps to reassure himself that it was really turned off.

"If I were you, I would be more … respectful … with Mr. Crawford. I have noticed that he seems to observe you with some close attention."

"Attention? What do you mean? … I always treat him with respect!"

"Of course!" He paused and smiled, flashing his white teeth in a distinctly feral grin. "I was referring to the need for a *salaam* now and then."

Finally I understood what he was getting at. "Oh, come on, Esmail, things are different with us Americans, you know that! He doesn't want that kind of response from me."

My friend shrugged his shoulders. He picked up the book I had just given him, a paperback copy of the writings of Seneca, the Roman stoic philosopher, and started to quote from the back cover. Something about accepting fate and learning to deal manfully with the inevitable trials of life. Something about happiness deriving from one's power to control the mind and the emotions.

A friend had sent the book to me from Europe and, on an impulse, I had decided to give it to Esmail. Not many months later, both of us would have occasion to return to this and similar texts.

Besides challenging my perceptions about what was happening in the Colony and at the consulate, Esmail gently corrected me when I made a mistake of tact or violated some unwritten rule of behaviour in that mad world. This happened usually in the office, but once when he was visiting me, sipping a drink and listening to some music, his eye fell on a small locally made rug I had put inside my door to serve as a doormat.

"Excuse me, sir. Please forgive me, but I've noticed that rug by the entrance. Are you aware of what kind it is?"

"I believe it's a prayer rug, isn't it?"

"Precisely. Don't take it amiss that I mention it — but some people might be offended that you have placed it there."

I sat up straight. I was embarrassed. The idea had never occurred to me. To me the rug was merely an attractive curio.

"I see. You mean a prayer rug is for prayers and shouldn't be used for anything else?"

"Exactly!" He seemed cheered that I had caught on so quickly.

"Are you offended by it, then, Esmail?"

"I did not say I was offended. I have a certain understanding of the situation. But others might be offended."

"What about on the wall? On the wall in the bedroom? Do you think that would offend anyone?"

"That would be a great improvement, I think."

I immediately moved the rug.

On one memorable occasion I believe I redeemed myself with Esmail for my insensitivity about the prayer rug. We had been working together on a difficult (and rather sensational) murder case. My friend was doing his usual impeccable job. At the end of a long day I suggested that we go to the nearby Crescent Hotel Bar and have a drink together. Esmail looked at me oddly, but shrugged his shoulders, smiled, and came along.

I have already described the Crescent Hotel and indicated that its bar was a very special place. What is it about such old, authentic bars that distinguishes them from those retro imitations that we see everywhere today? The older ones are usually spacious, but not too spacious, with something of the comfortable cave about them. They are seldom sparkling clean, but never grimy or sleazy. The lighting is usually dim or subtle. Nothing disguises the centrality of the bar itself; it stands up like an altar of truth, a wood and brass construction that for decades has gathered all the lost conversations, all the bright, sad reflections of a transient humanity. The bartenders are stunningly efficient, not too stagy, and seem to have been there forever. Drinks are of many kinds, but unpretentious in presentation, classic. There are snacks, but no cheap, greasy food. The clientele are unpredictable and varied, a parade of thirsty and momentarily convivial pilgrims who have, at that moment, found their favourite shrine on earth. Glasses clink and glitter, the conversation buzzes; happiness abounds in every corner. When you discover such a place you have come upon something like a sacred space, something to be wisely used and uniquely treasured.

In its heyday, the Crescent Hotel bar had just such a special ambience. I remember sitting there once with a friend new to the locale, taking it all in. I was about to make a rhapsodic comment about how perfect everything was when at the same moment he turned to me and said, "God, what a place! Is there anywhere else in the world like this?"

It would be appropriate, it seemed to me, that after some hard work together Esmail and I should have a drink in such a bar, and so we headed over there, passed through the familiar lobby, and entered the inner sanctum.

A few men turned from the bar, their glances lingering a little, but their conversation continued. Esmail and I took a table and I signalled the waiter. He looked in our direction but did not appear to see us. I signalled more vigorously. The waiter disappeared.

"I think it might be wise for us to leave, sir," Esmail suggested.

"What? What the hell's going on?"

"We can go somewhere and find a more congenial atmosphere."

"But I don't want to go anywhere else."

At that point the hotel manager appeared from the lobby. I have already referred to him — a laconic, middle-aged, balding European type of no fixed nationality who drove a Karmann-Ghia.

"You'll have to leave *now*," he said. He did not look at Esmail, but his expression was grim. I sensed that the men at the bar were taking in what was happening. Soldiers out of uniform, minor clerks, oil people — white faces all.

"I think we should go, sir," Esmail said.

But I refused to go. I stood face to face with the manager, who began to push me toward the door. The polite mask I had encountered many times before had fallen away and he was playing the tough.

"You know better than this." He cast an angry glance at Esmail.

"It was not meant to be provocative," my friend told him. "We can go elsewhere," he assured me.

I continued to protest, but suddenly felt the weight of the Colony's disfavour, its irresistible movement turned against everything I believed in. Don't get me wrong. As a white boy in New York, I was conflicted. Intellectually, I accepted equality for all races, but at the same time I had taken my stand with my own group in quite a few playground fights with "niggers." But when I went to Washington, where Afro-Americans were still made to ride in the back of the bus, I began to integrate head and heart. There, I started to escape from the conditioning that told me there was something natural and right about bigotry; I began to see race prejudice for the pernicious and inhuman thing it is. Now, in Aden, I myself was up against it, face to face with the serpent. It was not one man who was leaning against me and pushing me out of this public place, but a whole culture.

Dazed, I found myself in the Crescent Hotel parking lot, arguing with a man whom I knew deep down to be nothing but the instrument of a terror, one that had been efficiently sustained over the sad centuries. In the context, it was not an argument that could be won. Defeated, Esmail and I walked over to the shabby streets behind the Crescent shopping area and had a coffee together. We did not talk about the incident. I never knew if he spoke of it to others.

Later, Cathy and I were invited to the Sirah Club in Crater by Ali Muhammad. We played tennis there, but the Arab manager protested about my tennis shoes, ahead of their time in having patterned, deeply recessed soles, which had marked up the court surfaces. I was beginning to wonder if I could do anything in the Colony without coming into conflict with somebody's rules, but I didn't at that point know the half of it.

With Fuad, our slender and sad-eyed clerk and telephone operator, my contact was limited, although in him also I sensed something of a kindred spirit. We had some meals together and went a few times to the cinema, and after dinner one evening he produced a fine pencil drawing of me. Another time we drove out to Little Aden, had coffee, and walked the beach. It was one of the few times that I was the lone foreigner among Arabs and I relished the experience. I remember sitting in a shack, listening to Cairo radio's piped-in music sounding above the pounding of the waves, while, with Fuad as translator, I talked to the villagers about their lives in this bleak but splendid place.

Later, I remembered my reading of Frederic Prokosch, an American writer whose first novel, *The Asiatics*, published in 1935, was praised by Thomas Mann and André Gide, and who went on to turn out a body of superficial and essentially vapid fiction, some uninspiring poetry, and a book of memoirs that drops the names of famous people on every page without saying anything memorable about any of them. Prokosch's novel, *Nine Days to Mukalla,* describes the fate of four travellers, two British, two American, who attempt to trek to safety in Mukalla after their plane crashes in the desert. Some of the characters die on the way (but not enough). Pseudo-poetic and pretentious, the fiction presents the Bedouin as mysterious, sensual beings who talk very much like 1890s aesthetes. I used to read bits of this work to Esmail, Fuad, and Ali Muhammad in the office, and the passages where Prokosch's noble savages disclaim all interest in material gain and rave about the stars, the moon, the pure night, and so on aroused particular hilarity.

Of course, no living Bedouin ever talked such nonsense, nor did the villagers in Little Aden. They were practical, shrewd, worried about survival, and quite understandably full of complaints about the colonial system of the British. It was I who took in and relished the romantic splendour of the beach and the rocks, the picturesque shabbiness of the huts. The flickering shadows on the crude walls, the improvised rickety furniture, the thick, sweet, earthy taste of the coffee, the staring eyes of the beautiful children, the cynical resignation of the old men — all these made up a picture, and I saw myself for a moment at the centre of it, though as an untouched and objective observer. My meagre accomplishment at that point was to have overcome my own standoffishness, to have shattered the stereotypes I had carried with me from abroad, whether these were romantic illusions about the mysteries of Arabia or a cold sense of superiority derived from an over-valuation of the superficial achievements of my own world.

Sipping coffee with the villagers, I had no profound thoughts about how things might change, no solutions, but at least, in my newfound sense of what actually concerned them, I was making a small start toward breaking down the almost impenetrable wall that divided me from the real life of Arabia.

Later, when Fuad resigned from the consulate to work for an oil company (a move he would greatly regret), he organized a dinner, Arab-style, for the Americans. I bought an outfit for the occasion (local dress, not the Hejazi or Saudi rig of Lawrence of Arabia). The Adenis accepted this in good part and it was a pleasant enough evening. We took our shoes off, sat on piled-up rugs, drank coffee, ate local fish carefully roasted and seasoned with herbs, consumed chicken stuffed with spicy eggs, and devoured myriad sweets and dips. A small band played music, painted boys danced, and there was a generally brave attempt at connection on both sides.

Some days later came a letter from Fuad, thanking me for what he called my kindness to him and suggesting that we meet again. He obviously missed his contact with the Americans; and perhaps he was lonely. I was touched by this, but I had had a great deal of male camaraderie over the previous few years and it was not what I was looking for. I was self-protective, ungenerous with my own time, in search of some wondrous experience far beyond fraternal sharing. My duties and my dreams alike consumed me, and the imperious Cathy expected my full service and attention. As a result, I was cautious; I felt I had to ration my commitments. I saw little of Fuad after that. Did I have a sense that my struggle for survival in Aden was just beginning?

SEVEN

Plantation Owner and Yankee

While not exactly labyrinthine, the American Consulate building in Aden did have its hidden recesses. On the west side underneath the storage rooms where the Crawford's dogs roamed, and below the "secure" part of the complex, was a garage and repair facility, not very different in most ways from what one might find at a local gas station in any small American town.

This was where the Yemen expeditions began, where our Jeeps and the consulate sedan were repaired, and it was presided over by George Farnell Rodman, who, to his eternal chagrin, was not a "real" foreign service officer, but a support staff employee, in charge of supply and services.

George, who was from North Carolina, was a true southern gentleman, something of a cross between Senator Claghorn, a famous southern blatherer on Fred Allen's radio comedy show, and one of William Faulkner's hard-done-by backwoodsmen. He was a burly and substantial but rather soft-fleshed man in his mid-thirties, complete with sagging jowls and bald dome, and his world view was roughly comparable to that of the southern gentlemen in the Tara sequences at the beginning of *Gone with the Wind.*

"The Old Plantation Owner," as Ginger Crawford appropriately dubbed him, had put me up — with a little persuasion from on high — when I first arrived in the Colony, because the State Department's haphazard planning, while making sure I got there, had left me with neither a suitable billet nor funding to rent any.

Months later, as I staggered bleary-eyed toward my office after some late night carouse, I took a short cut through the garage. It was a place I seldom entered, an un-air-conditioned, grimy underworld of spare parts, tires, oil and gas cans, and bits and pieces of vehicles.

As I drifted through the place I heard voices, one of stentorian measure raised in anger, the other a pleading singsong clearly not made in America.

I stopped in my tracks. An oil can flew over one of the Jeeps and crashed into the wall. A brown-skinned man crawled out from the hoist and cast a frightened look over his shoulder.

A figure in colonial white appeared from behind a storage rack, a burly sweating man with bare fleshy arms and fists like paws. The menacing hulk stood over the cowering victim and denounced him with a passion that was all the more alarming for being almost out of control.

"*You dahr tuh tell me*" — George Rodman seemed to choke on his own words — "You dahr tuh tell me that you *lost* the distributor?"

The accused — it was Mr. Moggs, the consulate's mechanic — scrambled to his feet and stood as if ready to bolt, clutching at his ragged grey overalls and nervously eyeing his persecutor.

"I am so very sorry about this, sahib," he whimpered. "It was right there on the shelf last night, you know. You remember, you saw it there."

He pointed eagerly, but Rodman took a step forward and seized the hapless mechanic by the collar. "Don't you lie to me, you no-good little bastard. Don't you dahr lie to me!"

Rodman swung a meaty hand and began cuffing the mechanic on his shoulders and neck. He seemed to have lost all control. Mr. Moggs crumpled and cowered away, howling in protest and fear.

I ran forward, grabbed my colleague by the shoulders, and with a great effort turned him around to face me.

"For God's sake, George ..."

The southerner's grey eyes blinked. It was as if he were shaking off a spell. His lips trembled helplessly; he was speechless.

Mr. Moggs wriggled free and disappeared into the labyrinth of the consulate building.

Rodman glowered at me. "What in hell are you doing here?"

"What in hell are *you* doing? I was just taking a shortcut."

George wiped his bald dome with a sweating hand. "You don't understand ... Ah'm responsible for keeping our vehicles running. Bill Crawford relies on me. That no-good little bastard went and lost a distributor on me."

"You'll get in trouble if Bill hears about this."

George held me at arm's length. I could feel his body trembling. I was shocked to see that his eyes were full of tears. He spoke very softly now, intimately, and his voice quivered with emotion.

"You don't understand, Tom. He's a Cheechee, a bloody Cheechee. *A half-breed.* Even the local wogs despise him."

He turned, blinked away the tears, and threw up his hands in despair.

"And they hired him to help me keep the transport going!"

This was a very different George from the one I knew as a guest in his Khormaksar apartment. Everything there had been formal and correct, although congenial enough. The Rodmans' servant, Issa, an Ethiopian, was extremely well drilled, and within his own four walls George knew how to assume the lofty airs of a maharaja. It was riveting to watch him order Issa to bring a mint julep for "the memsahib." He could have given lessons in any British club in Darjeeling in 1875. At the same time the whole performance smacked of caricature, and as my time in Aden lengthened it grew increasingly hard to watch it with a straight face.

George and Penny Rodman were not, I think, united in their appreciation of life in Arabia. George rather liked the colonial style, but Penny missed the good old u.s.a. As house guest I witnessed a few tearful sessions, and when she got pregnant, George, who had grave suspicions about the British hospitals, decided that nothing was too good for "Mah Penny." It was decided that she would go home to have the baby.

He was indeed very protective of her, although sometimes she seemed to be barely aware of his existence. Once at a party on the consulate terrace I ventured an off-colour remark in the presence of the Rodman memsahib. George underwent a characteristic transformation: the genial old planter became an avenging spirit on behalf of southern female honour. White-faced and trembling, he approached me.

"Henighan, Ah want you to apologize to mah wife."

Thinking he was drunk, I greeted this with a guffaw, but seconds later, as his mouth firmed, his fist tightened around his drink, and his grey eyes bulged with outrage, I knew it was either apologize or meet him the next morning with my seconds on Khormaksar Beach.

Luckily, George was not within hearing range when Christiane, the chic wife of Tony Besse, a millionaire French businessman and a famous Aden character, referred to all the woman at a cocktail party, including the normally thin but very pregnant memsahib, as "disgusting fat cows."

I appreciated the Rodmans' willingness to house me in their apartment while the State Department sorted out my allowance, but this was perhaps not the best introduction to life in Aden, any more than my time with Cathy was. George's opinions about the imperial question were distorted by his indomitable belief in the white man's burden. At the same time, he achieved what must have been subliminal satisfaction for his not-quite-voluntary hospitality by fobbing off on me sundry used items that I didn't really want.

In those days I had much less sales resistance than I do now, so I allowed him to sell me a fairly hideous set of china, an old camera with a bellows that had a hole in it, and a few other castoffs. Given that I was also paying him for my time in his flat, this entrepreneurial revenge was really ungracious. It stopped when Michael Sterner heard about the camera and chastised George for taking advantage of me. Aden was a free port and I could have bought a camera ten times better for the price George had gouged from me.

Despite such irritations, my relations with George were mostly very cordial. I felt badly that the Foreign Service examiners had rejected his application to move up from the staff level, although I felt sure that they had made the right decision. I could understand that George's father, who was a judge, must have compared him unfavourably with his older brother, a captain in the navy, and that George suffered greatly from this.

Although his lordly airs could quickly turn into a boorishness that was equally disconcerting, there was a middle ground where George Rodman proved himself capable of camaraderie, wit, and a somewhat heavy-handed but genuine humour. And certainly, under the Old Plantation Owner's informed tutelage, Issa made some wonderful mint juleps.

The American south was not the only region represented at our outpost of democracy. New England also had a strong entry in the person of Gordon Browne, a fifty-eight-year-old superspy left over from the pioneering days of the OSS and the Central Intelligence Agency.

Gordon arrived at the consulate under the title of Foreign Service Reserve Officer. He was supposed to be opening a trade office to facilitate commerce between Aden and the United States, a somewhat laughable mission in itself, but one made especially absurd by his obvious lack of interest in anything connected with the mercantile world.

One day an unsuspecting Arab actually came to the consulate and asked me for some information about American-made trucks. I summoned our trade officer, who came bounding out of his backroom office, took in the message, and turned to me.

"Trucks — we have lots of trucks, don't we, Tom? How about the Mack, that's a pretty good truck isn't it?"

Long after the Arab had left, Gordon was still searching our office sources, in despair of ever figuring out how to get in touch with "Mack." So much for the "deep cover" of our intelligence agents abroad.

In fact, I could never fathom why CIA agents like Gordon were assigned to U.S. missions under the Foreign Service Reserve Officer designation. Invariably, those so designated were spies. This must have saved the KGB a lot of trouble, since a simple thumbing through of the consulate book would have indicated at once who our agents were.

In my time in the foreign service I met quite a few CIA agents, and although almost all of them were unusual individuals involved in obscure and sometimes dangerous missions, it is possible to divide them roughly into two main groups. First of all, there were those who were literally insane, a highly visible minority, one composed of the excessively paranoic, the compulsive-obsessive, the determinedly megalomanic, and the near-schizophrenic, not to mention those emotionally and mentally warped in unique and unclassifiable ways. During the Cold War, some of the mad ones advocated pre-emptive nuclear strikes, others revealed curious obsessions about our presumed allies, while yet others seemed to have been rendered cataleptic by the ingestion of too much secret information. In dealing with such people the best strategy was to humour them, preferably by saying absolutely nothing oneself while nodding one's head vigorously at their every word or glance.

The second and, thankfully, larger category of CIA agents included a whole range of operatives who, though they might be eccentric, did not give real cause for alarm. Gordon Browne was distinctly one of these. He was a tall, lean man, agile and tough, with a large inquisitive nose, sensitive lips, and a bald head fringed with sparse white hair. His glance was shrewd and direct and his opinions brusquely expressed, and once he decided that someone was too dull to take notice of, he sheathed his attention like an old falcon. Gordon was another Harvard man, but one of an older generation. I liked him very much and respected him immensely, and we got on well together.

With his wife Eleanor, a handsome, intelligent, and kindly woman, originally from Canada, he rented a villa with a great sea view on the Gold Mohur side of the Colony. I used to go there and drink the cinzanos and soda that Eleanor mixed, while all three of us talked about things that took us far beyond the gossip of the Colony. Gordon had had a long career in intelligence, and so had many adventures to relate and some fascinating friends (such as Carleton Coon, the anthropologist) to pass on stories from. To top things off, the Brownes were the only people in the colony who would listen to my excited talk about the mystical writings I was reading at the time. With the sun setting in a red blaze over the impossibly glittering ocean, I would sit on their balcony and raise questions that had occurred to me as I read the *Tao Te Ching*, *The Bhagavad Gita*, Thoreau, or Emerson, while Gordon, who was always pacing about, would interrupt me with some lightning-quick but shrewdly practical objection or qualification. It occurred to me later that as an old New Englander, connected, however distantly, to the world of Charles Ives and the Transcendentalists, and as one who had resided much in the East, he had a greater and more natural tolerance for my enthusiasms than anyone else in that cynical world.

Gordon himself, however, was fascinated not so much by mysticism as by mechanical things. He had shipped his own Jeep to Aden, and this vehicle was the focus of much of his special attention, for although the Jeep lacked any of the sinister refinements of a James Bond car, it had gadgets to spare. The rather elementary feature that seemed especially to delight Gordon was the winch. He demonstrated it to me with great glee, and I do believe that more than once he intentionally mired himself in sandy pockets just to show how the winch could accomplish what a mere four-wheel drive could not.

Gordon's Jeep took the two of us on a few local expeditions. Although Aden was obviously a good place to fish, until Gordon arrived it had never occurred to me to try. One day out of the blue he said in his characteristically laconic manner, "Like to fish, Tom? … Yes? Why don't we go?"

We would drive to the Arab village in Little Aden, hire a boat, and cruise out. It was a blissful time. The fishing was very good. When we had caught enough we would drift for a while, drinking beer and sharing a sandwich. Gordon would try to identify the fish, finding familiar names for some of the strange Arabian species.

For my part, I felt free on the water. The sunshine was powerful and seemed eternal. In the day's glitter, in the dazzling silence of those full and empty hours, the meaning of the mystical texts struck home. I was in the perfect place; there was nothing pressing to accomplish, and nowhere better to be. Imperialisms, revolutions, ambitions, the inner drive for love, or merely for power — these were foolish trappings, vain exercises. Time, a figment of the mind, coalesced and dissolved in each beam of light. I was happy.

EIGHT

Beach Flights

I was not always aware of it, but in Aden almost any occasion could be alive with social and political innuendo. Entertainment and duty often blended. The beach was not merely a refuge from the heat and dust, but a place to communicate news and opinions. Cocktail conversations could be calculated. Formal dinners, more guarded, were nonetheless an arena of personalities and values that were subtly in conflict. On those rare social occasions when nothing was at stake, a kind of saturnalia often reigned: pressures having been cast aside, one descended, with some relief, into mindlessness. In this, because of colonialism's power to distort the human psyche, there was occasionally a whiff of unpleasant tomfoolery — even an air of savagery.

When the consulate office closed at two every afternoon, I would eagerly climb into my Volkswagen, roll down the windows to let out the oven-like heat, turn the front panels round to direct a stream of air on my face, and drive off. On the back seat would be a towel and my bathing suit, a notebook, and perhaps a book or a magazine to glance through. I was headed for Gold Mohur Bathing Club, where there would almost certainly be acquaintances or colleagues to nod to, but perhaps no real conversation. I was always prepared for, and occasionally forced to enjoy, a solitary afternoon at the beach.

The Gold Mohur Road ran out of Steamer Point, beneath Chapel Hill, then wound its way around Telegraph Bay and through the promontory known as Ras Boradli, where the Cable and Wireless was located. A sharp turn led onto a high viaduct, which gave access to Gold Mohur Bay, a very large curving expanse of steep rock and rough, sandy shore. All of this was divided from the Crater settlement by the peaks of Amen Khal and Jebel Shamsan.

Gold Mohur Bay itself was cleft in the middle by a rocky promontory known as the Elephant's Trunk, and closed at the far end by another, dubbed the Elephant's Back, which was topped by a lighthouse. The club nestled underneath the lighthouse. It was a nondescript enclosure comprising a few changing shacks, a bar, and three or four scraggly trees. A paved terrace, steps leading down to the water, a shark net, a tiny float — these were its main features, yet it was the most popular meeting place in the Colony, one frequented by government and business residents, the military, the diplomatic corps, and many visitors. Needless to say, although staffed by Arabs, the club was off-limits to persons of colour.

On a typical day I arrive at Gold Mohur and park my car in the gravelled lot, making sure to leave the windows open; if I have stopped at Bhicajee-Cowasjee to buy some LPs I remove them from the back seat and store them in the trunk, to prevent them from melting in the heat. I find a place on the terrace and order from the unvarying menu: steak and sausages, eggs, chips, tea, beer or gin. I open up my book, perhaps the 1955 edition of the *Collected Poems of Robert Graves*, and aimlessly browse, gazing from time to time past the narrow beach enclosure and out at the inviting but forbidden sea.

From the club the view is spectacular. Cargo ships, the great P&O liners, bright rigged dhows like dream ships from the *Arabian Nights* — in turn they disappear in the distance or sweep toward the inner harbour. At sunset this great amphitheatre, an arena of water enclosed by black cliffs and opening up to the illimitable sky, will take on hues of indescribable splendour. Yellow, pink, rose and purple, deep blood reds, shades of violet and amber — how many home slide shows in Bromley or Tunbridge Wells reached colourful crescendos in the Nolde-like extravagances of the Aden sunsets? I have my share of such slides, but my Gold Mohur leisure was spent in mostly unproductive but energetic daylight glances in the direction of the daughters and young wives of empire, some of whom, with luck, might turn up at the evening's duty party. Astonishingly, my foolish quest eventually succeeded, and my reward was a night at Gold Mohur such as I had not even dared to dream of. But most days were uneventful, and I sat overwhelmed not by visions of beauty but by voices, by fragments of conversation that memory reconstructs as a chorus, arbitrary and unexpected, like some concoction of a musical modernist in love with the aleatory and the absurd.

"Colonel Jack killed two or three Arabs in a skirmish. The wogs respect him for that. His men think he's a god."

"What's that book you're reading, Tom? Poetry? My God, you have been in Aden too long. Wait a minute, I'll buy you a gin."

"MI6 is running things now. The navy is out. The Colonial Office is finished."

"Americans at the refinery — fat salaries but they're all just stupid. I never met so many stupid men."

"He's my third servant in three months. It's the smell I can't stand. I hate to think where he sleeps. I don't know what I'm going to do. I'll end up having to cook myself."

"I know she's in love with a certain person at the Secretariat. I can't name names, of course, but I know who it is. The two of them are completely transparent. They don't hide things very well. That one's going to get into trouble, he is, when his chief finds out."

"You can say I'm drunk, but I know what I'm talking about. I remember the days when the fucking ships came once a fucking week. We stayed upcountry for months and nobody asked any questions. I slept under a Land Rover, and went where I fucking well pleased. The wogs respected us then. Not like the damned prissy show we've got now."

Talk and more talk, as the afternoons leaked away. After a while, tired of listening, I would stretch myself, dive into the soupy water, and swim out to the float. Even from this rather close perspective, Gold Mohur looked insignificant. Gulls, pigeons, and some dark predator, perhaps a griffon vulture, wheeled above the rocks.

The barren rocks of Aden, indeed....

The British had come when Captain Stafford Bettesworth Haines occupied the port on behalf of the East India Company in 1839. When Haines arrived, Aden was a shabby little coastal town with around six hundred inhabitants. Haines had no reason to know of the splendid past of the South Arabian civilizations, but he did perceive the remarkable advantages of Aden as a transshipment area for goods from India and Somalia, and as a place that would connect Yemen and the Hadhramaut with those other mainstays of colonial trade and with England. His arrival, in effect, secured the position on the Arabian coast that the British Indian administration had begun to covet and negotiate for as early as 1802. Over the next several decades Indian and Somali merchants moved to Aden, and Haines succeeded in inducing American ships to load on coffee there, eventually diverting the trade from Mocha when the Imam of Yemen took over that port. Internal struggles among the tribal leaders continued, and this allowed the British to assume the role of peacemakers and to exercise a central authority over the whole vast Arabian southland. After Aden was declared a free port in 1850, there were many new settlers — British, French, and Italian merchants. Haines himself, who was appointed political officer, presided over the port's growth as a garrison and trading port, but he died tragically in Bombay in 1860 after being imprisoned as a debtor — a sad Dickensian end for this devoted and efficient imperialist.

Through the late nineteenth and early twentieth century the British tightened their control over the whole region, fending off the Turks and keeping the ambitions of successive Imams in check, eventually by means of air power. In 1937 Aden became a crown colony under the control of the Colonial Office. With firm administration came the whole apparatus of British colonial life: the racism, the class structures, the rule of Anglo-Saxon law, the power struggles, the exclusions, the deceits. The social round that the explorer Richard Burton had scorned sprouted colourful traditions: camel races, curry lunches, cocktail parties, the Aden Protectorate Levies' annual ball, the Aden regatta. And a curious motley of famous names or singular characters passed through or stopped in the Colony: not only Haines and Burton, but Luke Thomas, Rudyard Kipling, Arthur Rimbaud, the elder Kaiky Muncherjee, a legendary ship's chandler, and the elder Antonin Besse — not to mention Freya Stark, H. St.John Philby, Wilfrid Thesiger, Bertram Thomas, Evelyn Waugh, and Wendell Phillips. Although the ancient ruling powers, the Queen of Sheba, Abukarid Asad, and many other renowned names had faded into legend, and many of the ancient cities, Najran, Tarim, Shabwa, Ma'rib, Harib, and Timna, had declined or been forgotten — and while the hinterland remained remote for most of the British and Europeans — Aden itself offered a vivid spectacle of colonial hothouse life.

I sat on the float at Gold Mohur, in the middle of a colourful and sinister raree show, one that overlaid and concealed an even more marvellous local history. And because in the eyes of my young self the raree show quickly grew oppressive, I longed for the arrival of my own personal Joycean muse, for that magical birdlike girl who would appear by the seashore and earnestly charge my soul. On those days of dappled seaborne clouds, I longed, like Stephen Dedalus, to cry out in a burst of profane joy. Unlike Joyce's hero, however, I was no mere restless student. I had a job, and a fascinating one. But I was dissatisfied, for I wanted more than a job; I wanted a vocation — and poetry.

So the long afternoons at Gold Mohur waned amid middle-class small talk and colonial chatter. The shark nets divided me from the enticing deeper ocean as I downed my gin or beer and prepared to take on the eternal evening round of parties.

A handful of long-preserved invitation cards, quaint social markers, formal as tombstones, testify to the diversity of my social torture:

Aden Harbour and the Prince of Wales Pier area in the nineteenth century. [From an old print]

A View of Aden Harbour, 1959. The u.s. Consulate is the low-lying building, left, in front of the high-rise Rock Hotel.

The Crescent Shopping area in Steamer Point.

The Crescent Hotel, scene of many odd happenings during
Aden's colourful history.

Michael and Coco Sterner.

Ali Ahmad Esmail.

Consulate group.
Standing, left to right,
Eleanor Browne, Ginger Crawford,
Bill Wolle and Michael Sterner;
seated, Bill Crawford.

Native shops in old Crater.

Backstreets of Ma'alla.

Bags of qat awaiting pickup.

At the Khormaksar camel races.

Gold Mohur Beach on a placid afternoon.

U.S. Consulate, Aden, 1957.

Women chatting in a street in Shaikh Othman.

Crater, as seen from Khormaksar Beach.

A shanty town near Little Aden.

Salt pans near Little Aden.

The Colony, seen from the *U.S.S. Robert Craig,* the "death ship."

Agricultural station in Abyan.

*The Rulers of the Amirates of Baihan and Dhala';
the 'Audhali, Fadhli and Lower Yafa'i Sultanates;
and the Upper 'Aulaqi Shaikhdom*

request the pleasure of the company of

Mr. Henighan

*at a ceremony for the inauguration of the Federation
of the Amirates of the South at Champion Lines
on Wednesday, February, 11th, at 2.40 p.m.*

R.S.V.P.
*The Secretary (Inaugural Ceremony),
British Agency,
Western Aden Protectorate.*   [P.T.O.

Invitation to the ceremonies inaugurating the British-inspired
"Federation of the Amirates of the South" (1959).

DIANA MACDONALD

Tom on Khormaksar Beach.

Consulate team preparing to leave for Yemen.

Approaching Tai'iz.

MICHAEL STERNER

The Consul of France requests the pleasure of the company of Mr. T. Henighan at a reception given at the Shalimar Garden, on Tuesday, 14th July, 1959, on the occasion of French National Day ...

Prabhudas Purshottam requests the pleasure of the company of Mr. Thomas J. Henighan at a Cocktail Party to be held on the Crescent Hotel Roof in celebration of Derwali from 7-00 p.m. to 9-00 p.m on Monday, the 21st October, 1957 ...

Colonel and Mrs. P.H.D. Panton and the Misses Panton request the pleasure of the company of Mr. Tom Henighan to supper on Saturday, August 2nd, 1958 at 7:30. Dress informal. 5, Tarshyne ...

The Imperial Ethiopian Consul General & Mrs. Yacob Ianios request the pleasure of the company of Mr. T. Hennigaen [sic] at a reception on the occasion of the Coronation Day of His Majesty Emperor Haile Selassie on Sunday, 2nd November, 1958, at 7. P.M....

Mr. E.D. Carter requests the pleasure of Mr. T. Henighan for Cocktails to meet Mr. E. Lippa on Thursday, 26th September, 1957, at the B.P. Bureika Club ...

His Excellency the Governor and Lady Luce request the pleasure of the company of Mr. T.J. Henighan at a Cocktail Party on Thursday, the 9th December at 6:45 p.m. (dinner jacket or lounge suit) ...

Major E.R. Jolley M.B.E., & the Officers of "B" Squadron, 13th/18th Royal Hussars (Queen Mary's Own) request the pleasure of the company of Mr. T.J. Henighan and two ladies [sic] at a dance in the Community Centre, Little Aden, at 8:30 p.m. on Saturday, 30th August, 1958. (Dress: dinner jacket, buffet supper, carriages at 1 p.m.) ...

Even though my company was now and then a dubious pleasure, the invitations seemed endless. Nor could one pass up such delights — at least not without risking the label of "recluse" or eccentric. But on evenings when no such highlights materialized, there were other festive gatherings.

Horace Phillips, the Colony's brilliant and voluble Chief Secretary, was, beneath the thin cover of his title, the Colony's senior intelligence officer, a spy from the home country. Although he was careful to conceal his origins, he was in fact a Glasgow Jew, which must have made his role both difficult and especially piquant. Together with his ebullient wife Idina, Phillips hosted evenings of charades. This was singularly appropriate, since his role was itself in the nature of a charade. He was a small, lively, balding man, fiendishly witty and elusive, and was hated or resented by many. Bill and Ginger Crawford made sure to keep on good terms with him, and they played charades with all their might, as the occasion dictated.

The Phillips's parties were far more lively than most of those given by the Secretariat people or the military, and anything was preferable to cocktails at Government House or a British Petroleum reception at Little Aden. But the Chief Secretary's parties also made one uneasy, like the parties in the (much later) television show *The Prisoner*, where one is never sure what is really at stake, who is deceiving whom, and who is going to turn out to be Number One.

In the Colony, as in Shakespeare's plays, the social action took place on two contrasting levels. The official level, played out behind the scenes and subtly mimicked at the formal parties, suggested high stakes and important issues, the potential clash of powerful forces. At the other end, however, there was comedy, an array of odd and apparently meaningless actions, sometimes light enough to provide relief in the face of the intolerable daily grind, but all too often fierce and deconstructive, giving glimpses of the chaos that underlay the political and social order.

One night there appeared a British adviser, back in the Colony after spending too much time upcountry. Hyperactive from drink and isolation, like some character out of a Conrad story, he threw his shoes off at a formal party, repeating, as he wriggled his toes, giggled, and swore, tales of deadly wilderness encounters and savage camaraderie. Another evening spotlighted the local British tobacco representative tearing apart cigarette after cigarette to demonstrate, with a disproportionate and barely suppressed fury, that though not nearly as popular, the British brands were superior to the American.

And on an evening oppressive with humidity, in the dreary confines of the Khormaksar Club, a venerable but shabbily housed institution that overlooked the inner harbour, two old colonials, on a bet, conducted an experiment. Tying a sizable chunk of beef to a wire, they cast the bloody bait into the murky waters. Did sharks cruise the shores of their kingdom? They did not have to wait long to find out. Shapes materialized from the deeps, the thin wire trembled, the bait vanished.

I searched for my muse by the seaside, but events of greater moment swirled around me, and amid the serious politicking and the social comedy the whole facade of colonial life, carefully nurtured by the British on that barren coastline, trembled like a mirage and threatened to disappear.

NINE

Boosters and Detractors

After a very few months in Aden I was certain that I had mastered my often strange duties so well that no new challenge could daunt me. Personal life was another matter. The Joycean muse I longed for, the beautiful and subtle companion I imagined in the offing, had not materialized; folly and wastage of spirit and an aimless energy of libido spun me round in a squirrel cage of unfulfillment. But in the office and the everyday flurry of work, I seemed to soar. I was confident, rash to the point of hubris, truly, in Joycean phrase, "a hawklike man flying sunward above the sea, a prophecy of the end he had been born to serve."

My daily tasks, although hardly momentous, I performed with enthusiasm. I issued visas and renewed passports, took care of the visiting ships, revised the wage scale of the consulate's local employees, wrote economic reports, and travelled to interesting places like Mukalla and Bayhan. I had many British acquaintances, and had begun to know persons of other nationalities, the French, the Italians, and the Greeks. When an Indian student walked into my office and asked for help in enrolling at an American university, I arranged things. This led to an invitation to meet his family, the owners of one of the Aden salt-producing firms. It was my first real contact with the Indians in Aden, and it gave me a sense of the Colony's roots in the past, for these Indians were from Bombay, and Aden had originally been part of the Bombay administrative district of the British colonial service.

The young student's name was Dinkerrai Harishanker Joshi, and his uncle was manager of the Little Aden Salt Industrial Company Ltd. After Dinker's acceptance by the University of Missouri, where he was going to study business administration, I received the following letter from him, carefully typed on thin green-tinted paper, and dated April 11, 1959.

My dear Mr. Henighan,
From the books, cinemas and radios the picture of an average American I have is that he is full of energy, always with new ideas, cool and calculating

and still full of humanity, intelligent and obliging. You are the first American I met and you fully justify my concept, so I shall always be glad to remember you.

I had long cherished a desire and that was to invite you at the Salt Works which is very near the refinery, and where we reside.

My self, my father and my uncle Mr. H.N. Pandya, Manager, Salt Works, are very much pleased to invite you and your family at the Little Aden Salt Works, Bureika, on Saturday the 18th of April, 1959, in the evening. I shall be pleased to come and receive you in our car at the time and place suggested by you. I am not going to accept your no under any circumstances.

If it is not possible for you to come on April 18, you may suggest me a date suitable to you.

Sometimes it becomes difficult to convince the other person how much we wish through the medium of language, spoken or written. At this moment, I find the same difficulty. I feel, however, that you are not going to disappoint me.

Very truly yours,
D.H. Joshi

While I was later to meet more sophisticated, more Anglicized, and more cynical Indians in Aden, the charm of this letter has hardly faded. Even my callow youthful self recognized in it a summons that could not be refused. Off I went on the appointed date to visit the Joshis. The whole family received me: Dinker, his father and mother, their three daughters, a son-in-law, and Dinker's uncle. I was treated to my first Indian dinner; every dish was explained and I was warned about the super-hot spices. Since I was quite ignorant of the traditional rivalry between the Indian merchants and the native peoples in Arabia and East Africa, the conversation at table was fascinating. Dinker's uncle soon set me straight on his idea of local politics. The Arabs were like locusts, he assured me, swarming over everything and devouring everything. The situation in Aden was difficult, and would become hopeless, unless the British could contain the militants, especially the Aden Trades Union Congress. If nothing could be done to squelch Arab nationalism, it would be impossible for Indians, French, Greeks, and the others to do business in Aden. Nothing good would come out of independence. I drank tea, devoured the wonderful food, and nodded. Later I was shown the salt works.

That was another of Aden's odd surprises, for the "factory" consisted mostly of great flat rectangular salt pans, expanses of unruffled water that reflected the sky and the clouds. These perfectly empty, perfectly still containers were as beautiful as Zen gardens. I walked around them at sunset and marvelled at their mirrored light, shifting between orange, gold, rose, and violet, at first dazzling then soft and soothing, as the sun dipped below the horizon and the day faded.

I was glad to meet the Joshis. Dinker later visited me in Michigan, where I had started my career as a university professor. He seemed quite disappointed by my new option, and told me that I should be overseas representing my country. He was rather disillusioned with the American students he met in Missouri — their attitudes seemed frivolous to him and their work habits rather slack. His image of "the average American" had obviously changed with experience; I was pleased that he thought I might be able to sustain his earlier vision.

Because I had been successful in dealing with the crazy assortment of tasks thrown at me by everyday events in the Colony, I felt myself buoyed up with confidence. At one point, while Crawford and Sterner were both in Yemen, I was left in charge of the consulate. Just then an uprising against the Lebanese government of Camille Chamoun took place and United States marines, followed by other forces, invaded that country. The reaction of the pro-Nasser Arabs was immediate and strong. Stirred up by Cairo's *Saut al Arab* radio, a small mob of protestors appeared at the consulate. Abdullah, our uniformed but unarmed consulate guard, was powerless to do more than stand by and watch them. I made an appearance and gave a stirring speech defending the American action (which privately appalled me). Some spirited debate followed, but when the leaders had had their say and the mob quietly dispersed, I felt very satisfied, but at the same time rather disgusted with myself. The protestors had a point; on the whole, I agreed with them. Out of duty and the desire to show my stuff I had argued the contrary, and my defence, although agile enough, was lacking in conviction. Did I want to spend the rest of my life defending causes I only half believed in?

Bill Crawford returned. I would have liked to discuss my inner conflict over American policy with him, but he carefully avoided playing mentor. He took little notice of my handling of the protestors, although he did manage to find a small error in one of the official telegrams I had drafted. The hawklike man was still flying high, but far too close to the sun. Shortly afterward, the first crash came.

One sleepy afternoon, just five minutes before closing time, I was lounging at my desk, already imaging the delights of a dish of fresh crab at the nearby Rex Restaurant, when a slight disturbance in the vicinity of Esmail's usually placid territory caught my attention. I looked up through my glass-panelled door and saw a tall, rangy man, European or

American, leaning over the wooden railing, head to head with my assistant in some kind of argument. After a few seconds, Esmail got up and strode back in the direction of my office.

He slipped in, closed the door behind him, and gave me a painful look. "Sir, there is a gentleman here who says he must see the vice consul. He says it is urgent, but he will not say why. I told him we were just closing, but he insists. And, if I may say so ..." — and here Esmail lowered his voice to a grating harshness and bared his teeth in a distinctly feral grin — "he is *very rude.*"

I groaned. By this time I was rather fed up with some of the more absurd demands put upon our consular service at all hours of the day and night. Why couldn't the fellow wait until the morning?

"God!" I said aloud. "Who the hell does he think he is? Tell him to come back tomorrow."

Esmail carried away the message; I started packing up my papers. The next thing I knew our visitor had vaulted over the railing that divided the inner from the outer office and was heading my way. The Arab staff gaped at him. Was the man a loony? I reached for something, anything, in order to defend myself. All I could find was the consular seal of the United States of America.

As I stood, clinging tightly to this heavy metal, the visitor stormed into my office.

"Put that goddamned thing down!" he commanded. He was a very tall man, wiry but well built, and — short of braining him — it seemed the best thing to do.

"What in hell's going on?"

The man bristled and glared at me. "Are you the vice consul?" he asked doubtfully.

I noticed that he had a fine craggy face and was wearing an expensive white cotton shirt. A gold emblem representing crossed tennis rackets adorned one of the heaving breast patches.

"I'm here to see the consul," he said, still not looking very friendly — and his request had gone up a notch.

I sat down; he remained standing. "Cigarette?" I suggested. It was like trying to break the ice with a paper napkin.

"I don't smoke," he informed me. "I'm Fred Kovaleski."

A glimmer of recognition now flashed in my almost paralyzed brain. I had once listened regularly to the sports news on the radio and Kovaleski's name had surfaced now and then on those long Sunday lists of tennis match results, usually at the point where I had lost patience and was about to flip to the music station.

Light began to dawn. Mr. K.'s leap over the wooden railing was maybe not so strange. Still, this wasn't the Davis Cup. His hostility had not abated one iota. Well aware that I had already blotted my copybook, I tried to redeem the situation.

"Out here for a match?" I ventured.

"No. I'm the new local representative of Stim Cola. Is the consul here, or not? I'd like to see him right away."

I knew Bill Crawford wasn't in, so I called Michael Sterner on the intercom and told him that Mr. Kovaleski, the new Stim representative, was awaiting his pleasure. I closed my door and we moved uneasily to the outer office. Neither of us leapt the railing. Esmail asked if he could go home. I said, yes, that I was just leaving too.

Kovaleski erupted again. "I want *you* to introduce me to the consul," he insisted.

Now I was more than fed up. I didn't answer; I grabbed my briefcase and pushed through the door into the fierce Aden heat. Only when I reached my car, parked behind the fence outside, did I turn around. Through the glass windows of the consulate I could see Esmail and Kovaleski in heated discussion. Then Michael Sterner came out of his office and listened while Kovaleski went on, gesturing in my direction. I drove away as quickly as possible, but my fresh crab luncheon was spoiled beyond recovery.

I knew that consequences would arise from this absurd incident. I had not lived up to Dinker Joshi's image of me: I had not been "cool and calculating." I had certainly not been "obliging," and hardly even "intelligent." While Michael Sterner would be able to put such an incident in its proper place — as an unfortunate and accidental misunderstanding, best forgotten — it was, I knew, precisely the kind of slip that Bill Crawford would find unforgivable, and would use to discredit me. I wasn't wrong on that count either.

Mr. Kovaleski took his place as the representative of Stim Cola in Aden, played some tennis, and very soon disappeared from my ken. Years later, however, *The New York Times* did a story on him, using the now aging athlete as an example of a man who had maintained his excellent conditioning well into old age. As the *Times* story noted, Kovaleski had been a runner-up in the American national "over-sixty" tennis championships. More interestingly, though, the story referred to him as a "former State Department official." How could that be, I wondered? Had Mr. K. eventually graduated from pop to op, or had Stim been merely "sim," a clever cover for something else? Perhaps I had offended not merely a recognized American sportsman, but one who was even then an unrecognized American agent.

The truth I never learned. What's clear is that the incident marked a turning point in my working time in Aden. I had been sailing through my job, many things had gone very well, and I had avoided any grave mistakes. Day by day I could look Bill Crawford in the eye and challenge any hostility on his part. Now, it seemed, the situation had suddenly changed: the wax wings had melted a trifle and things did not look so good for the high flyer.

TEN

The Warning

When I arrived in South Arabia, the region consisted of the Kingdom of Yemen in the north, a "closed" country ruled with medieval wilfulness by an ailing and irascible Imam, and, in the southern desert regions, a multitude of petty Arab states, over which the British exercised an increasingly nervous hegemony. The Colony itself was a kind of Arabian Gibraltar, a fortress and a watch post. From its vantage point the British could oversee their Protectorate states, while at the same time keeping an eye on developments in the Persian Gulf. They could also monitor events in Yemen, a country to which, thanks to the animosity of the Imam, they were largely denied access.

What struck me immediately when I got my bearings in Aden was the whole area's complex ethnic and religious mix — a patchwork of allegiances and interests that made simple political solutions nearly impossible, even before the rise of Arab nationalism and the intervention of the Soviets. Yemen, at that time an isolated and undeveloped country of some ten million people, was ruled by a Shiite sect of Muslims known as Zaydis, who traced their origins to the immediate successors of the prophet. The ruler of Yemen, the Imam, was both a religious leader, a captain in the Holy War, and a secular leader, whose political connivings were designed to regain "the lost southland." Despite this dynastic entrenchment, a slight majority of Yemenis were not Shiite Muslims at all, but Sunnis.

The evolution of South Arabian politics followed a classic pattern. British intervention disrupted the traditional society by introducing Western values of material gain, social mobility, and democracy. The British espoused, although they did not always practise, a pragmatic rationalism, and, as with other such interventions around the world, this helped break down the local order. What the British failed to provide was ideological enthusiasm, a gospel to stir the masses. This arrived with Nasserism, which in some ways was the polar opposite to the British doctrine of sensible development, and it opened the door for a third force,

Marxist revolutionary thought, which appeared to combine rationalism with enthusiasm. Thesis-Antithesis-Synthesis — a Hegelian logic of historical development took hold of the Aden Arabs and swept them toward an unexpected future, one in which the Marxist Synthesist phase, however, also proved to be unstable.

At the centre of all this was the Colony itself. Thanks to the policies of the British it was socially and politically developed, and it possessed a considerable infrastructure. In the late 1950s it boasted a population of nearly 140,000 people, of whom more than 100,000 were Arabs, either native or from Yemen or the Protectorate. There were approximately 16,000 Indians, 10,000 Somalis, and barely 5,000 Europeans. The Protectorate population was much larger, nearly 800,000, but was scattered over an area of 112,000 square miles. Its social structures were complex but quite traditional. In that vast region elitist groups ruled, including the tribal families of the shaikhdoms, emirates, and sultanates, and, in the Eastern Protectorate, the Sayyids — descendants of Muhammad's family via his daughter Fatima, originally from Basra in Iraq. Although there were some challenges to the power of these entrenched elite groups, and many subtle checks and balances, the Protectorates were a much more stratified and reactionary society, and, paradoxically, a far more unstable one, than the Aden of the more urbanized Arabs.

The advent of Gamal Abdel Nasser and the British-French-Israeli conniving in the 1956 Suez crisis had not only stirred up a new phenomenon, militant pan-Arab nationalism, but had completely undermined British credibility with the Arab peoples. Even reactionary rulers like the Imam could ride the wave of Muslim contempt for British policy. Despite minor attempts by the British to modify the old colonial system, to make their rule more flexible and give it a more progressive image, they convinced almost no one that the future lay with them. Apart from a few collaborators and local rulers anxious to maintain their ancient privileges, the Arabs did not accept the British version of their future. The situation grew more and more unstable and, almost inevitably — after some years of escalating terror — the British did lose Aden. A new and more inclusive southern Arabia began to emerge, but only after monarchist, Nasserite, and Marxist-inspired factions repeatedly clashed through several decades, and terrorism, civil war, party infighting, shifting borders, and political restructuring — as well as foreign intervention — disrupted the old ways forever.

In the 1950s and 1960s the Soviet Union and China, mindful of the strategic importance of the Colony and of the possibility of new sources of oil, were actively working to extend their influence in the area. Yemen was soon to be flooded with eastern bloc aid personnel, engineers, and economic and military advisers, and to become yet another scene of confrontation in the worldwide front of the Cold War. From the consulate in Aden, American diplomats and spies monitored the situation, cooperating with the British and trading information with them, but maintaining a certain independence of outlook.

As a result of these developments, foreign service officers at the American consulate spent a great deal of time in Yemen, and full diplomatic relations were established in 1972, even before the final unification of South Arabia. It was inevitable that even a young vice consul, whose assignments were mostly non-political, should go at least as far as Ta'iz, and one day Bill Crawford decided that it was my turn.

I drove up with Ali Muhammad, the suave and rather reticent consulate political adviser, an Aden Arab, and Ali Ahmad, the consulate's Somali chauffeur, a fine man and a wonderful driving instructor who had helped me get my first licence. Ali Muhammad was a very sophisticated and well-informed young man and totally committed to the panArab revolution instigated by Gamel Abdul Nasser. Because of his efficiency and his knowledge of local politics, he was most useful to the consul and Michael Sterner, and they consulted him frequently. The Sterners in particular became quite close friends with Ali and later met him in Egypt. What his political connections in Aden really were I do not know, but I suspect he was much more than an interested observer. Of course he was far too wily to reveal anything to me, although we played tennis occasionally, and he had even once admitted to me that he had a wife, but that he had not "intercoursed her yet."

Ali Ahmad was a jolly fellow, a little older than Ali Muhammad, but agile and very eager. He lived in Ma'alla and referred frequently and with helpless humour to his cornucopia of children. I was told that he had been lectured about birth control by one of the previous vice-consular wives, but he was obviously enjoying life far too much to bother about other people's ideologies.

At that time the road to Ta'iz was mostly a desert track, but as such tracks go it was quite easy. One could relax and fall into the bliss of sameness that makes such travel unique. We were driving through an area that since ancient times had been marked by intermittent and small-scale tribal warfare, and would see tank and artillery battles in the near future. But these were colonial days. The British were still masters; the Aden Protectorate Levies still patrolled the desert; Russian advisers had not landed in Aden; and Carlos the terrorist and the Baader-Meinhoff gang had not yet taken refuge there.

On the way to Ta'iz, cocooned in the air-conditioned comfort of our green Willys Jeep, I began to enjoy the experience of travelling in the desert.

Some of the wonder of the old stories, the *Arabian Nights*, lies in the power of transport: one flies instantly from wish to fulfillment, from a village hovel to many-towered Baghdad, and the intervening miles are abolished. Yet part of the charm of travel in Arabia is the sheer monotony of the landscape, the endless miles of slow progress through wadis and across rocky escarpments, the infrequent arrivals in some shabby village or oasis, the appearance of a border checkpoint where borders are inconceivable, the seamless brilliance of the sky, and the absence of variety in vegetation or animal life.

We were moving toward the heart of the old *Arabia Felix* — "happy Arabia," as the Romans designated it, perhaps because they had never settled there. On the barren plains that lie south of the Yemen mountains, however, it was hard to conjure up images of past glory, to recall the ancient spice trade, to remember that not far away was the land of the Queen of Sheba. What one experienced was relentless heat, milky white sunshine, an unending hazy horizon, blistered rocky outcroppings and irregular shifting patches of sand: the very paradigm of emptiness, the Tao of unmeaning.

But not quite. The process is strange but almost palpable, and for many quite inevitable. You grind on; the scenery barely changes — hardly a plant, a sprig, not the least stir of life. The mind says "empty," "barren," "boring"; but something in you responds. You feel yourself undistracted, undeceived by conventional beauties. Your soul, your senses are liberated. You suddenly realize that you are perfectly happy; there is nowhere else you would want to be.

In *Seven Pillars of Wisdom*, a book that subtly — and not so subtly — influenced British attitudes even as late as my time in Arabia, T.E. Lawrence constructs a dramatic myth of the desert. It is the desert, Lawrence suggests, that is the purifying vehicle for the prophet, the carrier of the new creed, the visionary. Kept simple by circumstance, the Bedouin, for example, are like an empty vessel, ready to be fired with a new vision, even as they were by Muhammad's original Word. This desert faith, this receptivity, is impossible in towns. As Lawrence puts it, "To live, the villager or townsman must fill himself each day with the pleasures of acquisition and accumulation, and by rebound off circumstance become the grossest and most material of men."

I thought of this as the three of us passed through the Lahej settlement in the heart of the Western Protectorate's most important sultanate. This was a grim, sprawling village of warehouse-like buildings, with an unappealing marketplace, a few shabby trees and benches, a petrol station, and the inevitable border checkpoint where our permits had to be pulled out for inspection.

On the trail again, the mystique of the desert reasserted itself: everything seemed placid, dreamlike. All around was a landscape of moon-rubble and heat-blasted rock; yet it was not many miles further on that we came upon a system of wadis, dry riverbeds that made excellent natural roads for the Jeep. Scrub bush sprang up everywhere; the Yemen hills were visible in the distance; the sparse rains that would fall in force later, though intermittently, had already lured clumps of dark-green shrubbery out of the resistant rock. Here and there we could see stunted, twisted acacia trees, the red-stemmed *abb*, thorny plants, and rough grass like a prickly carpet.

Soon we entered a series of deeper-cut wadis. The hills began to rise around us, barren and smooth mostly, though with increasing vegetation; a rich tawny brown at first, the colour of a deer hide, they greened as we climbed into Yemen.

Terraced hillsides appeared, swirling patterns of cultivated land; eucalyptus trees stood out against the hazy sky; travellers walked along the road, one or two carrying black umbrellas. A series of hairpin turns and a sight of pleasant valleys; then finally, Ta'iz itself, gently set among the hills. This was old Ta'iz, before the hoards of American engineers, Russian pilots, and Chinese road builders had descended upon it, to change it forever, and I was immediately struck by the sight of its white triple spires, graceful minarets rising above the dreaming city.

"Look, sir!" Ali Ahmad cried out. He slowed our vehicle and pointed at the road ahead.

He wasn't referring to the apparition of the city, but to the crowd that had appeared in front of us, streaming out from what seemed to be a large field, well beyond the Ta'iz gates, a crush of bodies blocking the road, men in brown, black, or striped jackets, with skirts and turbans, many wearing the curved dagger or *jambiyah*, a few, perhaps guards or soldiers, carrying rifles. One or two veiled women could be seen among them, while a host of boys scurried among the throng, playing tag between the parked cars, the trucks, and the donkey carts.

Ali Ahmad leaned on the car horn, attempting to bully his way through. The crowd parted a little, but not much. He rolled down the window and began a shouted conversation with some passers-by. The conversation went on a long time. Ali Muhammad — who had begun to feel ill some time before — stirred from his lethargy on the rear seat and stopped groaning. He too shouted questions at the crowd.

After a while, Ali Ahmad rolled up the window. He and Ali Muhammad exchanged a few words in Arabic. The latter turned to me with an expression I knew well. Like Esmail, my Somali friend, he loved to shock me with revelations about his world, one in which I was so much a stranger and a novice. He smiled wanly — obviously still feeling ill — and announced in his smooth, precise voice, "It's an execution, sir. A man killed a woman's only son, and the judge — you would call him a judge — gave her a choice. She could get some restitution or else the man could be executed. His head was cut off just now. Too bad! If we had arrived twenty minutes earlier you could have seen it."

I sat back, gazing numbly at the crowd; at moments like this, moments of sudden estrangement from everything I took for granted, I would fall into a dreamlike daze. I was both thrilled and horrified. This was what travel existed for: to stun one into a new sense of the variety of the world and of human nature.

It was a joy to be twenty-two, to have escaped from North America and to be in the presence of such wonders. I had left the tedious routines of everyday life behind. I had entered a charmed circle where nothing commonplace could touch me. That someone should die to entertain me — that was not the issue at all. I was destined to experience henceforth only magical things.

I swallowed hard; Aden had often been dreary and full of restrictions — this was what I had been waiting for. This was more like it. Ali Ahmad chuckled and leaned on the horn.

Our destination, the Ta'iz guest house, lay near a shallow ravine on the outskirts of the city. It was a low-slung two-storey structure of grey stone with a crenellated roof; the entrance was an arched drive-through porch, jutting out like a stunted castle tower. As we approached the place it started to rain, a strange miracle to an Aden resident. The road adjoining the place was bleak; one or two Land Rovers were parked there and beside them a few pye-dogs lay scratching themselves, yelping incessantly, perhaps in protest at the brief shower. Somebody had left a half-full jerry can of gasoline in the entranceway.

We unloaded the Jeep and settled Ali Muhammad in one of the guest rooms. Ali Ahmad went off for some medicine for our friend's upset stomach. I decided to walk down to the city market.

I strolled through the impressive gates and into a noisy scene: cars and camels, beggars, labourers in loincloths, merchants' stalls laden with pots and beakers, rugs, sandals, hats, baskets of bread and brightly coloured pastries. And everywhere dogs and children, a pleasant din of real life, but for me incomparably exotic.

I had lived many months in the fierce heat of Aden, where I had fallen into a lethargy of both body and spirit; my political and social idealism had been tested, my naïveté about social life exposed, and I had defended myself by establishing the persona of a jaded, scornful young man of the world. This was curiously appropriate, because an air of boredom really did afflict the Colony; everyone, and especially the political activists on both sides, seemed to be marking time, waiting for history to explode in their faces. The parties and excursions, the boozing and play soon grew wearisome; yet it was difficult to organize oneself for any serious work. From time to time I would feel in myself a kind of wanton energy, which could hardly be expressed in any creative way. Rare but sharply painful glimpses of the brutalities of colonialism goaded me toward an activism that my official position rendered unthinkable.

Now, walking down through the gates of Ta'iz, even though I was there on no special mission, I felt a changed (and much more liberated) sense of purpose. This country, although ruled by the medieval theocracy of the Imam, did not have the same whiff of unreality that one felt in the Colony. I resolved to try to come back, to persuade Bill Crawford to allow me to undertake some real mission, for there was a pleasant sense of anarchy in the air here, one that entirely suited my twenty-two-year-old self.

Back at the guest house Bill and Ginger Crawford welcomed me. They introduced me to the German consul from Jidda and to Brunnhilde, an odd if free-spirited woman whom I've already mentioned. She was clearly one of those characters who hang around in exotic places and begin to lose touch with any coherent reality. I bought her a dinner, during which she kept alluding to mysterious events in which she was involved without actually telling me much about them. Yet she was by no means the strangest person I was to meet on my visit.

That night I didn't sleep well. The air in my small, shabby, first-floor guest house room was stifling, the bedbugs were ferocious, and, despite the medicine, Ali Muhammad groaned so loudly that I could hear him through the thin walls.

Next morning I had breakfast with the Crawfords and went for a walk with Ginger, who had adopted one or two of the pye-dogs. We sat on a hill above Ta'iz and talked about life in Aden. As usual, I was critical of the absurd facade of jollity that masked the psychological oppression in the Colony. I was also furious about the U.S. invasion of Lebanon, which had led to the protest in front of the consulate that I have already referred to. I then launched into general criticisms of American policy in the Middle East and elsewhere. To the Crawfords — even though they partially agreed with me — this was merely undergraduate speculation.

They of course had inside knowledge I lacked and this put them beyond such palaver. It's the mission of diplomats to work with existing policies, they informed me, but I was a little too naive to back off.

Later I walked around Ta'iz and took some photographs. I began to wonder just why Bill had wanted me there. Through Cathy, I knew that he had been somewhat unsatisfied with Michael Sterner's performance when the latter first arrived in Aden, and that Michael's first trip to Yemen — to Bill's relief — had transformed things and focused everything for Michael. Perhaps Bill was hoping for the same result in my case. The idea seemed plausible at the time, but what I didn't know was that he had already made up his mind about my professional suitability and had acted accordingly.

Lunch was served in the hall of the guest house and I ate with the Polish ambassador, a sly man who kept trying to probe me about the American attitude to British policy in Aden. I had dinner with Amadeo Guillet, the Italian chargé in Ta'iz, and his long-suffering wife Bice. (Besides his Aden "air hostesses" Signor Guillet had "harems" in various parts of Yemen.) I was never as impressed by Amadeo as Coco Sterner was — his boastful philandering seemed to me comical, and his constant demonstrations of "personality" inclined to self-caricature.

Besides, I had just met a far more interesting character, none other than Bruce de Bourbon Condé, a resident American who claimed to be a lineal descendent of the great French royal house, and who had come from somewhere like Arkansas or Oklahoma to live out his wildest fantasies in the heart of Arabia.

Bruce Abdul Rahman Condé — for that was the Arab name he had chosen for himself — turned up at the guest house and invited me to visit him at his place later in the day. His apartment, which occupied part of a house at the edge of the Ta'iz settlements, faced a steep hillside; a spectacular road could be seen near the peak. When I arrived, he greeted me with that restless manner, that nervous expectancy, that I soon saw as part of his nature.

A thin, handsome man of about thirty-five or forty, with a wispy moustache and goatee, originally blond but dyed black to mimic the Yemeni style, Condé was dressed in a white shirt, an Arab *futah*, or skirt, and expensive sandals. He spoke in a high-pitched voice, in rapid-fire sentences, and was constantly moving, gesturing, pulling out this or that diary or notebook, and dipping into his box of slides and photographs — all this to illustrate one point or another in his running discourse.

Condé, I had been told — or perhaps warned — was queer, but I soon realized that he was also a very special kind of lunatic. He was suffering from that "upcountry" madness that I had seen in a few British officers who had resided in some remote Protectorate outpost much longer than was good for them. This involved "going native," or achieving a nearly complete identification with the local culture. In such cases the persona becomes a caricature of the native type, and a desperate unconscious energy fuels a performance that is often manic and can be comical.

That day Bruce Condé simply couldn't sit still. He paced up and down his "writing room" popping little white pills — something for his nerves, he explained. His apartment was in the Arabian style, with camel saddles, Bayhani rugs, and *jambiyahs* much in evidence, while the walls were hung everywhere with excellent photographs, mostly of Arab boys, a wonderful gallery of beaming, provocative young faces.

Condé showed me slides of several visits he had made to Ma'rib, reputedly the Queen of Sheba's ancient capital, located in northeastern Yemen. In fact, he was probably the first American to visit the place in the wake of Wendell Phillips's abruptly terminated archaeological expedition of 1951–52. My host had his own version of the Phillips fiasco; he offered to take me to Ma'rib (whether he really could have done so is another question). He also showed me many of his travel articles, mostly published in small-town American magazines, or in philatelic journals — for one of Bruce Condé's passions was stamps.

"This piece was in the *Butte Examiner*," my host explained. "They'll publish anything I write. I get letters all the time from little old ladies in Topeka. They all envy what I do. Look at this piece, on San'a, from the *Arkansas Courier*. San'a is more interesting than Lhasa, Tibet. Stay here a while and I'll take you there."

Condé grew more and voluble. He began to gossip about the westerners in Ta'iz. He had many secrets, many scandals to confide, and I prepared myself.

"This is my country," he kept assuring me. "I knew it right away. My mother wanted me to settle down at home, to become a suburban zombie, with two cars, kids, and a cute little wife. The good old American death sentence. Just look at those faces" — he waved at the beaming boys. "Did you hear about the execution this afternoon?"

"We just missed it," I told him.

"Old-fashioned justice," he sighed. "Not like Kansas!" He peered at me and smiled. For a minute he was silent, as if measuring me for the final confidence. "You're a sensitive guy," he said. "How do you like working for Billy Crawford?"

I stared at him. Despite some clear warning signs, I was still in my first blush of enthusiasm for Bill Crawford's intense professionalism. My naïveté was boundless and unshakeable. My chief, I knew, was demanding, and perhaps just a little cool in manner. But I seemed to have no reason to fear him.

Now I sensed that Bruce Condé was about to tell me quite a different story. I almost dreaded to hear it. He popped a few small white pills. His nervous hands moved. His blue eyes pinioned me. When I didn't respond, he continued unabashed.

"Billy Crawford hates me. He's trying to get me kicked out of Yemen. I love the people here, and that bothers him. He has no passion for anything — except himself. Don't you see how he operates? He tells the State Department exactly what it wants to hear. A little Boy Scout for America — but if you cross him, watch out. He's ambitious, full of anger underneath the smooth pelt. You notice the white hairs? He'll be an old man when he's forty… "

Condé went on for a while like this; a man clearly obsessed. I didn't know how to answer him. I sat stunned by the irony of it: had Bill Crawford brought me to Yemen to hear this? But then I didn't believe a word Condé said. After all, he was unreliable, "queer." He embarrassed me, and I groped to change the subject. I knew I was in the presence of a madman, of a man who boasted about being a lineal descendant of the Bourbon kings of France!

All of sudden I was desperate to get out of there. Condé's babble, the "native" trappings, the pictures of the smiling boys that covered the walls, everything seemed oppressive and unreal.

Yet I must have known, however much I repressed the knowledge, that this madman spoke at least part of the truth. I was simply not ready to face the fact that Condé's words had suddenly evoked for me aspects of "Billy Crawford" that I had sensed but refused to see. Conde's excesses prevented me from accepting it just then, but my chief did espouse a near-puritanical work ethic, applying rigorous and sometimes narrow standards to others in the name of a tightly defined esprit de corps, one that he had secretly appointed himself to uphold. Had I been more experienced, or less naive, I would have recognized right there that I could never follow such a path, or work with ease under such a man's direction.

I let Bruce Condé rave on, pretending to be sympathetic. But I also felt uneasy. Did I recognize my kinship with him as an outsider, as a self-willed seeker after experience, as something of a romantic fool?

Two years later, in Hamburg, Germany, a colleague handed me a press clipping.

It was from the Paris *Herald Tribune* and read as follows:

Cairo, Egypt. November 19. Bruce Abdul Rahman Condé, a free-lance journalist and long-time resident of Yemen, was once again refused entry to Egypt today. He had recently been expelled from Ta'iz, but claiming his papers were not in order, authorities here refused to allow him to stay in Cairo. He was placed on a regular flight and returned to Ta'iz, Yemen, via Jidda, Saudi Arabia. But Yemen also refused to admit him. For the past several weeks he has been flying back and forth between these destinations, unable to land in either country. Reputedly, he owed the airline a large sum for his flights and his considerable excess baggage, but could not pay because he was carrying only uncashable gold coins. It is not known how the situation will be resolved.

Bruce Condé, expelled from his mythical kingdom, his private Oz, had landed, not back in Kansas, but nowhere. It seems that in a characteristic outburst he had attacked one of the Yemen Royal Guards and had been given a choice between expulsion and staying in Yemen and having both his hands cut off. Because he had renounced his American citizenship and was unable to obtain a passport, Condé had no travel documents. He eventually settled in Beirut, finding a niche in the fanatical but ever-tolerant East, and no doubt spent many years telling his sad story to all who would listen, recounting a cruel fate, one hardly appropriate for a true descendant of the great Bourbon family of France.

Three days after my encounter with Condé I drove back to the Colony with Amadeo and Bice Guillet. Guillet dropped his wife off near the Crescent Hotel and went off to see some of his lady friends. I soon fell back into Cathy's orbit, and she and I resumed our madcap non-relationship. The silly parties, the riotous nights continued; even so, I enjoyed my work, entertained fleeting images of possible princesses, and met new friends. With a few of the latter I more than once shared my amusement at Bruce Abdul Rahman Condé, who, to my still innocent and unsuspecting mind, seemed wholly out of touch with reality.

ELEVEN

A Prisoner on Socotra

Long before the real terror began in the Colony, local resistance to British rule had become visible. The South Arabian League, founded in 1950, was a sign of change in the region. Its leaders, although in origin part of the old Sayyid elite, with connections to the Western Protectorate area of Lahej and Yemen, were educated middle-class intellectuals. The chief of them was Abdullah al-Giffri, who, with his two brothers, advocated an independent South Arabia, to be unified with Yemen in the new movement toward pan-Arabism. They attacked British policy and tried to create a coherent nationalist front. Popular support for the SAL was minimal, and it soon gave way to more radical and better-organized movements, but the British viewed it initially with some alarm.

When, in 1958, the al-Giffris tried to stir things up in Lahej, the Aden government quickly cracked down. They arrested the brothers for subversion, and although two of them escaped to Yemen, Abdullah al-Giffri was captured and flown off to Socotra, a bleak windswept island in the Indian Ocean some 525 miles from the Colony. This British version of Devil's Island was officially ruled by a sultan, one of the Mahri people, who inhabit the area around Mukalla and have been connected with the island since ancient times. The sultan's power, however, did not reach far on the mainland, nor was he really independent. His actions were monitored and effectively controlled by the British through their resident "advisers." It was not difficult for the Aden government to arrange Abdullah al-Giffri's banishment to Socotra.

To my surprise and delight I was assigned to fly down and report on the conditions of his imprisonment. Early on the morning of June 7, 1958, I woke, climbed out of bed, packed a few sandwiches and a camera, and drove out to the British military airfield near my flat in Khormasar. It was a typical bright Arabian day and the temperature even at that early hour was already 85 degrees Fahrenheit. I boarded a two-engined RAF Valetta transport packed with soldiers, and we waited in a cabin resembling a Turkish bath for the rather creaky but reliable vehicle to groan and shudder its way into flight.

Once aloft, however, my sense of confinement gave way to a feeling of exhilaration. To be lifted suddenly out of my everyday office routine, to escape a dreary social life, to have a full view of the great harbour from the air, to soar along the divide between ocean and towering cliffs with the whole mass of Arabia stretching away to the north — this was more like living, more like the adventure I had imagined my time in Aden would be.

Two hours went by very swiftly. Rocks and sand, sky and water — I was in the midst of a great and pleasing emptiness, and, except for an occasional tiny village or a coastal vessel on its way to one of the nearby ports, everything looked new-minted, fresh, and natural. It was like some vast arena awaiting a unique and spectacular presentation, and when Mukalla came into view, a gleaming array of white buildings, mosques, and warehouses set under black, towering cliffs, the dramatic effect was perfect.

On flew our Valletta, however, and came down at Riyan, an airstrip located at a village further up the coast, a bleak dusty place with a few white buildings, set between the sea-girt cliffs and the desolate inland plateau, or *djol*, that leads, after long miles, to the fabulous cities of the Hadhramaut.

When the plane had lumbered to a stop, we got out. I followed the pilot, co-pilot, and two officers of the Buffs Regiment. We climbed into waiting Land Rovers and were driven to one of the white buildings. Inside we found a table set for tea. There sat Arthur Watts, the British political adviser, Lieutenant-Colonel George Coles, the local military adviser, and his wife, together with an RAF Flight Lieutenant named Rudd, apparently the Colonel's assistant.

It seems that Colonel and Mrs. Coles had come over from Mukalla because they wanted to attend a Catholic service in Riyan. This was one of the oddest moments in all my time in South Arabia. Here I sat, in a hut on the edge of a shabby airfield beside the Indian Ocean, in the heart of old Islam, drinking tea with a trig Colonel and his chic and very attractive wife, who had come to hear Mass, while beside them lounged the chief British political representative in the whole area.

We had a chat, which turned out to be for me a kind of briefing. Watts explained that I was about to see one of the most interesting parts of the Arabian southlands. He was flying down to pick up the Sultan of Socotra in order to deposit him in Mukalla; I could visit al-Giffri and photograph him, although he would not be allowed to speak to me. The

Buffs officers explained that the soldiers on the Valetta were being transported there in order to relieve the contingent that watched over the exiled radical. Accommodations on the island were pretty rough, and the men, who had been on guard duty for six weeks, would be eager to get out.

Having drunk my tea, I boarded the plane again with Arthur Watts and the Buffs, and we took off and headed straight out over the empty ocean. It was another wonderful flight, a three-hundred-mile trip down to the island that left the coast far behind. We soared over white clouds, with the very blue sea glittering far below.

All the way there, Watts rattled off facts and ideas about the history, politics, economics, and geography of the area. He was a plump, dark-haired, restless man, sharp-eyed, quick of gesture, with a fluent, insinuating voice, a fascinating talker whose transparent surface and generous airs ("Come and stay with me in Mukalla any time — absolutely any time!") obviously concealed several dimensions of complexity.

The name Socotra, I was told, comes originally from Sanskrit and means "isle of the blessed." Some considered it to be the island where the hero Gilgamesh found Utnapishtim, the Babylonian Noah, who told him of the events of the flood — although nowadays we think of Bahrain as a more likely original. The island was also reputed to be the home of the legendary phoenix. Another etymology, of Arabic derivation, connects the name with words referring to a poured liquid, suggesting the island's production of precious fluids, notably frankincense, and the sap of the dragon's blood tree, *dracaena cinnabari*. This tree, its tentacled branches twined within a bushy umbrella-shaped top growth, also has mythical associations, for its crimson resin is called "the blood of two brothers," a reference probably linking it to some half-forgotten saga of ancient combat. This resin has long been used for many purposes — as a pigment, a glue, and a healing medicine.

If you look at a map you will see that the Socotran islands — there are four of them — lie just off the horn of Africa. Until ten million years ago, they formed part of that continent. Anciently isolated bird and plant species abound on the main island, and the seas around it are still being explored for unknown types of marine life.

Watts explained to me that Socotra was also linguistically isolated. The sultan and his close advisers were the only people in the world who could speak Arabic, English, and Socotran, an ancient dialect of Arabic, related to the Mahri language.

The island, which is about eighty miles long and twenty-two miles across, was the home (at that time) of only about 5,000 people, according to the very rough (and perhaps too low) British estimates. The original inhabitants, the Socotran-speakers, dwelt mostly inland, some in caves. A pastoral people who kept cattle, sheep, and goats, they had light skin and straight hair and looked rather European, possibly thanks to historical contact with Greek traders. On the coasts lived fishermen, mostly of African descent, ex-slaves from the Swahili coast, while resident Arabs, related to the Mahri, occupied the wadis and cultivated the date palms. Socotra's tiny capital, Hadibu, in the north of the island, sits among palm groves in a great semi-circular plain surrounded by mist-shrouded mountains.

As our flight brought us ever closer to this remarkable island, Arthur Watts continued his briefing. "Although we'll only be there for several hours, you can at least get the feel of the place," he told me. "You can look around a little, after you've had a glance at al-Giffri."

We flew on, he fell silent at last, and I was able once again to sink into the experience of gazing down on that tranquil ocean. Before Socotra appeared, I felt almost hypnotized by the glittering water, lulled half-asleep by the hum of the plane's engines, but I was completely receptive to the sight of that long narrow island rising up out of the sea like the arched back of some half-submerged ancient sea beast.

A beautiful place, it seemed, but in no conventional sense: reddish rocks that dissolved under one's gaze in shimmering sunlight, bursts of green foliage, dusty plains, and mountains swathed in mist. The island appeared both mirage-like and very solid, with a touch of the other-worldy about it. We might as well have been landing in the heart of a newly discovered Martian landscape. We circled the airstrip several times; it was a mere track on a vast plain stretching away to the mountains. It appeared to be quite empty.

When we bumped down, I saw the camp, five or six green army tents with soldiers and native troops lounging about. They looked disorganized; it turned out they had not been advised of our exact arrival time.

The plane taxied to a stop, the door opened, we stepped down; heat and dust enveloped us. A strong wind was blowing, whipping at the tent flaps. The temperature was nearly 98 degrees Fahrenheit.

A line of native soldiers sprang up. They wore khaki uniforms enlivened by colourful red-and-white headdresses. Arthur Watts reviewed them in practised fashion. All around milled many native Socotrans, who had come to see their sultan off. Buff Regiment officers appeared, greeted their replacements, and led me away to one of the tents, where they offered me some "jungle juice," which looked like warm and fly-blown Kool-Aid and tasted equally foul. When they explained that there was quite a bit of malaria and typhoid about, I lost some of my eagerness to explore. It would take several hours to unload, reload, and service the plane, but not long enough for me to get away from this desolate plateau, which resembled nothing so much as an exotic Purgatorio, where al-Giffri and his guards were sharing, almost equally, the misery of an absurd punishment, decreed by nameless, distant powers.

While the soldiers who had flown down with me were unloading their equipment, including a much-needed gas refrigerator, I was taken over to al-Giffri's barbed-wire enclosure. There he sat, moustached and grinning, perched on a camp chair just inside a large, shabby tent. He was having his hair cut, and it was a vision that for me confirmed the complete absurdity of the whole situation. The British imperial style, often ruthless, was occasionally marked by a touch of unintentional jocularity, deriving no doubt from a strenuous attempt to remain human and civilized while enforcing policies that guaranteed the very reverse.

I took my photographs and was driven some way across the plain, from where the Valetta, the tents, and the lounging figures of the Arabs and the British were nearly swallowed up by the vast landscape. I picked up some reddish stones and put them in my pocket, plucked a few plants to send home, and rejoined the surprisingly good-humoured British soldiers.

After a while the sultan himself emerged from his tent. This was Isa ibn Ali ibn Salim, a skinny little man with a bony, hawk-like face that peered out from under a black and white headdress. He was attired in a purple jacket and wore a sword in a gleaming solid gold scabbard — the next-to-last sultan ever to rule over the island of the blessed. The Mahra Sultanate of Qishn and Socotra, dating back to 1549, the time of the Portuguese occupation, would end rather suddenly on October 16, 1967. A few weeks later, the People's Republic of Yemen would take over, and the era of the hereditary petty chieftains would officially cease to be.

At that moment, however, as the sultan's considerable baggage was loaded on the Valetta, his people saluted him, both uniformed guards and a crowd of loyal subjects, huddling in the howling wind to say goodbye to their master. Isa ben Ali took note of this homage, then, with a burly, grim-faced man, his official executioner, and a few shrewd-looking Arab advisers, he climbed on the plane. From his tent al-Giffri watched stoically, the figure of a doubtful future gazing on the embodiment of a shabby, sleepy past.

Landing again at Riyan, we waited for the sultan to review an honour guard sent to welcome him, after which he departed in a limousine for

Mukalla. I went back into the white hut by the airfield for another bout of tea and conversation. In the background a phonograph played Rachmaninoff's Prelude in C Sharp Minor, a composition without much sunshine, but in its relentless grandeur appropriate to the day's scenery, and lugubriously presageful of the gloomy things to come.

Back in my Khormaksar apartment, settling down after a shower and some solid food, I felt a kind of sadness take hold of me. Just then the political struggles I had caught a glimpse of seemed fascinating, but from one point of view pretty irrelevant. The sea and the land, those deserted beaches I had looked at all day, the coastal heights beyond, the amazing island vistas — surely they would outlast the memories of plots and prisoners, of individual sultans and their colonial advisers? Already I missed the spectacular openness of that littoral scenery, its resonant emptiness, its elemental contrasts of light and dark, of hard rock and surging pliant water. I missed red-hued Socotra and prayed it would never be marred by a resort, a tourist hotel, or a superhighway. Yet having delved into much science fiction, and taken in many dystopian visions of what might turn out to be our overcrowded and mechanized future, I knew that whatever political die was cast, the Arabian coast and the islands would surely be transformed. I also knew that such changes would be called progress, as they always are, especially when they are most destructive.

None of this, of course, would go into the dispatch I would write next morning for the State Department. There I would report on al-Giffri, paraphrase some of Arthur Watts's thoughts on the political situation, and speculate about the upshot of the British repression of the nationalists — whereas what really obsessed me was the thought that I might well never see the island of Socotra again. I was clearly an over-pessimistic twenty-two-year-old, the victim of my own comfortable kind of *Weltschmerz*, with far too little trust in my own capacity to make new discoveries during my remaining time in the Colony. In fact, I needn't have worried. All was not lost. I still had quite a few singular experiences ahead of me.

TWELVE

The Death Ship

Friday morning, October 31, 1958. "Here's something interesting," Cathy O'Hara announces, waving a telegram at me. It is a signal just received from the captain of an American military transport ship, the *U.S.S. Lieutenant Robert Craig*, anchored in Aden's outer harbour. The captain's message is not the usual perfunctory request for some minor consular intervention; on the contrary, it sounds distinctly frightened. One of the ship's crewmen, an electrician named James T. Hill, has disappeared and may have been murdered. The *Robert Craig* is in a state of terror.

I climb on board a launch at the Prince of Wales Pier and head for the outer harbour. It is a beautiful Aden morning, sunlight glittering on the water, oil tankers and a few cargo ships floating lightly at anchor. We motor past these, the gulls soar and cry, and, as we move, the rocky cliffs that encircle the harbour take on a purer definition. I try to recall a few lines from a poem by Oliver St.John Gogarty about the "lapsing, unsoilable whispering sea," although right now there is no whispering, and not a touch of roaring majesty: the sea is merely companionable, comforting in its bright, low-keyed equanimity.

When I catch sight of the *Robert Craig*, however, my blithe mood darkens a little. This is not from any conjured-up melodrama of expectation; the grey ship, lying low in the water, is actually a grim sight — sleek and almost menacing, with a high bow that slopes down amidships, a white bridge topped by a single stack, steely cranes fore and aft that rise like jury-rigged crosses or bare gallows trees. From stem to stern, right down to its brick or blood-red paint border at the water line, this ship is an instrument of pure utility, but lacking any Bauhaus charm.

I go up the ladder, survey the nearly empty deck, and greet the second officer, who takes me at once to the captain's cabin. The skipper's name is Claus Lampe. A middle-aged man, slightly bowed, with a grey careworn face, he speaks with a slight German accent. My youthful appearance does nothing to reassure him, while for my part I am surprised to find the panic of his telegram perfectly expressive of the atmosphere of the ship. As we leave the deck, faces peer from behind containers, figures move between the cargo booms. From time to time, recounting his story, Lampe glances nervously around, then pauses and listens intently, as if he were expecting a visit from the Gestapo or the Golem. Mr. Benson, the second officer, stands guard outside the cabin door.

Lampe's story is simple, at least on the surface. Jimmie Hill, a seaman-electrician, has been missing since about 12:30 p.m. the day before. At that time the ship was on the high seas at 14° 50' north latitude, and 49° 50' west longitude. What were later to be verified as bloodstains had been found at the stern on the port side near a door leading to two levels. The upper level held the carpenter's shop and two storerooms, and the lower was occupied by the ship's steering engine room. The bloodstains led from the ship's side railing across about fifteen feet of deck and down the stairwell, stopping on the upper landing. There were two smudged fingerprints in blood on the bulkhead by the stairs. On the deck and the stairs were rag marks where someone had attempted to wipe up the blood.

Most of this I verified for myself, after reassuring the captain that we could help him. By this time my own delight and excitement were as vivid as Lampe's gloom. I could hardly wait to get back to the consulate and report.

Before I departed, however, the captain led me to his cabin, closed the door, and addressed me with a ferocious intensity, speaking in a whisper. What he said was quite clear, but I felt as well something lurking behind his words.

"We've searched everywhere. Somebody murdered Hill and threw him overboard. You've got to bring the police. Whoever did it might kill … any of us. I don't want anything to do with him."

"You sound as if you know who did it."

He shook his head, wiped his sweating face. "I know what I know. And, believe me, the crew are afraid. Can you get the police on board — right away?"

"I hope so … Today, I hope. Don't worry, I'll come back as soon as I can."

"Tell them to bring some weapons. If you knew what we were up against, you'd understand. Everyone's afraid. We don't want to spend another night with a murderer."

"Captain Lampe, I'm required to conduct an investigation."

"You're going to question these seamen? Do you know what you're up against? These are tough men …"

I smiled, left him there, and returned to the consulate. I could hardly wait to report to Bill Crawford. Esmail, however, intercepted me. When I told him the story, his eyes beamed with anticipation. Before I could blink, he was reading me the appropriate regulations of the consular handbook. His conclusion, that it was well within our authority to conduct the investigation, pleased me no end. We needed a police guard, however — it was the captain's specific request. I put through a call to R.H. Stewart, the Assistant Police Commissioner, with whom I had a good rapport. He was quite willing to supply the guards, but there was a problem. That morning there had been labour protests and marches in Crater. All available men were assigned. Perhaps we could try the army?

This was something Crawford would have to approve. He did so, to my delight, and even paved the way with a call to the local British commandant. Since the situation on board seemed a bit ambiguous, the British decided to take no chances. I would meet that evening with a contingent of soldiers and together we would board the ship. With the soldiers keeping order, I would conduct an investigation beginning that very night.

We telegraphed Captain Lampe to this effect and at the appointed hour I met the soldiers at the staging area. This was at a dingy barracks shed in Tarshyne, just beyond the Prince of Wales pier. In a dim, small room Esmail and I — along with one junior naval officer — stood by while a young lieutenant briefed eighteen soldiers. The whole scene had a Jack Armstrong quality about it — an air of bravura adventure and unreality — but I enjoyed every minute of it. The lieutenant's briefing, however, was deadly serious; we might have been about to board an enemy destroyer. When he had finished, he gave the order to fix bayonets; we made our way in near darkness to the jetty, where the Royal Navy launch waited for us.

As our launch churned through the murky harbour waters the lieutenant continued to give orders. We had asked Lampe to leave a ladder for us. The lieutenant would go up first, I would follow, then the soldiers. Esmail would wait on the launch, together with a couple of guards and the naval officer, until everything was secure on board.

By night, the *Robert Craig* looked even more sinister than she had by day. Inwardly, I kept questioning my own reaction to the ship. Surely I was simply projecting onto her my own foreboding, my own excitement. Surely she was just a good solid working transport ship. But no, when I studied her at that moment, her masthead light shining above us, her bridge, deck, and hull gleaming dully in the Aden night, it struck me again how bleak and somehow heartless she looked: a perfect setting for a mean or spiteful act of inhumanity.

We hove to; the ship towered above us, waves slapped at metal. We cut the engine and bumped close to the swaying ladder. The lieutenant drew his pistol and started climbing; I followed. The soldiers came up behind me. They scrambled aboard and deployed precisely as the lieutenant had specified in the briefing. Captain Lampe and the first mate stood by, their relief quite apparent. They did not seem to think this show of military force excessive. To me there was a touch here — although only a touch — of comic opera.

The questioning would take place in the captain's cabin. Esmail came aboard and he and I, together with the lieutenant and two soldiers, followed Lampe there.

With armed guards at the door, the captain began to confide in us.

"You have to arrest him now. We're all frightened. It's Robinson for sure that did it."

"Who's Robinson?"

"The chief electrician. He's got a violent temper. He's a black man from Brooklyn. They were gambling — four or five of them. Hill was a big winner, almost a card sharp."

"Wait a minute! How do you know Robinson did it? We're here to take evidence, not to arrest anyone."

"I saw him that night. He was carrying a bucket. At the port side after-end. Washing away the bloodstains, I know that. I didn't want to go near him. Why don't you talk to him right away?"

I considered this and said, "No, let's do it this way. We'll talk to his roommate first, then anyone else involved in any way. We'll get Robinson's testimony later when I know what questions to ask him."

"Sounds like a good idea," said the lieutenant.

Esmail and I took over the captain's cabin and began to interrogate the crew.

I enjoyed this very much. It had a touch of Perry Mason, but thanks to the eerie night atmosphere and the almost palpable fear on board the *Robert Craig*, there was a whiff of *Macbeth*. I swore in each witness and read them the following statement:

I am a Foreign Service Officer of the United States of America. I desire to question you under oath concerning the disappearance of Jimmie Hill from aboard the U.S.S. Robert Craig. *Any statement that you make must be freely and voluntarily given and may be used by the government as evidence in any proceedings against you or any other therein. Do you understand?*

Following this introduction, I asked the questions; Esmail took dictation, typed the statement, and each witness in turn read and signed it.

I still have the transcripts of my interrogation and I can vouch for its thoroughness. My object was to establish everyone's whereabouts, to probe into the relationships among the gamblers, and to establish some kind of motive for the murder. I succeeded in pinpointing the gambling group, uncovered some of the animosities among them, and made clear by my questioning that the murderer could have ambushed Jimmie Hill without showing himself for more than a few seconds on any of the main decks.

After the first night's questioning, Captain Lampe approached me. "Mr. Henighan, you must have legal experience."

Over the next few days a motley cast of characters appeared before me. I sat behind the captain's desk and questioned everyone from Charlie the Wiper and "Sparks" to most of the engineers, carpenters, and firemen on board. Esmail recorded their testimony and occasionally suggested a line of questioning. The British guards were eventually replaced by u.s. sailors from visiting warships. And when the u.s. vessels departed, a few days later, these men were assigned to the consulate, so that Captain Lampe had guards on board during the whole time of our investigation.

I quickly extended the scope of my interrogation. Reports were coming in that Chief Electrician Cecil Robinson, the captain's prime suspect, was behaving rather strangely. On the way to Aden, one crewman reported, he had declared, "I feel like killing someone tonight." Before Hill was discovered missing, Robinson had asked one of the officers to examine a bucket, possibly the same one that the captain had seen him carrying near the scene of the crime. In Aden, Robinson reportedly suggested to his mates that information about the gambling be suppressed; he was also seen peering over the side to monitor the arrival and departure of the investigators, myself included.

Quite early in the game we questioned Robinson himself. He was a large well-built man in his mid-thirties and he answered most of my questions in a pretty matter-of-fact manner, but without making very much eye contact. He could not, however, establish an alibi, since no one testified to having seen him during the crucial hours of the night of the murder. He claimed to have won money during the poker games with Hill that preceded his assistant's disappearance — although it was eventually established that he lost something like a thousand dollars.

After the interrogation Robinson declared that the next time he appeared before us to answer questions he would insist on being represented by a lawyer.

A couple of days later I got a call from Commissioner Stewart. A body had been pulled from the harbour. Could I come over and have a look? I met Stewart and examined quite a few photographs of what was left of

Jimmie Hill. It was not a pretty sight. Most of his face had been eaten away; both arms were missing and a leg. The lively sport of the midnight interrogations gave way to some serious private reflections on mortality. Aden had a way of stimulating such moments. Would I like to see the actual remains? Stewart asked. I thought not.

Reports of the murder were spreading through the Colony. I was suddenly very popular at cocktail parties. The armed intervention seemed especially to delight the British. Someone suggested that this was the first time a British military force had boarded and occupied an American ship since the War of 1812. *Newsweek* picked up the story, garbling some of it, and I wrote a corrective letter, which was published in the magazine on May 18, 1959, at the time of Robinson's trial. My letter was quite straightforward but elicited a reminder from Crawford that all such correspondence should be submitted to the State Department for approval. This struck me as rather pedantic.

My inquiry lasted nearly a week. At that point the Naval Commander of Middle East Forces, who had been kept informed of developments by Captain Lampe, ordered two naval intelligence agents flown down from Naples to take over the investigation. Those were innocent days in so far as forensic science went, and despite the arrival of the professionals there was no striking breakthrough in the case. The agents simply ran a few lie detector tests and coordinated and expanded the information we had developed.

The naval men were generous in their praise of what Esmail and I had done and suggested that Bill Crawford place some kind of commendation in my file. I don't think he did this, but at the time it hardly seemed to matter. The real issue for me was an internal one, one connected with my personal values, and with my sense of reality.

For I was certainly convinced, as was Esmail, that Cecil Robinson had murdered Jimmie Hill. The motive was there, the opportunity was there, and Robinson's actions betrayed his guilt at several points. Yet despite my belief and conviction I made little real attempt to press Robinson all the way to the end. Why?

For one thing I was struck by his position as a black man among an otherwise white crew. The good Captain Lampe's fearful allusions to "what he might do," although far from overtly racist, seemed to conjure up, however indirectly, the stereotype of the dangerous, prowling black killer. Then, too, I had been trained by the example of a thousand detective stories to expect the murderer to be fairly hard to identify. (We demand that the solutions of our literary mysteries be less than obvious. As one of my friends exclaimed in disappointment after finishing

Dostoevsky's *The Brothers Karamazov*, "Seven hundred pages and the butler did it!") The Robinson solution seemed far too easy.

These things I saw at the time. But there was much that I missed. For one thing, although I partially sensed that the *Robert Craig* story held an image of the outcast seaman worthy of the tales of Joseph Conrad, I overlooked the symbolic power of that white man's corpse washed up on the shores of the Colony. That mutilated corpse, Captain Lampe's fears — these were a link, however tenuous, between the racism at home and the racism I had found in the colony. Cecil Robinson's undoubted isolation and rage were surely more than personal burdens. When I left Washington, blacks were still forced to ride in the back of public buses; America's major civil rights battles were just beginning. With the arrival of the *Robert Craig* and the disclosure of its secrets, the Aden shore had become an uncomfortable passageway between far distant and nearby scenes of oppression and conflict.

Stories of the murder spread beyond Aden. Several of my young State Department colleagues — the ones I had met at the Foreign Service Institute — saw my letter to *Newsweek* and kept me posted of later events in the Robinson case. At the time of the trial, the New York *Daily News* ran the typically graphic headline, "CHARGED WITH TOSSING PAL TO SHARKS AT SEA." The news services also highlighted the story. The prosecution argued that Robinson had clubbed Jimmie Hill to death and thrown him overboard "into waters teeming with sharks." Robinson finally admitted disposing of Hill, but claimed he had been dead when he hit the water. He had thrown the older man down a hatch and killed him, he said, after Hill made "a homosexual advance" to him. Robinson pleaded guilty to voluntary manslaughter and was sentenced to ten years in prison.

The truth underlying the grim outcome may never be known. Fear and desire, Freud intimated, are the two underlying elements of any good story. The third is perhaps mystery, or ambiguity. Life and literature meet at certain depths to suggest how inconclusive is our "factual" knowledge, how tinged with uncertainty all our profound experiences. The "uncanny" is no mere literary trope but a very real potential of human experience. Nor should this surprise us, since, as the Russian writer Ivan Bunin once affirmed, "the creepiest thing in the world is the heart of man."

THIRTEEN

Bonjour, M. Besse

Many months after the conclusion of the *Robert Craig* affair, I arrived, very early one morning, at the Crater office of A.B. Besse Red Sea Ltd., the largest of the Aden import-export firms. Tony Besse, heir and master of this powerful and far-flung trading company, greeted me with a smile and signalled his servant to bring some coffee.

"I see you've been writing to *Newsweek*, Tom." He was referring to my corrective letter to that magazine on its coverage of the trial of Cecil Robinson. We talked about the murder for a while. This was the first time I had interviewed Besse alone.

Young Tony — dark, slim, intense, bursting with barely suppressed energy and anger — the son of a famous father, and the most important of the Red Sea merchants, could veer suddenly from opinionated ferocity to a world-weary, blasé manner that would have done credit to any decadent poet.

Self-contained and often silent, Besse had no use for stupidity, slovenliness, or indecision. A Frenchman whose birthright included an anglophile heritage of increasingly dubious political value, Besse constantly railed at British policy in Aden, without necessarily having a coherent alternative. Perhaps inwardly he knew that the real alternative would have meant the end of his empire and the destruction of the very system that had made his family rich.

While Michael and Coco Sterner saw Tony and his wife Christiane fairly often, my encounters with Besse were rather limited, but that morning he was direct and considerate in a way that almost surprised me. This may have been the result of the Sterners' good will toward me, but no doubt I also owed it to my central role in the *Robert Craig* affair, and to the fact that I had, with the confidence of youth, contributed some pretty strong opinions on literature at one of the Besse dinners, given for a visiting Parisian intellectual in their villa at Ras Marshag. It may also have had some connection with the Aden regatta of the previous January, in which Tony and I had raced together.

Although I had never been in a sailboat before, the Sterners lured me into joining them and the Besses for the annual race in Aden harbour. This was a typically "colonial" event, jolly and serious at the same time, and a good excuse for sporting on the water, a fairly rare occurrence in the colony. I suppose it was the ever-present sharks that prevented sailing from really taking hold in Aden, for otherwise the conditions were perfect, and that day of the regatta was no exception. The sky was a blazing blue and the water calm and beautiful. Sails dotted the harbour like the wings of white butterflies. The Sterners had naturally decided to race together, but for some reason — perhaps because she was pregnant — Christiane Besse did not participate. I was therefore chosen to be Tony's sailing partner.

The shore was alive with activity, cars and Land Rovers parked by the water, a battle dress of bathing suits and cotton T-shirts visible everywhere, various crews scrambling on board. I scrambled with the rest, although with some trepidation, wondering if I would succeed in spoiling things for my imperious captain. I needn't have worried. Tony Besse was a ferocious martinet, an Ahab by way of Captain Bligh. He took this race *seriously*. I didn't have to think; all I had to do was shut up, pay attention, and jump when he said to jump. In fact, my main job seemed to be to drape my body as far out over the side as I could, and to duck under the swinging boom whenever we tacked.

Although several boats capsized, including the Sterners', and others dithered along to no effect, the Besse team leapt bravely ahead. After a while I realized that I might actually cross the finish line without falling out of the boat. Or let me put it this way: I knew I wouldn't *dare* fall out of the boat until I was signalled to do so by the master. I hung on, and at last — to my utter astonishment — we found ourselves in a small group of craft that were running for the prize.

I remember that race as vividly as I remember anything in Aden; it seemed to go on forever. If the harbour was beautiful from the shore it was ten times more appealing as we flew across the water. There were glimpses of sails, of the sky, of the wavering shoreline, of bodies splashing in the water, and the sound of Tony's voice barking at me as my body twisted, stretched, leaned, and shifted, in response to tersely delivered orders.

At last we came near the finish. I blinked; I gulped. We were heading the pack. In fact we had only a single competitor, the boat of Paul Ries, another Aden merchant and the great rival of Besse, with whom we were running neck and neck.

Tony *could not* lose. A final straining effort, a last barrage of shouted instructions, and, incredibly, we were there, slipping across the finish line a few yards ahead of Ries. I could hardly believe it. Besse relaxed and nodded his satisfaction. When we landed, he showed me his hands, which had grasped the tiller with such intensity, with such clutching power, that the skin had rubbed away, leaving the flesh of his palms raw and bleeding.

We stood on the shore. I was a bit dazed, but it was off for drinks and lunch at the Besse villa. And since my trousers and bathing suit were both soaked, I was lent a pair of my captain's pants to wear for the occasion. A suitably ritualistic gesture, marking my rite of passage into the Aden community and the great world.

I knew of course that more famous carcasses than mine had been exhilarated and stressed out beyond belief by the Besse intensity. Tony's father Antonin, the originator of the family dynasty in Arabia, was a man of strong charisma. He had known (and disliked) Rimbaud. While the famous poet — working as a clerk in Aden — only dreamed of wealth, M. Besse senior amassed a great fortune by staking and preserving his claim as the leading entrepreneur in the whole Red Sea area. Besse senior lived until the 1960s, and rumour had it that his sons Tony and Peter had fought over the succession, with the younger son's unquenchable ambition triumphing eventually over Peter's less urgent claim. In 1950 the aging Antonin Besse had founded St. Antony's College at Oxford, this being only the best-known of his many worthy educational projects. A commemorative statue to him still stands in the college.

Antonin comes across vividly in a hilarious account written by Evelyn Waugh, who visited Aden Colony in 1930. At that time Waugh was already the celebrated author of *Decline and Fall*, while *Vile Bodies*, his second comic masterpiece, had just appeared. Waugh's account of his Aden trip appeared originally in *Remote People* (1931), but is more easily accessible in his collected travel essays, *When the Going Was Good*, which came out in 1945, just after *Brideshead Revisited* had added to the writer's fame. In his preface to *When the Going Was Good*, Waugh predicts the hippie travel era, which was more than a decade away, and anticipates our present mania for "international cultural relations." He also explains that he "never aspired to be a great traveller. I was simply a young man, typical of my age; we travelled as a matter of course."

Waugh delighted in Aden, and no wonder. The Colony, tinged by absurdity, seems to have been specially created by some malignant sprite to serve the purposes of a Waugh satire. Visiting an open-air cinema and noticing that most of the patrons are asleep, Waugh declares that it is "one of the odd characteristics of the Aden climate that it is practically impossible to remain both immobile and conscious." The hotel food has only two flavours, "tomato ketchup and Worcestershire sauce," while "the bathroom consists of a cubicle in which a tin can is suspended on a rope.... The bather stands on a slippery cement floor and pulls a string releasing a jet of water over his head and back; for a heavy extra charge it is possible, with due notice, to have the water warmed."

Waugh's account of an Aden Boy Scout meeting, which fails miserably every known canon of political correctness, is nonetheless treasurable. His story reaches a climax, however, in his encounter with "Mr. Leblanc," in whom one immediately recognizes Tony Besse's famous father.

Mr. Leblanc entertains his visitor ("It is not a luxurious wine, but I am fond of it; it grows on a little estate of my own in the south of France"), then invites him for a stroll, which turns out to be an ascent of Shamsan, Aden's highest peak, forming — as I have explained — one rim of the crater in which the old city lies. The terrified Waugh watches his host, "whose whole body seemed prehensile," scramble up sheer rock faces. He follows and, after a few hours, reaches the highest point of the crater. They descend to the beach on the other side and Waugh notes that "variety was added to this last phase by the fact that we were now in the full glare of the sun, which had been beating on the cliffs from noon until they were blistering hot." The whole experience "is kept fresh in my mind by recurrent nightmares." On the beach Mr. Leblanc goes for a swim, expressing his preference for bathing there and not at the club. "They have a screen to keep out the sharks — while in this bay, only last month, two boys were devoured."

Quite a different picture of Antonin Besse emerges in the letters of Freya Stark, certainly one of the best writers of her kind in modern times. (But what exactly was her kind? I hesitate to call her an explorer, for she did not bring hitherto unknown regions to the attention of her European contemporaries, yet "travel writer" seems quite inadequate. Whatever term we choose, Stark's books are unique and full of interest.) Born in Paris of British parents, she began her career as a reporter in Baghdad in the early 1930s. While there she visited the Luristan region and produced her first important work, *The Valley of the Assassins*, in 1934. She was in Aden between 1935 and 1938, travelling mostly in the Hadhramaut. *The Southern Gates of Arabia*, published in 1938, tells a fascinating story, very much from a woman's point of view, of life in the old Protectorates. Stark rode her donkey from the coast inland, taking pictures everywhere, visiting the harems, and capturing landscape and people in sharply etched and memorable prose. More than once she got seriously ill, and in the end had to be airlifted out by the RAF. During the early part of the Second World War she returned to Aden as Assistant Information Officer.

The Southern Gates of Arabia is vivid with impressions of a vanished world, but in a curious way impersonal. Reading it, one gets little sense of Freya Stark's emotional life, which just at that moment was far from placid. Her letters tell a different story. There we learn of her association during her Aden visits and residence with Antonin Besse. Freya Stark and Antonin Besse became very close; in fact they certainly had a "romance," which, partially out of consideration for Madame Besse, she seems to have wanted to continue on an elevated and purely "spiritual" level. When this proved impossible, Freya Stark backed away. None of this appears in The Southern Gates of Arabia, although in her letters she is quite frank about her feelings. What's more, her descriptions in her letters of her excursions with Besse have a poetry that is not matched in her travel book.

> We motored down to the port; found the launch and Somali chauffeur waiting with the rising moon, and were off with a most delightful feeling of escapade. It was such fun. We passed by all the lights of Aden — people dancing in bungalows, sailors feasting on the ships: we made for the entrance point; the sea and wind freshened, we were round the corner under the black hills and rocks, Orion above and Taurus and the Pleiades. Then no lights at all, except three yellow and a green from some ship travelling at sea; the spray in a light rain on our faces; M. Besse and I lying in great comfort on cushions, while he kept the tiller with one hand.

When I sat in Tony Besse's office that Aden morning, however, I knew very little of this romantic family background. I drank exquisite coffee, and was treated first to a near-boastful exposition of his strenuous daily working routine (designed to banish any notion I might have that he was a dilettante playing at empire). Then followed the Besse indictment of British policy in Aden. Here his exasperation reached a high pitch, and I could see that it did so not because he was anti-British, but because he knew that the success or failure of the British in Aden would determine the future of his company there.

Too many of the colonial administrators, Besse told me, were incompetent. British policy was ad hoc in the wrong way; there was still too much of the romantic schoolboy tradition among the resident officers. The British had mistakenly put their faith in a federation of the South Arabian shaikhdoms, antagonizing the Imam of Yemen in the process. This was the twentieth century; new ideas were needed. Nasser was in the ascendancy, and Radio Cairo beamed its message of Arab brotherhood, its anti-western slogans, to the Aden streets, messages that the Soviets were cleverly reinforcing. It was quite clear that Aden's original status as part of the Bombay administration continued to taint British policy. The British were still acting as if they were the guardians of Empire on the northwest frontier of the old Raj. Besides, there were struggles among the administrative factions: the intelligence people wanted one thing, the Colonial Office another, and the armed forces demanded something else.

"But what should the British do?" I asked him. "What kind of policy should they have?"

"A clear and definite policy based on the idea that the ultimate goal is an Aden democracy based on rule of law, accompanied by the notion that for the immediate future they are here to stay. They should point to the progress already made and indicate that certain reforms are possible, but not tack with every wind that blows from the desert or from the United Arab Republic."

I listened; I took notes; the coffee dwindled. An Arab secretary arrived to indicate a pressing appointment. I shook hands, mumbled a few words of thanks, and was shown out of Besse's headquarters. I headed through the dusty Aden street toward my Volkswagen, parked just off the Aidrus Road. An Arab, dressed in a *longhi* and sandals, drifted past. He was using a stick to drive his goat down an alley. I dodged a man on a bicycle. Down the street I could see a mosque, and a school. On one side, far above, rose the old fortifications, behind which lay the Hindu burial ground. Beyond that was Ras Marshag, where in the Besse villa I had dined on gazelle shot by Tony and Christiane themselves and served with a sauce poivrade and a purée of chestnuts. The wine had flowed that evening, and the conversation had been about Parisian intellectual life.

The impact of Tony Besse's strong personality stayed with me. I thought of the regatta, of his hands rubbed raw by fierce clutching, of his exasperation, of his determination to endure whatever history thrust on him in Aden. It would take more than the Besse tenacity and arrogance, however, to survive in the fiery cauldron that Aden would soon become. With a final glance upward, at the white ramparts of the Parsee tower of silence, I climbed into my car and headed back to Steamer Point.

FOURTEEN

Moving into Terror

February 11, 1959, a bright winter day in Aden. I sat with hundreds of others on uncomfortable improvised chairs at the Champion Lines, British Forces Headquarters, Khormaksar, and watched the official inauguration of the Federation of the Arab Emirates of the South.

It was a curiously hollow ceremony. The Government Guards marched onto the parade ground. Sir William Luce, the Governor, accompanied by the Secretary of State for the Colonies, A.T. Lennox-Boyd, took the seventeen-gun royal salute. Then more marching, a few speeches and the signing of the relevant documents, a symbolic change of headdress by the Government Guards, still more marching, a *feu de joie* from the guns, and it was over.

In my notebook I wrote later that day, "What does all this mean? Everything so forced — seems out of touch with anything. Just another British charade?"

In fact, the creation of the Federation brought the British very nearly to a point of no return in Aden. It was like a move in the middle of a chess game that, in retrospect, can be seen to have led almost inevitably to an impossible position, to checkmate.

The weakness of the British position lay in the disparity between the territory they ruled in Aden Colony and the much vaster territory they controlled in the Protectorates. The Protectorates were tribal, relatively undeveloped, and backward. Roads and airfields were primitive, poverty and famine almost endemic, educational opportunities circumscribed. True, the Qu'aiti and Kathiri states in the Eastern Protectorate, largely because of remittances from abroad, had developed to a rudimentary urban phase. But even they fell far short of what had been created in Aden itself, which had a full infrastructure, hospitals, schools, a diversity of business investments, modern conveniences, and an educated middle class.

The Federation signing brought together six Western Protectorate states — one shaikhdom, three sultanates, and two emirates — which agreed to the central control of certain services, such as customs, communications, education, and health. But the new structure had been imposed from on high, by the tribal rulers and the British government. It had nothing to do with the will of the people of the Protectorate, nor did it create a means to ascertain that will.

In order to convey how inadequate, indeed how disastrous the British plan was, it is necessary for me at this point to go beyond my personal story and mention a few events that took place during the next several years.

Once it had set its course, the Aden government moved with determination to overcome the difficulties surrounding the entry of the Colony itself into the new political structure. In the background was the fiasco of the Suez invasion, the continued rise in the prestige of Nasser, the Cyprus crisis, the Kenya troubles, radical regime changes in Iraq, uncertainty in Jordan, Lebanon, and Kuwait — all of which seemed to cry out for a shoring up of British power in the strategically important Aden base. Furthermore, in close proximity to Aden, the Russians had been establishing more and more influence in Yemen, supplying arms to the Imam, while the inclusion of that country as at least a token adjunct in the newly formed United Arab Republic increased pressure on the Protectorate rulers.

Clearly, the British could hardly rest easy with the loose Protectorate Federation of 1959. If South Arabia was to have any substantial unity, Aden itself had to be brought into the picture.

That, however, was a very difficult task, plagued by many problems internal to the Colony, including religious differences: many Shia-Zaydis had come from the north to work in Aden port amid the Sunni-Shafti majority. It was further complicated by the fact that in 1962 a revolution in Yemen ended the Imamate and installed a pro-Nasser regime. This, in the eyes of some Aden Arabs, opened up new possibilities for the south, while others saw it as a threat. Britain refused to recognize the new Yemen government (although the United States did so), and passed the merger bill on November 13, 1962, which was implemented in Aden in January 1963. The federation of Amirates (or Emirates) became The Federation of South Arabia, and the passage of the new measure was accompanied by a more stringent British intolerance of the Aden opposition, including the imprisonment of one of Federation's most vocal opponents, Abdullah al-Asnaj, a union leader and head of the People's Socialist Party (PSP), as it came to be known, at the time the most popular political group in Aden.

Overseas criticism of this strategy extended far beyond the Yemen and Egypt. A 1963 United Nations report condemned the Federation plan as part of a transparent attempt by Britain to retain control in Southern Arabia. In the same year the u.n. General Assembly, by a vote of 77 to 11, called for self-determination for the Colony and the Arab south. The British replied with a reaffirmation of the principle of "independence as soon as possible," and suggested that the Protectorate states themselves had initiated the drive toward federation, while the inclusion of Aden Colony was but a logical step toward pre-independence unity. This of course begged the question of what portion of the population of the Protectorates actually had a stake in what had been established, and overlooked the fact that the majority of people in the Colony viewed the union with the tribal rulers as undesirable and incompatible with the Colony's more forward-looking development.

In December 1963 an attempt was made to assassinate High Commissioner Kennedy Trevaskis at Aden airport. An innocent bystander was killed and one of the High Commissioner's aides mortally wounded. Urban violence, which had been sporadic, began to escalate.

In the early stages, the British completely misread the situation. Obsessed with the opposition of their known Aden opponents, al-Asnaj, the psp, and — after April 1965 — al-Asnaj's newly formed Organization for the Liberation of the Occupied Sousth (olos), and with the dissident factions within Aden and the Federation, the British failed to counter the terrorist threat with appropriate measures. Above all, they failed to follow the shift in terrorist power from one group to another, or to understand — until it was too late — the coherent nature of the assault on their power in Aden and the Protectorate.

In January 1966, al-Asnaj had succeeded in establishing a unified resistance group, the Front for the Liberation of Occupied South Yemen (flosy), combining some members of the rival National Liberation Front (nlf), also created in 1965) and his own olos group. Hard-core members of the nlf, however, rejected this unification, and the nlf continued to act independently, and with ruthless effectiveness, until the final showdown with flosy immediately following British evacuation in November 1967.

The nlf program for achieving independence, although it overlapped at some points with that of flosy, was far more comprehensive. As Julian Paget has noted in his book *Last Post: Aden 1964–1967*, terrorist methods in Aden included 1) intimidation of the population by propaganda and assassination, 2) neutralization of government sources of intelligence by similar methods, 3) disruption of everyday working life by means of strikes and protests, and 4) a massive propaganda campaign with independence as the watchword.

Although Egyptian militancy played in a multitude of ways into the dynamic of the South Arabian revolution, it was not the only basis of the Aden insurgency — a considerable number of Arabs who wanted independence also feared Egyptian domination. The Syrian Ba'ath Party was influential in Aden Colony, and the Qawmiyyun-al-Arab group (forerunners of the Popular Front for the Liberation of Palestine) — radical Islamic forces that sometimes clashed with the more moderate Nasserist groups — also formed a source of inspiration, especially for the NLF.

Between 1963 and 1965 the NLF built a strong organization, one that cut across ideological lines and that maintained direct connections with sympathetic Arab states. It fully embraced violent revolution. The NLF perceived that this would — as the Arab scholar Joseph Kostiner notes — "play into the Arab propensity to react violently to foreign rule." It was also assumed, as theorists of the Algerian revolution had previously argued, that it would raise the morale of the people and unify them against the imperialist enemy.

As a young foreign service officer, one whose time was largely taken up with consular matters, I had little access to information that would have enabled me to comprehend, never mind anticipate, such events. Even those British and American officials who specialized in such matters failed to find a way to stop the Colony's drift toward chaos and violence; nor did they even imagine the worst that was to come. In fact it would have taken the prophetic vision of a Percy Shelley, as displayed in "The Masque of Anarchy," to envision the events that unfolded in Aden preceding and following the British departure.

Diplomats must often shake their heads over the strange twists and turns of history, and lament the fact that unpredictable events can make nonsense of a country's best-laid plans. They are like those philosophers whose fanciful ideas keep bumping up against a recalcitrant reality. Luckily, I was no diplomat, but a mere consular officer. Consular officers are not required to have extensive knowledge of grand plans, nor expected to offer many opinions on them. Their good fortune is to practise a craft that can bring order with a signature and closure with the imprint of a seal.

Among the everyday Aden consular duties that pleased me most was calling on the American naval ships that visited the port. Every few weeks the consulate would get a telegram informing us that a destroyer would soon be arriving. Occasionally they came in pairs; at other times, although rarely, a whole squadron, complete with admiral, turned up, but single ships were the rule.

Some of the naval officers and sailors who arrived in Aden had done their homework; others could only be described as baffled by what con-

fronted them. Occasionally, when I talked to educated junior naval officers who had come ashore for lunch or dinner, they would tell me how
exciting it felt to be visiting an old British colony, a place that reminded
them of a novel by Conrad, or a poem by Kipling. Most of the commanding officers I met, however, had no such associations.

On the day the ship was due, I would be deposited at the Steamer
Point jetty, where, if the destroyer did not send a launch, I would pick
up a small craft myself, chug out through the harbour to where she was
anchored, and climb the ladder. The ride out was short and never boring; Aden harbour was always active and colourful. There were sleek
tankers in abundance, supply ships and grubby lighters, coastal vessels of
all descriptions, sailboats and small launches, dhows that evoked
Sindbad the Sailor — possibly a British naval vessel or two, not to mention an occasional P&O Line passenger ship, busy disembarking its
soon-to-be-disappointed tourists among the unspectacular shops of
Tawahi and Crater.

Dressed in suit and tie for the occasion, and possibly sweating a little
despite the harbour breezes, I would board the ship, leaving the launch,
with its identifying u.s. flag, standing off. Nine times out of ten the
boatswain would be ready as I stepped on board and would pipe me on.
Strict protocol, based on rank, dictated who got what salute when coming on board, and American ships, distinctly less punctilious in drill than
the British, managed occasionally to adhere to it. This gave a special air
to some of my visits, and allowed me to feel that I was part of long sea
tradition.

When I climbed on board there was often a small reception party,
mostly very informal, although a few times I landed on a deserted deck
and had to ask directions, and once, probably by mistake, I got a full
dress welcome and a request to "review the guard." Most commonly I
would be greeted by a second-in-command and led away to the officers'
mess to meet the skipper, a commander or a captain, and brief him on
the situation in Aden. I would explain that I would take him up to
Government House so that he could sign the Governor's guest book. I
might invite him and his officers to a party, or recommend a trip to Gold
Mohur Beach or a restaurant, and I would give them tips about shopping and explain a few of the basic Islamic customs.

I would caution them, for example, that the small round-domed buildings in town were not public toilets, but usually mosques, and that it
would be advisable for sailors who had drunk a bit too much beer to avoid
relieving themselves inside them or even in their vicinity. I made a point
of this because several sailors from previous ships had taken liberties, and

after being rescued from a near-murderous mob of outraged Arabs had been fined several hundred dollars in the local British court.

Once such information had been passed on and admonitions duly spoken, I would get down to what for the consulate was the really important business of my visit. With a discreet cough, perhaps, I would reach into my pocket and pull out my list. I was no Leperello, and this document had nothing to do with anyone's sexual conquests. Neither had it anything to do with informing the captain about Aden. It was, on the contrary, a request for something humble and life-sustaining, something that the destroyer, we hoped, would generously supply. It was a request for chickens.

It will come as no surprise to most readers that the British — although unshakeably confident that their customs and way of life were far superior to anything that even the Americans could boast of — consumed food that was generally abominable. The great British food writer, Elizabeth David, later to be one of my shining lights of cuisine, had barely come on the scene, the London restaurants had yet to be transformed, and the food in Aden was, if anything, markedly inferior even to the dreadful stuff consumed in the home country.

While the colonial Italians and the Indians, with their usual magic, managed to produce some wonderful dishes, and the French millionaire, Tony Besse, dined like Lucullus, we Americans were stuck with our plain old North American recipes. Unfortunately there could be no joy in cooking, since the local produce, especially the chickens, were nearly inedible, British mayonnaise a joke, and tinned vegetables generally revolting. The American destroyers, on the other hand, had huge freezers full of frozen chickens, real chickens with meat on their bones; they had steak and roast beef and frozen vegetables, ice cream, and all sorts of treats that, if one only asked, they were quite willing to dole out at cost to us non-military personnel.

As a result, for a good part of the time I hobnobbed with the American ships I functioned as a procurer. And it was not only the consulate I served. I also managed to supply Wendy and Mark Veevers-Carter with many a tasty treat, even though I had to arrange transshipment of the stuff to Mukalla, or else carry it up there myself. Most of the letters Wendy and I exchanged refer to such starkly important items as cases of lima beans, cans of whipped cream, sides of roast pork, and whether the chickens should be sent completely gutted or wrapped whole with parts included. Our correspondence shows us always to be treading on delicate ground with each other, for neither of us wanted to suggest that the food served as a bribe for a bunk on one of my Mukalla visits. Actually, the advantage was all mine, because arranging to send the food caused me little trouble and made me feel quite good about myself, whereas providing lodging on short notice, especially in a place like Mukalla, must have been troublesome for Wendy, and surprise guests, I know, were downright irritating.

My conferences with the captains, then, would eventually become confabulations with the supply officer, and a launch from the destroyer would duly arrive at Prince of Wales Pier bearing enough supplies to last us until the next visit. On subsequent days and nights British guests would be wowed by fat roasted chickens, distracted by lima beans, or bowled over by salads dressed with Kraft or Hellman's mayonnaise.

Our contact with the ships did not end there, however. I would still have to turn up with my Volkswagen Beetle to drive the commanding officer up to Government House to sign the book. This was an experience like no other. First of all, most of these naval men did a double take at the Beetle, not having seen such a vehicle before (they spent a great deal of time at sea, I suppose). On these occasions, too, they often felt they had to reassure themselves about my identity. I had acquired some British speech patterns and a bit of an accent in Aden, and of course "consuls" in bygone days had usually been locals who represented the United States, not Americans. Curiously enough, when I explained to the various captains that I was from New York, they seemed generally satisfied, if not reassured. Their searching questions about life in Aden also often astounded me.

"Do all the A-rab guys wear skirts?" they frequently asked.

"How do you like serving in Saudi Arabia?" was another favourite query.

And one scatologically minded old sea dog, gazing at the harbour's huge oil storage tanks, guffawed, "What does BP stand for? Big Prick?"

Once I had whisked these conversationalists along the corniche roads and up to the Residence to sign the book, the question of entertainment arose. Many of the captains simply wanted to get back to the ship, one or two gung-ho careerists insisted on consulting with the consul, while others fell readily into the spirit of the colonial customs.

One of the latter, a commander who had had more than a few drinks with our Cathy at Gold Mohur, and must have fallen, as so many did, under her unique spell, turned up at two in the morning and attempted to batter her door down. He was removed from the premises as discreetly as possible, and fed coffee until he was capable of staggering back on board.

I had many adventures with the navy, the most dramatic of which I shall recount in due course, but these were not the only intriguing visitors to Aden that I had to deal with. One day an official arrived on rather short notice from Washington. A quiet, grey-haired man with antiquarian tastes, he was scheduled to be flown up on a visit of inspection to some areas of the Protectorate. While he waited, I took him several times to the excellent little museum of antiquities belonging to Kaiky Muncherjee, the reigning scion of a famous family of Aden-based Parsee ship's chandlers. The elder Muncherjee had a standing offer of baksheesh to Arabs who brought artifacts from the desert and sea, and had amassed a small collection of coins, statues, giant cowry shells, and other material, all housed in a rickety building that formed part of the Muncherjee establishment in the Crescent shopping area in Steamer Point. In the words of one of Kaiky's advertisements, *If you are in Aden, don't fail to see the Museum of Antiquities of Ancient Arabia (2400 years old). Mermaids also on show.*

I don't remember the mermaids (which were probably figureheads from old ships), but I do remember how my Washington visitor walked around Kaiky's exhibits, pointing out the many inaccuracies in the listings. The so-called "Crusader coins," for example, were, according to my guest, pieces of eight from the Spanish Main. Our sessions reminded me of *What in the World*, one of my favourite American television shows, on which archaeologists were challenged to identify obscure artifacts from many cultures. Despite his skepticism, however, the man from Washington was impressed by what Kaiky had on display, and, in fact, although major expeditions were few, British policy since before the Second World War had been to preserve local antiquities, and not ship them off to overseas museums, as had happened in Egypt, Greece, and elsewhere. For this reason alone many important local artifacts remain in Aden to this day.

Soon after, I learned that the scholarly gentleman and amateur archaeologist from Washington had come to the Colony on a mission for the Atomic Energy Commission, which at that time was searching out desolate places in the world for the purposes of nuclear testing and waste disposal. I felt that an irony lurked somewhere in this juxtaposition, given that a nuclear exchange in those years seemed particularly likely to reduce our modern civilization to a pile of rubble that future archaeologists (if any) would inspect with some puzzlement. It also struck me as unreasonable — for I was then unaware that it is the usual practice — that a ruling nation should impose on the ruled such a terrible burden as that of being an atomic testing ground or a dumping place for nuclear wastes. Back in my flat, however, as I was reading the Roman historian Tacitus, I came across a memorable saying summarizing the effect of the

Roman Empire's imperial policies on the conquered. *Solitudinem faciunt, pacem appellant*, Tacitus wrote; "They make a desert and call it peace."

Whatever the dark side of his mission, the man from Washington was a polite guest and visitor. That was not always the case in Aden.

As the political situation heated up, more and reporters turned up. Most of these, like Osgood Carruthers and Randolph Churchill, were British, but some Americans also came, and in one case two *Stars and Stripes* reporters descended on us and managed to produce their own unique version of theatre of the absurd, one quite in line with the general insanity that pervaded the Colony in the those days.

Our Pozzo and Lucky — more proactive than Beckett's pair — flew in on a military plane and announced that they were doing a "major story" on life in Aden, focusing on the consulate as a bastion of democracy in one of the world's troubled regions. It was clear that we must cooperate — and we were happy to be singled out — so the resources of our office were put at their disposal. George Rodman and I drove them around, Cathy took them to the beach; we posed for endless photographs. Not only did we show them the "real" Aden, we also arranged that they should have a couple of flights to the Protectorate. It was the old red carpet treatment all the way.

At one point I remember driving them through Crater while they sat in the Jeep and simply clicked their cameras at everything in sight.

Naive though I was at the time, I queried one of them about this. "Can you really get good photos by that kind of haphazard shooting?" I ventured to ask.

"Oh, sure," replied Pozzo. "Just point and shoot down any old street. Never know what you're going to come up with." Lucky nodded his head in agreement. They hinted that it was time for another drink.

A few days passed, during which the duo continued their assiduous probing of our mission in Aden and deepened their experience of the local politics. They shuttled, or rather we shuttled them, between restaurant and bar, from back alley to beach. They shot hundreds of dramatic photos, mainly of us, posed against all kind of colourful local backdrops. They flew out to the Protectorate and returned. Then it was time to leave. They promised to send us the story, the huge and flattering spread that would soon appear in the pages of *Stars and Stripes*.

Unfortunately, they went for a last nip at the Crescent bar. One drink led to another, and they grew amiable and talkative. There, possessed by some demon of hubris, they confessed — or rather boasted — to an unimpeachable source that their visit had been no working trip at all, but merely a little vacation they had cooked up to get themselves out of

Ethiopia. There would be no story, for they had only pretended to write notes. And there would be no flattering photos, because — at least when shooting us — there had been no film in their cameras.

They managed to get out of Aden before this was reported to us. When the news did reach us, George Rodman and I vowed to pursue them and kill them, if only we were given departmental leave to do so. This of course was not forthcoming. Then we swore that we would complain to the highest journalistic authorities about this swindle, this colossal waste of our time. We did so, but our authorities were clearly not high enough. Or perhaps they were too busy creating anti-Communist storylines, or trying to get out of Ethiopia. So we laughed; and we cried. In particular Rodman, the Old Plantation Owner, for whom hospitality was a fetish, cried. He had bestowed quite a few mint juleps on them, and posed for more than his share of "action" photographs.

In my second year in Aden a whole expedition turned up, a ship carrying scientists from the Woods Hole Oceanographic Institute of Massachusetts. They were taking part in an international survey of the Indian Ocean, and stopped for several days at Aden in order to make some final preparations for their trip. I got on well with them, and spent many creative hours in the Crescent Hotel bar listening to fascinating yarns and questioning the scientists about some of the experiments they were planning after they sailed south. They liked me and invited me to accompany them on the voyage, which proved impossible, since they would be at sea many weeks, but I did help to organize the storage of their cargo of high explosives. These were necessary, the officers claimed, for some of their undersea work, though I never quite understood why. At any rate, off-loading explosives required fairly lengthy negotiations with the British and culminated in a dramatic operation carried on at night along hushed Aden streets.

At ten o'clock one stifling Saturday evening we began to move the dangerous cargo. It was conveyed in a lighter to a dock at Ma'alla, then off-loaded, container by container, into army lorries, while we stood by sweating — and not only because of the heat. Any mistake might have resulted in a small catastrophe, and in the confined spaces of Ma'alla such a mistake would have been amplified in the worst possible way. We had guards with us, too, just in case Arab dissidents took a notion to hijack the shipment.

Once the trucks were loaded we began our painfully slow run up through the pass and down into Crater, where the British storage depot was located. I remember the yellow arc lights, the shadowy hills, the glare of lamps, the tense faces glimpsed in a harsh chiaroscuro. Half-sleepy, curious Arabs peered out at us from alleyways where they had bunked down, as always, on their rope beds, but pedestrians were excluded from the danger zone; I never again saw the Aden streets so empty. I rode ahead with the Aden police, and from time to time glanced back at our entourage. To me it was a romantic excursion, something out of Clouzot's *The Wages of Fear*. With frequent stops to check the cargo or to chase away curious onlookers, the trip seemed to last forever, but at last we came to the barriers, where armed guards awaited us.

It was five o'clock in the morning when the last truck was unloaded. I stopped in a small shack inside the compound watching the first sunlight flood the city and drinking tea with the police commander and a couple of army men. By this time my suspicions about the shipment were aroused. Why the large cargo of explosives and why all the secrecy? At this point in my Aden stay I was growing suspicious of everything, realizing how little I knew of what was going on. But I had also learned that to ask certain questions would be a waste of time.

In retrospect, the whole episode takes on life not only as a vivid memory, but as a metaphor. In fact, although few suspected it, the Colony itself was soon to explode beyond all imagining. The careful repression imposed by the British proved insufficient to prevent the foul cache of centuries from blowing up in the faces of the Colony's semi-benevolent masters. Later that year the first bombs of the terrorists, who were also, to begin with, freedom fighters, started to explode in the streets of Aden.

FIFTEEN

Playing Cardinal Puff

The insurgency campaign in Aden accelerated after the British Labour government put forth its Defence White Paper in February 1966, a document that specified the date of British withdrawal as 1968, and suggested that the United Kingdom would not thereafter maintain a military base in the area. As Julian Paget has shown, in Aden itself the number of terrorist incidents increased at a constant rate between 1964 and 1967, reaching a total of nearly four thousand. Casualties amounted to just over two thousand dead and wounded, a number that included civilians and local nationals. The terrorists struck upcountry as well; the British had to fight an extensive campaign in the Radfan area of the Western Protectorate, a region with terrain as inhospitable and difficult as the worst in Afghanistan. As a former Aden resident, however, I found the incidents in the Colony the most disturbing, since they played out in my mind against the days of peace and rather innocent folly I have described as typical of the period before 1960.

I will give only three examples.

On December 23, 1964, the sixteen-year-old daughter of an air commodore was killed and several other young people wounded when a bomb was thrown into a dance party held in a "secure" area near the airport.

On June 17, 1965, a hand grenade was thrown at a group of British schoolchildren waiting at Aden Airport for a flight to the United Kingdom. Five children were injured.

In 1967, during the last months before the British withdrawal, a series of assassinations took place in Steamer Point, some of them very close to the Tawahi police station. As reported by British journalist Stephen Harper, the victims included a Danish sea captain who had been shopping at the Crescent stores, a German TV reporter, and, on October 20, a British official, Derek Rose, who had been taking photographs of a Muslim procession. These deaths were not the result of bombs; the murdered men had been directly targeted in close-up gang-style executions.

The British were unable to mount a successful anti-terrorist campaign for several reasons. They had lost the support of the population; the Federal forces and the police had been infiltrated by the enemy; British intelligence contacts were systematically murdered; and an order of "minimum force" restrained the military during most of the troubles, which meant that turning the Colony into a rigorously controlled police state was almost impossible.

Some of the frustrations resulting from these handicaps, and the ensuing terror, resulted in a few reprisal killings by British troops and the alleged harsh treatment of many prisoners at the Fort Morbut detention centre in Steamer Point, which resulted in a condemnation by Amnesty International in 1966.

All of this, to those of us who had experienced life in the Colony just a few years before, seemed an inconceivable nightmare. Yet more was to come. The NLF and FLOSY, after years of bitter infighting, signed a truce agreement in Cairo in October 1967. This was largely ignored by both sides. While the British were mulling over the terms of their departure, however, serious fighting between the terrorist groups flared up again, and British troops stood by while the Colony became a battlefield. Four days of fighting resulted in thousands of deaths, including many women and children. This time, however, the NLF, with the South Arabian Army on its side, won a clear victory, one made irrevocable when FLOSY's Nasserist allies in Yemen were neutralized by a coup. The British turned over power to the NLF delegates in Geneva on November 29, 1967. The People's Republic of South Yemen came into existence. One hundred and twenty-eight years of British rule in Aden had ended.

The evacuation was not simple. Many people, and goods in great number, had to be moved to the airport or to the ships offshore under conditions that were extremely volatile. According to Julian Paget's vivid account, a few mementos of British rule, including a statue of Queen Victoria, were merely relocated: two red, white, and blue harbour buoys were deposited on the top of Shamsan and chained deep in concrete; a car was dropped on another peak, and a huge white ensign moored on an unscalable cliff overlooking Ma'alla.

Thus, despite their military superiority and their enormous political experience, despite the best efforts of a number of well-intentioned and capable administrators who served in Aden, despite even their very real self-interest in doing so, the United Kingdom failed completely to provide the means for a peaceful evolution toward independence in South Arabia.

What betrayed them was first of all their inability to commit themselves to a true democratization of the peoples under their control. Instead, they took the way out sanctioned by their own mythology of the noble desert Arab. They chose to co-operate with the decadent and historically irrelevant tribal leaders, afterwards coercing Aden Colony, which possessed at least the rudimentary elements required to begin building a progressive state, to accept the ultimate misalliance by joining the Federation. Behind this, no doubt, was a geopolitical opportunism that suggested that an embryo state centred in Aden — one that would satisfy world scrutiny as to independence — could eventually be co-opted for Britain's strategic purposes. Yet when resistance surfaced, the British misread the nature of their opposition and, lacking both accurate intelligence and a strong policy of counter-terrorism, withdrew from their erstwhile territories in humiliating circumstances, abandoning what remained of their local supporters.

Because of the failure of British policy, thousands of innocent people — Arabian and British; soldiers and civilians — died, and South Arabia to all intents and purposes fell for more than two decades into the Soviet orbit. Even when it shook off Soviet influence and was incorporated, after its defeat in the 1994 civil war, into the larger Yemen union dominated by the north, it continued to be a birthing ground of terrorism and radical movements that even now threaten the West.

In 1962 the Conservative government of Harold Macmillan had argued that Aden was "essential" to British interests, and linked it with England itself and Singapore as one of the three indispensable British military bases. Aden had in fact been selected as a unique offensive launching pad for operations in Arabia, the Persian Gulf, and East Africa. It was also the third largest fuelling port in the world, and a useful link to Middle Eastern oil sources, which were vital to the British.

By 1966, Harold Wilson's Labour government had decided to dispense with Aden, stating in its White Paper of that year, "Although we have important economic interests in the Middle East, Asia and elsewhere, military force is not the most suitable means of protecting them. Outside Europe, we can act (1) only with Allies (2) only with facilities." There was to be "no maintenance of bases in independent countries against their desires."

The British left Aden because they no longer had the will to impose their rule at all costs on a people that did not want it. To do so would have required the creation of a regime that had few precedents in British colonial history, a virtual police state, and the creation of a puppet government in the manner of Stalinist eastern Europe. This might have been feasible in the past, but it was a difficult and desperately uncomfortable role for a democratic state in the post-Second World War era of open communications and consistent United Nations monitoring of "troubled areas."

What I observed during my time in the Colony was not a British power bent on control at all costs, but a fading and rather chastened imperium, unable to find a comfortable way to exit from the burden of vanished dreams and once-cherished responsibilities.

I sensed this at the time, even though as a young vice consul my great fear was not the threat of terrorism, but the spectre of boredom. I was not alone in this anxiety. Ennui was an ever-present burden, victimizing everyone who lived in the Colony. Options were limited, and the days stretched out in a discouraging sameness. Oppressive heat, blank sunshine, a barren landscape, the unrelenting sea — we tried to ignore them, to do our jobs, to amuse ourselves, to get out. It wasn't easy. Colonial officials, soldiers in from desert duty, businessmen, housewives — all looked around nervously for the next thing, for the perfect distraction. Something haunted us, something not quite tangible, although we feared it all the more for that. It was nothing so simple as violence, nothing so concrete as armed rebellion — more like the reflection of our own hopelessness in the dark-skinned faces around us. Inertia, futility: the psychic landscape of colonialism was a troubled one. In Aden, Sisyphus ruled.

Our choice of entertainments expressed our predicament. "Cardinal Puff" was a favourite pastime. I learned this bibulous ritual — to call it a "game" is misleading — from Terry Caitliff, the embittered Irishman whom I have already referred to as an off-and-on admirer of Cathy O'Hara. This reckless ritual was a perfect one for Aden, since it involved drinking the health of the imaginary Cardinal Puff, but in a prescribed manner, according to a set script. Mistakes forced one to repeat the ritual (and all the drinks) from the beginning. The idea was to let go, but within strict boundaries, to combine licence and discipline. Getting drunk by playing a ritualistic game later struck me as a singularly perverse activity.

Aden thrived on formality. Receptions at Government House, cocktail parties at British Petroleum (usually in honour of some dreary messenger from Texas or Oklahoma), diplomatic parties to celebrate Ethiopia's or India's national day — to a twenty-two-year-old all such events seemed forced and rather stilted. The premier military party was probably the Aden Protectorate Levy Ball, held in a Khormaksar field, barren, yet decorated with tents and banners as if the occasion were a medieval tournament. There were double rows of camels and guards at the entrance, elegant gowns, full military dress, and medals everywhere. The formality of the occasion did not prevent some quite drunken scenes. Throughout the evening, eager eyes probed to find out who was with whom at the other tables, and shifts of social allegiance and new liaisons were noted.

Other rituals were more unbuttoned. On Saturday afternoon, also in Khormaksar, camels raced at the club. Formal dress was required, but guests milled about, sipped pink gin, and made informal bets on their favourites. Arab jockeys attempted to induce the poor beasts to circle the track, but typically one or two of them went scurrying away toward the beach or the parking lot, fed up with the whole charade. It was a dispiriting event.

In Khormaksar as well took place most of those gastronomically satisfying but debilitating curry lunches, typically also held on Saturdays. These feasts began with beer and gin (often in the form of Number 2 Pym's Cup). After extensive libations, the table was spread with a huge number of small dishes, which contained finely chopped green and red pepper, tomato, hardboiled egg, and pineapple, as well as nuts, raisins, and other tidbits, which one could add to the main curry and rice dish. Deep-fried popadums and chutney were also served, leading me to conclude that this was a bastardized cuisine drawn from both Indian and African sources. These lunches were wonderful, but the gin and beer flowed so uncontrollably and the food was so abundant that one had to stagger home immediately afterward, usually collapsing in bed and waking up just in time for that evening's party.

Living in Khormaksar was itself dispiriting. In ancient days Crater City had been an island and the isthmus had been a sea channel (or *khor*). Sitting in my flat I could sometimes imagine that strong disruptive currents still flowed beneath our sandy foundations.

One day, in a fit of tedium, I wrote a long satirical poem on the houses of Khormaksar. Esmail liked it and suggested I send it to *The Aden Chronicle*, a rather dreadful Indian-edited paper, published in English. Thank God, I never did, but Esmail and I concocted an Arabic pseudonym for me, Qurad, which he claimed was the closest he could come to the English "gadfly."

The British, of course, were given to similar effusions, only they often sent theirs through the Protectorates by wireless. In my leisurely verses I address the British children of Aden, Hilaire Belloc-style, and take pains to characterize the major edifices of my charming seaside suburb:

> Brown and squat, in a reek of beer
> Are the seedy lines of Seedaseer,
> And the Al-Kaff's yellow, 'gainst the sky,
> The color of a jaundiced eye.

The Nurses' Compound on the beach,
All major arteries within easy reach.
And standing apart from that non-U band,
The haughty broad-beamed Casa Strand.
The Shell House, as I hear tell,
Is more or less an empty shell.
The hospital itself a merry
Air-conditioned mortuary.
The Beach Flats towering grey and stark
Where strange things happen after dark.
The Buff tents' khaki, shining bright,
Where strange things happen in daylight.
The villas of the Royal Air Force,
White as the souls within, of course.
And the airport whose warm tarmac
Welcomes the damned, speeds parolees back.
Last of all, children, is the place
That you with your little bodies grace,
The Isthmus School, where you must stay,
While mummy and daddy spend the day
In that perishing endeavor,
Keeping the Commonwealth together.

Camel races, curry lunches — if these seemed closer to the world of Kipling and Burton than to mine, they would soon end. Philandering and folly might continue, but within a decade the language of Khormaksar would be Russian. Soviet advisers — military personnel, economic experts, diplomats, and spies — would inhabit the houses and walk the beaches of the old British enclave.

None of us anticipated such a turn of events, least of all the young vice consul who had become more and more enmeshed with the ebullient Cathy. For I had finally capitulated to her unexpressed wish and taken on the role of companion, sidekick, and confidant.

Our evenings often began with drinks in her apartment, or at the Rodmans', after which we would join her friends or perhaps drop in on some tedious duty party, from which we would escape at the first opportunity. Later we would cruise around looking for entertainment where we could find it. On less hectic evenings we went to the Astra (outdoor) Cinema, where the shadows of copulating lizards flitted across the whitened screen.

Our time alone together was spent in endless conversations about our Aden friends, about our failed stateside relationships, about love and religion. Cathy was glib and I was stubborn and opinionated, so our discussions often ended in huge arguments, insults, and "irreparable" breaks. We were like a married couple, full of unspoken frustrations, but our consummations were largely verbal.

Once or twice we nearly crossed the boundary and became lovers. I kept her company one evening while she waited for a call from Terry Caitliff, a call that never came. We drank for an hour or so and talked, then suddenly found ourselves kissing and clutching on her sofa. This happened quite often, but Cathy would usually think better of seducing her youthful sidekick and pull back. That night was different; she didn't pull back and I had neither the desire nor the power to do so. The point of no return had been reached when something absolutely unexpected intervened. Carmela Natale called up from downstairs to say that a merchant ship's captain was in the main office below with a crewman he wished to sign on. I simply couldn't believe it. It was 11:30 at night, but it was indeed my responsibility to witness and record such signings, so I had to pull on my half-discarded clothes and readjust my body and my psyche to deal with this onerous duty. The captain seemed unhappy to see a bleary-eyed and half-drunk vice consul turn up to do the signing, but he didn't know the half of it.

On another occasion Cathy and I were visiting the Rodmans' apartment along with Carmela. The memsahib, Penny Rodman, had returned to the States, however, leaving George to be attended to by his sedate Ethiopian houseboy Issa. Cathy began swallowing mint juleps as if they were ice water, and I had a few myself. All of a sudden she seemed to lose control and virtually attacked me. We spent an unconscionable time writhing on the floor in various intimacies, as Carmela wailed warnings like some post-Freudian Cassandra and George sat stupified, mumbling complaints about this violation of his genteel southern ambience and insisting that we were shocking Issa. After a while the storm passed. I managed somehow to drive home. Cathy telephoned to apologize and we talked for an hour and a half about the mysterious workings of the human libido and other matters.

By far our most dramatic encounter, however, took place on the occasion of my first introduction to the demon vodka. Despite the conclusions the reader may draw from some of these anecdotes, I was (and am) a fairly moderate drinker and generally handle my alcohol very well. Because of the tropical heat, beer and gin were my favoured Aden drinks, but, like

James Thurber's legendary brown bear, I could "take them or leave them alone."

Once again, the mischief started at George Rodman's apartment. After some dreary official reception, the Old Plantation Owner had invited Cathy and me back for drinks, but on that occasion he served not the traditional julep, but vodka cocktails. I had seldom tasted the stuff and put away quite a few glasses, seemingly with little effect. Cathy and I staggered hilariously through the streets to her apartment. There our peripatetic intimacies turned into something far more serious. We were mostly unclothed and doing our familiar dance when a hammer from nowhere knocked me into state of total unconsciousness. I remember a scream and a slamming door, and then came blackness.

The next morning I woke up, my body sprawled across the floor of Cathy's tiny living room. Hardly aware of what I was doing, I crawled to the door and out onto the balcony, where I managed to get to my feet. My head seemed ready to explode. I rubbed my eyes and looked around. Not ten feet away on the same balcony, outside the main entrance of the consular apartment, stood Ginger Crawford. The consul's wife took one look at me and, overcome by a fit of hilarity, retreated inside. Only at that point did I notice that I was wearing Cathy's bra and panties.

This incident was never mentioned, but in retrospect I count my blessings, grateful that Bill Crawford, so imaginative in his evaluations, never reported this to the State Department as a "tendency toward transvestite behaviour" in his young subordinate.

Getting out of Cathy's clutches wasn't easy. My obsession with finding my destined Joycean muse, one who would lead me to a life of poetry, caused me to undertake an unhealthy over-analysis of almost every woman I met. Few of them seemed quite up to my notions of perfection, and this inhibited me. More inhibiting still — the real crusher — was my own lack of self-confidence. I was anything but proactive, yet I fantasized daily about intimate dinners with my dream partner. I imagined exchanges on art and poetry, discussions of Zen, evenings listening to Rachmaninoff, and dangerous midnight swims, culminating in captivating sexual adventures.

Such shameless romanticism was put into perspective by my brief friendship with Derek, a rather suave junior civil servant only a few years my senior. He lived in one of those pseudo-mod beach flats in Khormaksar that I alluded to in my poem, and drove a sweet blue Triumph. One night he latched on to me at a party and invited me over to his place. We downed quite a few beers, and he started telling me about his adventures with the women of Aden. I had been paying fairly close attention to this subject myself, so every name he mentioned was familiar to me.

The gist of it was that poor Derek was dissatisfied. The eligible women did not please him at all, despite his intimate contact with all of them. *All of them?*

I grew skeptical. "But Patty G. You surely haven't slept with her."

"A couple of times — a real bore."

"And Cynthia S.?"

"Just last night. She's off to Nairobi."

"And Vanessa Y.? Unapproachable, I hear."

"Threw herself at me. She's a tigress, but empty-headed."

This was an Aden I hadn't known existed. I sipped my beer and wondered: *did it exist*, or was this cardboard Romeo putting me on?

"Fascinating!" I confessed, then added, "Of course, I haven't been dating that widely. I've been going around with Cathy O'Hara from the consulate."

"Cathy? Not very discriminating; she's slept with almost everyone."

"Including you, I take it."

"Naturally."

I learned later from one of his friends that Derek was bitter because his fiancée in England was betraying him — many excuses were made for misogyny in those days — but his cynical narrative did spur me into action. My near misses with Cathy now seemed even more ludicrous and I began to wonder about my future with the opposite sex in Aden.

Somehow these things got around, and before I knew it a few sympathetic older women were busy trying to set me up. One was Mrs. Merry, the wife of the naval commandant; another was Mrs. McGinnis, the wife of a Caltech executive. The latter informed me of the imminent arrival in the colony of a "charming young girl from Scotland." Possibly I overreacted to this news. "That's tremendously exciting!" I told her, as if she had just promised me salvation. "It's not that exciting," she cautioned. "The girl's only seventeen."

I was duly introduced to Diana B., the daughter of a local bank manager. She was blonde, verging on plain, and chatty-British. At first I found her not to my taste and went back to playing Cardinal Puff with Terry and his cronies. At the same time I began eyeing a few of the young consulate wives with great enthusiasm. There were some beauties among them — Mrs. Kazimi, a lovely dark-eyed Syrian, and Mrs. Schaefer, the wife of the German consul — but they seemed quite unapproachable. So when Mrs. McGinnis reminded me of the existence of Diana B., I ventured to ask her out.

A two hundred-shilling date followed, with dinner at the Crescent Hotel and a movie at the Astra Cinema, but the evening was not a success. Diana B. refused an invitation to attend my next party, and when

Carmela inadvertently introduced me to her at an official reception, the sweet young thing commented, "Isn't he the one that runs errands for you at the consulate?"

Diana B. soon fell into the spirit of Aden social life. She gave a fine performance in the Little Aden Theatre production of *The Importance of Being Earnest* and pursued the feckless soldier Angus Cameron until he was forced to divide his time between her and Cathy.

By day I played tennis with Ali Muhammad at the Sirah Tennis Club in Crater, took to rock climbing, and haunted Gold Mohur Beach. By night I made the rounds of the parties, but real intimacy, the encounter with the longed-for muse, seemed unobtainable.

At this point a young married woman named Alison materialized in the apartment next to mine in the Al-Kaff Flats. She was dark-haired and pretty, and her husband, an oil prospector, spent virtually all of his time in the Protectorates. With her I began a comical flirtation and wooing that lasted a few months. We went about everywhere together, although not to official parties, since her origins were lower middle-class, and by the colony's egregious standards she was distinctly declassé. No matter, evenings I would knock on her door and we would have drinks — often quite a few — followed by dinner. At some point things would grow passionate — at least on my side — and she would respond with flirtatious zest, giggles, and a kind of wanton complicity, but she always managed to stop things short of what to me would have been a logical and satisfying conclusion. I couldn't understand it. It's not that I had any competition. My only rival was a bald-headed middle-aged rake named Neville, who, despite the fact that he drove an MG, was — as I saw it — far too worn-out and stodgy to compete with me. In desperation, I resorted to more and more extravagant means — endless trinkets, a nightly bottle of champagne, and, finally, a lobster dinner, which I intended to cook with my own hands and serve up as the grand prelude or postlude to my final storming of the citadel.

While the lobsters were in the pot, the champagne flowed. Things seemed to be going very well; there was great congeniality, some spirited touching and clutching, a pursuit through the apartment, and clothes shed everywhere, as the giggles amplified and became little shrieks of pleasure. At last I had her where I wanted her, nearly naked and in my bed.

All of sudden she stopped resisting, gazed up at me with her enchanting dark eyes, and exclaimed, "The lobsters!"

I had forgotten about the damned crustaceans. What could I do? I ran back to the kitchen and rescued the wretched things, but when I tested one I found that I had let them boil far too long. I had nothing but a pot full of empty shells. Alison found this hilarious. When she stopped laughing, she insisted that we get dressed and go out to dinner.

As I now realize, there was clearly something symbolic in this fiasco. I never came so close to seducing my pretty neighbour again. Soon her husband returned and she invited me to endless parties with Neville and several dreary hangers-on. At one lugubrious event, from which I escaped after forty-five minutes, she accompanied me to the door. "Why don't you have them stuffed and start a museum?" I asked politely. "Are you being nasty again?" she queried. I was and I didn't care.

Such absurdities were not mine alone: similar experiences marked the lives of most of Aden's foreign residents, colonial officials, and visitors. And such explosions of nonsense surely betokened an underlying political decadence. While the British rulers desperately sought a coherent policy for South Arabia, one that would extricate them with both grace and profit from the increasingly visible political morass that they themselves had created, Cardinal Puff looked on and smiled. That mythical fellow — not the Queen, not the foreign office — was surely the patron saint, the grotesque éminence grise, who mocked all their well-intentioned plans, and chuckled with pleasure at their rapidly shrinking dreams of empire.

SIXTEEN

Some Muses and a Cat

One night at a buffet dinner hosted by Signor Nardone, the Italian Consul, I met a British woman who surprised me by cutting through the pervasive social chatter and striking up a conversation about literature. Her name was Joan Pepper; she was a writer, and I soon found myself in a special pleasure dome, talking about what I had recently read, exchanging ideas on the contemporary novel, and hearing about the "writing scene" back in London.

Naturally, I confessed to her that my great dream was to write fiction, that in fact I was already taking notes on my Aden experience for that very purpose. At one point, just before the requirements of social exchange forced us to pay attention elsewhere, Mrs. Pepper fixed me with a serious glance and told me, "Don't give up the idea of writing. If you persevere, I'm sure you'll publish something."

I went home, my contact with James Joyce's "ecstasy of profane joy" renewed and revivified. My typewriter clicked and clacked, my notes multiplied. I began wrestling with the demon Plot. Thinly disguised portraits of my more colourful Aden acquaintances emerged, often with absurdly chosen literary names: Sally Roehart, the promiscuous innocent who was the American consulate secretary; Roderic Eastby-Monk, a local writer (based on a real one named Westby-Nunn, whom I barely knew); Mr. Pailoscopolou, the Greek Consul; André Rivière, the suave, youthful, and vastly wealthy French merchant — you get the idea. Luckily, so far as sustained literary effort was concerned, I was a flighty and disorganized youth, and I never got to the point of inflicting this stuff on anyone.

While I was struggling to produce something worthwhile, another unusual personality appeared on my horizon. This was Clara Montenegro, an Italian woman whose husband Mirko worked for the Aden Port Trust.

I met her at a party and we were immediately drawn to each other. She was then in her thirties, strong and intense, with a beautiful face — the face of an intelligent, ironical madonna — and she exuded a breezy sense of entirely approachable competence. She was vaguely reminiscent of the cinema's Anna Magnani, but lacked any peasant aura. A sophisticate born in Rome, she was brilliant, lively, enthusiastic, talkative, and hugely imaginative. When I told her how much I had loved visiting Italy, and confessed that since childhood I had wanted to learn the language, she offered to give me a few lessons.

Somehow Ali Esmail heard about this, and for many weeks thereafter at the close of business he would wink at me and inquire, "Going to your Italian lesson, I presume?"

It was Esmail who told me about Clara's involvement with John McGrath, who, it seems, had also undertaken to study some Italian with her. As I have already mentioned, McGrath was an American vice consul who had served in Aden some years before my time. While in Mogadiscio, he had been featured in a *Life* magazine spread about Americans serving at outposts and trouble spots around the world. That article, with its vivid photography and its sense of an American enjoying a real adventure, had stirred up all my romantic notions about life in the foreign service. These were only magnified when I read McGrath's witty and colourful political reports, and heard the stories still being told about him in Aden. (For one thing, he had once failed to negotiate the turn on the corniche road leading down into Gold Mohur Bay. His car struck the barrier but ended wedged in the shattered wooden railing, a few hundred feet above the rocks and the sea. McGrath had climbed out, dazed but unhurt.)

The fact that McGrath had been attracted to Clara further inflamed my enthusiasm. Things became a little eerie later when I followed in McGrath's footsteps to a Hamburg posting. There I had a harmless little romance with one of the German staff, only to learn that my phantom predecessor, the ubiquitous John, had also been her close friend.

Very soon Clara took me home to meet her husband and son. Mirko, a large, hawk-faced man, greeted me with an eloquent, cynical look that said clearly, "Oh, not another of Clara's protegés!" I was shocked at this, for I had walked quite innocently into the situation; now it seemed more complicated than I had anticipated. Their son was a beautiful child of six or seven, with lovely green eyes.

So began a few months of close companionship of a kind that was new to me. Despite Esmail's jibes and Mirko's look, there was no physical connection whatever, only wonderful conversations about life and art, and an exchange of dreams and plans. We shared the desire to write a book while travelling around the world on a tramp steamer; we listened to music together; Clara talked about psychology, Zen, Professor Tucci, and Tibet. She had a beautiful, rich voice and I listened, like a student or a faithful dog, verbally stroked into submission and a state of bliss. It was a classic case of sublimation; the sexual energy that was bursting out elsewhere was tamed. Of course it's possible that Clara was surprised at this, or even disappointed, but I doubt it. I think she enjoyed our meetings as much as I did, and for the same reason — as islands of healing repose in the unsatisfying and sometimes wounding routines and frivolities of Aden.

One of the things that made this restraint possible — and even easy — was the arrival of a third muse, who materialized, as I always hoped she would, in true Joycean fashion, on the beach. This was Diana C., a blonde, quintessentially Anglo-Saxon girl of seventeen, as different from Clara in her looks as she was in her personality and life experience. Diana C. was in Aden as an au pair, or "nanny," to look after her cousin's children. He was an MI6 operative who was to die shortly afterward of a brain tumour. This was a solid British middle-class family from southern England, with several Lord Mayors of London in its fold. (Virginia Woolf wrote about one of them in her diaries.) Diana herself was lively, well mannered, and confident in her sphere, but rather unformed both in mind and body. Although she was very clever she had been tagged as "not the brainy one" in her family, and had not been considered for university, or even A levels, in her private girl's school. She was chatty, much more intense and complex than she appeared to be, and somewhat directionless. Looking back, I am rather amazed that we connected at all, but despite many problems, this became one of the few Aden relationships that actually lasted beyond my time in the Colony, and it was the one that changed my life in the most profound ways.

There was nothing magical about our first meetings, however. At Gold Mohur one afternoon I noticed a young girl who was soon to enter my diary as "the chubby blonde." (She had the bright good looks and the solid fleshly form of a Busby Berkeley dancer.) She sat on a beach blanket nearby, together with another young woman, the two of them obviously in charge of some children who were frolicking in the water. A few days later, again at Gold Mohur, I saw them again, this time sans kids. At the end of yet another afternoon during which Mrs. Panton, a socially active colonel's lady, and Mrs. Merry, the genial wife of the naval commandant, busied themselves consoling me with tales of young beauties who would soon be arriving in the colony, and with whom they would certainly "fix me up," I trudged out to my car, secretly preparing myself for yet another few months of disappointment in love. In the parking lot appeared the two nannies, for some reason stranded, so I offered them a ride back to Khormaksar. I got the blonde's phone number, and thus began several months of intense romance, punctuated, as I will relate, by several comical interludes.

All the while male friendships were developing — with the Arabs at the consulate, with Jean Portal, the French Consul, and with a male couple, Sam and Nigel, who were in Aden as part of the aftermath of "Operation Magic Carpet," a plan to secure the emigration of the remaining Yemeni Jews from South Arabia to Israel.

By any standards, Sam and Nigel were an odd couple. Nigel was a handsome young Englishman from a moneyed urban background. He was an Oxford man, polished, sensitive, artistically aware, and genuinely devoted to helping others. Sam was from Chicago, an older man, bald, bespectacled, and hairy-chested, with a slightly bulbous nose and a pleasantly gruff manner. He reminded me of a character actor in the movies, destined always to play the part of a small-town doctor or druggist. I saw quite a bit of the two of them and we got on famously, despite some typical 1950s heterosexual blundering on my part.

When I first met Sam and Nigel I made a few scoffing remarks about the Arabs and their "queer" customs, going on to generalize my dislike of this orientation, whether sighted in New York or elsewhere. This outburst was not typical of me, and surprisingly I had no overt knowledge that Sam and Nigel were gay, which suggests that my "shadow" unconscious was working overtime that evening.

I had been perfectly aware of the general Arab tolerance of male love and of the existence of gay couples among the British in Aden. Two gay men who lived in Little Aden shared a sumptuous flat decorated with oriental rugs, original paintings, and antique furniture. One of them drove a magnificent Bentley. I rode with him one night across the causeway, fascinated by the dashboard's mysterious violet illumination. As the motor purred softly, I looked around and thought that in the middle of all that darkness, emptiness, and silence, we might as well have been in deep space. Another gay man, my Khormaksar neighbour and quite a character, even among the Aden British, had an equally interesting apartment, although in the art nouveau mode. One wall had a bright Beardsley-ish mural with the single word *Decadence* artfully scrolled across it. The subject of homosexuality never came up in Aden, although Bill Crawford and Horace Phillips once dressed up in pink shirts and shorts and went hand in hand to a military costume party, smirking mightily and wearing placards announcing that *Boys Will Be Boys*.

On the occasion of my blunder, without actually declaring himself homosexual Sam made a very patient and gentle reply, explaining that if some people felt inclined to associate thus and thus, where was the harm? Surely it was a restriction of personal freedom to take great exception to this? Logically, I had to agree, and would have backed off even if I didn't, since the truth of the situation had suddenly dawned on me. I was terribly embarrassed, but this bad beginning didn't prevent the three of us from becoming good friends for the rest of our time in the Colony.

We had several meals together and many lively conversations. Cathy sometimes joined in — which made for a fascinating mix. Nigel visited me alone and we read bits of poetry together and listened to music. At that time I was in full flight with the elusive Alison and my stories about our various fiascos served to amuse him.

I soon learned from Sam and Nigel something about the long and creative history of the Jews in Yemen. They had probably migrated from Palestine between the ninth and sixth centuries B.C.E. That is, between the time of King David (which was also the era during which the Adam and Eve creation story was set down) and the writing of Genesis 1, the magnificent priestly myth of creation that opens the Christian Bible. In Yemen, the Jews developed in a singular way, although they were not altogether isolated from the rest of Judaism. So potent was their influence that for a brief time the Yemen kings converted to Judaism. Periods of persecution occurred later, and during the twelfth century Moses Maimonides wrote a famous letter of encouragement to the Yemen Jews, urging them to hold fast to the faith despite their troubles.

The Yemen Jews had a distinct dialect and culture. They produced poets, philosophers, and students of language. Their religion was based on the Talmud and they were devotees of the Kabbalah, the famous text of Jewish mysticism, and partial creators of the medieval Aggadic Midrashim (biblical commentaries). They were also notable artisans.

Even today, many Arab silversmiths attribute their knowledge and skills to their Jewish predecessors. When I got my first Aden apartment in Khormaksar, I looked for a screen to serve as a divider in my somewhat cavernous living room. Esmail referred me to an old Jewish man, who agreed to make me a bamboo screen for one hundred East African shillings — about fifteen American dollars. Since Esmail told me that my screen-maker liked to tipple, I threw in a bottle of Beefeater gin. Within a few days the man brought in a doll's house model for my approval. I suggested a few adjustments, and before long I had a fine, unique, full-sized bamboo screen, which I still treasure.

There were not many Jews left in South Arabia when I got there. (Sam and Nigel estimated twelve hundred.) The Yemenis began to emigrate to Palestine in 1892, and before the arrival of the post-Holocaust European immigrants constituted one of the most influential groups in the Jewish homeland. There had been a pogrom in Aden in 1947, and as part of Operation Magic Carpet some fifty thousand Jews had subsequently left South Arabia.

Sam and Nigel's task of persuading the remaining Jews of Yemen and Aden to leave was no easy one. Given the new post-Nasser Arab nationalism, the migration was clearly a good idea; not many Jews were destined to survive the internecine fighting that began even before the departure of the British, and that grew horrific thereafter. Those who did were severely restricted and forbidden to leave the country. But the Yemeni Jews had deep roots in South Arabia and constituted a very conservative society; many of them had no interest in risking a new life elsewhere, even in Israel. Others refused to leave behind relatives who could not travel.

It had occurred to me more than once that, under cover of their humanitarian task, Sam and Nigel may have been doing some intelligence work in Aden, but I could hardly hold that against them. Everyone in the Colony seemed to have a variety of masks and disguises. In such a context my innocent and unguarded enthusiasms took on an aura of temerity.

One day my two friends invited me to celebrate Passover with them. There were only a few of us; I may have been the only non-Jew. We met at their house in Crater; there were prayers and blessings, and some fine informal words from Sam. Then we drank wine, ate the matzahs, and followed with a festive roast chicken dinner. Afterward came more blessings and music. A few Yemenis mingled with us British and Americans. There were rugs, oversized chairs, the smell of spices, the taste of heavy, sweet wine. Fans twirled; outside, the streets swarmed with Arabs, most of whom had been brought up to despise us all. It was like a secret meeting, a testimony to something, perhaps merely to survival, and to the possibility of connection across ancient gulfs. It contrasted sharply with the previous time I had visited my friends in Crater. Then Carmela and Cathy had come along, and a small group of RAF musicians had appeared, to swig beer and to record some rhythm and blues numbers, mournful songs from Appalachia, or pseudo-Appalachia, about lost sweethearts and self-pitying drunken binges. On both occasions I had sat there wondering about the strange world I had landed in, like nothing I could have imagined in my wildest New York fantasies.

Sam and Nigel obviously trusted me, and when the time came for them to go on leave they asked me if I would look after their cat, a splendid pure white shorthair named Middlesex. I agreed, and wrote home enthusiastically about my temporary acquisition, bowdlerizing the cat's name to "Mickey" to avoid jokes or questions.

Mickey duly arrived at my Khormaksar apartment and so began several weeks of torture — almost certainly for both of us. I had a huge sense of responsibility to my friends, and wanted to take good care of their cat, but my Aden routines had already been set and were fairly inflexible. Also, I'd had no pets since childhood, so I was by no means experienced in the ways of cats. I found it impossible to set up a comfortable routine. My cook and houseboy were no help; they were dismayed by the cat's arrival and disapproved of its habits. Knowing the environment to be unfavourable — the sands of Khormaksar held a thousand perils for a cat, or so I thought — I was fussily obsessed with its whereabouts and welfare. For his part Mickey seemed restless and discontented. He seemed to dislike his food. He clamoured to get out at unsuitable times, often waking me at night. He wandered away, and sometimes even disappeared for a day or so. On those occasions I had to tramp around the neighbourhood after him — in Khormaksar this was not a pleasant pastime — fearful that I'd lost him for good.

I must have complained to others about this; I must have received advice. It never occurred to me to write to Sam and Nigel — perhaps I simply didn't want to bother them. But one day I picked up the phone, called the Agriculture and Veterinary Department, and had the cat put away.

When Nigel and Sam returned a few months later, we had a fine reunion — there was lots of news to exchange. It was only some minutes into the conversation that they asked about Middlesex. Clearly taken aback at what I told them, they responded with their usual calm and tolerance. They listened sympathetically to my explanation of my weeks of misery. The subject never came up again.

As the great novelist Ford Madox Ford wrote, in his best book, "the death of a mouse from cancer is the whole sack of Rome by the Goths." In the complex pattern of my Aden experience the sacrifice of Middlesex seems a trivial thing. Yet it affected me; I was suddenly aware that for many months in the Colony I had been indulging myself, nourishing thoughtlessness, developing a much too thick skin about some of the very dubious things going on around me. I ended up being horrified at what I had done. (I'm still horrified.) It was the betrayal of a trust.

Very soon after, I myself experienced just such a betrayal, but I was lucky: I was the one who had nine lives. I also had a confident sense of what I was worth and where I could take my life. That stood me in good stead — as did my incurable insouciance — when judgment day came round for my young self.

SEVENTEEN

Contretemps in Mukalla

During 1958 and 1959 the Chinese and the Russians were increasingly active in Yemen. It soon became evident that the State Department required a much closer view of what was going on in that country. Thus began the process of creating a permanent American mission in Yemen, one that would not only provide a much better perspective on the course of events there, but would also play an active role in the diplomatic cold war that was rapidly developing. Once the foothold had been established, an embassy could follow, with all the advantages that would give us in our strategic struggles with the encroaching Communist powers.

The State Department's chosen representative for the new Yemen post was Charles "Chuck" Ferguson, an animated, energetic foreign service officer, who was almost as ebullient and forthcoming as Bill Crawford was reserved and reticent. None of us at the Aden consulate, however, had any illusions about Ferguson; there was altogether too much blather and showy bonhomie about the man. Needless to say, Bill Crawford disliked him intensely, which was unfortunate for the effective creation of the new American post, as well as for Ferguson himself, since his Yemen mission was dependent for nearly all things on the co-operation of the Aden consulate.

Although I had little to do with the Yemen operation, one of the details involved in setting up the new post was to change my perspective on Bill Crawford and his methods. The Aden consulate was the obvious transshipment port for materials destined for Ta'iz, and a logical place in which to keep track of what the State Department provided for the expanded operation in the north. Inevitably, in such a hastily improvised situation the bookkeeping gets somewhat compromised. Vehicles and communications equipment, office supplies and household items were soon flying about as if a poltergeist or two had descended on us. It was up to the very competent consulate accountant Carmela Natale to find ways to bend the rules without breaking them, and she began to do so with great aplomb.

This was precisely the kind of situation that was certain to disturb the meticulous Crawford, especially in view of the fact that he neither liked nor trusted Chuck Ferguson. Characteristically, he took quick action to protect himself.

One day I was called into Crawford's office. In his usual low-key way he told me that I was going to play my part in the consulate's expanded mission. I was to be given a new responsibility. He was appointing me — to replace himself — as the consulate's certifying officer. As such, I would have signing authority for every single one of our official business transactions. This was news indeed. It seemed as if my chief was finally taking me seriously, as if he were recognizing me at last as the responsible and efficient fellow I thought I was.

I wrote home to my parents, informing them with some pride of this promising new development. For a while I was elated, but I soon found that my fellow employees didn't share my rosy view of things. Michael Sterner, after hearing the news, looked a little grim, and Carmela took me aside and told me in a tone of almost maternal solicitude that she would be my guardian angel. "Don't worry, Tom," she said, "I'll protect you. I'll make sure that nothing bad happens."

I was surprised, too, when the State Department balked at this appointment, citing the fact that junior officers are (and should be) excluded from such honours. Bill Crawford's influence was strong enough, however, to induce them to make an exception in my case.

Then Carmela and George Rodman informed me of something Crawford had obviously forgotten to mention, or had downplayed so carefully that I had missed it. They told me that the certifying officer was legally responsible for the whole financial operation of the consulate, that it was up to him, or her, to sign for and approve all transactions, in particular all purchases and transfers of goods and materials. If anything went amiss, if the books did not balance, or if some procurement came up for criticism, it was the certifying officer who was responsible and who, in case of irregularities, might well be prosecuted in court.

That certainly put Bill Crawford's choice of me in a different light. The financial improvisations involved in setting up our new establishment in Yemen made the situation of the certifying officer in Aden a little precarious. I suddenly felt like the point man the sadistic sergeant had "honoured" with the task of stalking the German bunker. There was, however, nothing much I could do about it. To refuse the title would have been to lend support to Crawford's notion that I was somehow uncooperative and ornery. (How much he was privately playing up that notion I hardly then suspected.) I simply had to trust Carmela. To her mind Bill Crawford could do no wrong, and my new assignment was an ingenious plan her boss had devised to protect the consulate and confound or control the erratic Ferguson. For that reason — and because she was forthright and fair-minded — she would certainly protect me.

Such clever administrative shifts, or machinations, would put most young vice consuls out of their depth, and I was no exception. I was much more eager to get out and explore South Arabia than to take steps to defend myself from a consul I continued to write glowing letters home about.

At last it came time for me to make my first trip to Mukalla, a place that had fixed itself in my mind as the epitome of Arabian exotica, perhaps because such diverse writers as Freya Stark, Lowell Thomas, and Wendell Phillips had either alluded to it or described it in detail. No doubt in my enthusiasm I exaggerated its uniqueness, but given that the wilder parts of North Yemen seemed out of reach, and since I had already had a glance at Mukalla's white towers on the way to Socotra, I looked forward to my first visit with real excitement. From there I would go by truck up and over the *djol*, the high plateau that rises almost from the sea, then into the legendary Hadhramaut itself.

Accordingly, a cable went out to Wendy and Mark Veevers-Carter, to wit:

ARRIVING SATURDAY. ANY CHANCE OF A BED?

YES, DELIGHTED, came the immediate reply.

As I've explained, Mark was the British Fisheries Officer in the Eastern Protectorate and Wendy a New Yorker of distinctive charm, poise, and spirit, who was later to live in the Seychelles and write about those special islands. Thanks to their generosity, the Veevers-Carter residences in Mukalla served as a kind of impromptu B&B for visitors, a situation that sometimes got out of hand and caused them irritation, although it was natural to want to stay with such a colourful couple, and there were in fact very few alternatives.

Of course I would not have dreamt of dropping in on the Veevers-Carters unless I could arrive bearing some of the American food they valued so much, so I packed in my small travelling bag a few chickens and other items procured from my destroyer visits, and threw in for good measure a bottle or two of bourbon — an impulse that was to have unfortunate consequences when I arrived in Mukalla.

The trip began with a bad omen. The regular and usually reliable Aden Airways plane, after a successful take-off and a flight of twenty minutes or so, had to return to Aden to effect some mysterious and unspecified repairs. We took off again and this time there were no problems. I sat back and enjoyed the splendours of the coastal highlands and the sea.

My excitement grew as we landed at the Riyan airport, the same one I had stopped over at on my way to Socotra. This time, however, I had arrived on a commercial and not a military flight, and there was no one to point the way to the government transport that must have been there for passengers like myself. When a turbaned driver beckoned me into a small van that he assured me would take me straight to Mukalla itself, I willingly went.

After a short drive toward the sea over a bumpy road, the city hove in sight. It was everything I had hoped for: something like a stage set for an exotic film, but with many shabby edges that anchored it to an undoubted reality. The massed white buildings created a totally different atmosphere from Aden's grim brick and stone. The Colony always had the air of having been designed by a half-humane prison board; Mukalla, capital of the Eastern Aden Protectorate's Qu'aiti Sultanate and head-quarters of the British Agent and Resident Adviser, was much more fanciful, lighter, more spectacular in its shoreline vistas and curving stretches of white sandy beach.

Instead of Aden's goat-infested back streets I saw camel caravans loaded with cargo and escorted by men in loincloths, sporting rifles and elaborate curved daggers, or *jambiyahs.* These long-haired nearly naked men with indigo-dyed bodies and fierce eyes were Bedouin from the desert and the *djol,* the barren plateau that rose above the city and stretched east, west, and north, until cleft by the great wadis where the Hadhramaut cities lay.

Mukalla's winding streets were full of cars, trucks, ancient battered bus-transports, and swarms of humanity. White plastered multi-storeyed buildings rose everywhere, all with high narrow windows, some with great balconies screened by awnings, or topped by roofs elaborate with balustrades in arabesque patterns. A sea breeze stirred the dust and made the oven-heat bearable, dissipating the inevitable stink of the alleys.

I was relaxing, enjoying myself, and very eager, when I noticed that the driver had turned off the main track into a big open space, a shabby compound surrounded by barbed wire and littered with boxes piled up near some old buildings and a rather down-at-heel shack. Two uniformed Arabs stood nearby and loiterers were everywhere, gazing at us with only mild interest. I was puzzled. "Veevers-Carter," I murmured doubtfully, a name that clearly meant nothing to my driver.

Surely Mark and Wendy were not going to meet me here?

My Land Rover stopped. The driver pointed at one of the uniformed men who approached and pronounced in English a word that was at first puzzling: "Customs."

I gaped at him. Then it dawned on me. I was of course in the semi-independent state of Qu'aiti. They collected customs all right, and with some fervour, as I recalled from reading about the bad experiences of Wendell Phillips and his expedition in Mukalla.

I jumped out and nodded that I understood. Then I pulled out my diplomatic passport and repeated the time-worn phrase, "Nothing to declare."

The official did not crack a smile. Instead, he pointed at my travelling bag, stuffed, as I have explained, with chickens and booze for my hosts, and commanded, "Open!"

"No, no, no," I insisted. "Diplomatic."

"Open." He reached out for my bag; I pulled it away.

"No," I said. "Absolutely not."

The loiterers were now crowding in on us. Perhaps it was the wrong time of day, perhaps they were bored, or irritated by something the British had laid on them — at any rate I was soon surrounded by a small mob of forty or fifty Arabs, screaming at me and gesticulating wildly.

Was I frightened? Not in the least. I was loving every minute of it, watching myself being threatened by an angry mob of Arabs. *Is this really happening?* I wondered. Youthful insouciance is a great buffer.

Now we were face to face and shoving. A few men grabbed my bag and half-wrestled it away from me. I hung on valiantly to one leather handle. The men pulled hard and the other handle separated from the bag. *Granny bought a dud at Wanamaker's,* I thought. My grandmother had presented me with the bag on my departure from New York. I wondered what she would have thought of this scene.

Things were getting a little desperate. The mob was pressing on me and driving me toward the customs shed, but I refused to let go of my precious bag. If they found the whiskey they might confiscate it or even send me back to Aden. Where the hell were Mark and Wendy when I needed them?

I don't know how it happened — perhaps some Britisher heard the ruckus, or perhaps a cool-headed Arab official telephoned. At any rate an official-looking Land Rover displaying a small Union Jack roared up — a very welcome sight. A stocky, lively, bespectacled young man hopped out and made his way toward me, shouting various things in Arabic at the crowd and the officials.

When he reached me, he extended his hand. "Michael Crouch," he announced. I managed to shake hands, identify myself, and explain my problem, all without releasing my bag.

Crouch listened and interjected a few comments, then palavered energetically with the officials, obviously referring to my claims to diplomatic immunity. The crowd still milled about, there was a lot of shouting, and the officials seemed determined to see inside the bag.

"Tell you what," Crouch suggested. "Just offer them something, say fifty shillings, on the contents, and we'll see if we can get you out of here." Fifty East African shillings was only about seven U.S. dollars. A lot of palaver followed, and eventually I had to pay one hundred shillings, and sign a (quite false) customs declaration. Only then, disgruntled and complaining, did they let me off without opening the bag. (Nemesis struck much later, when, on a routine Channel crossing from Holland to Britain, I ran into the worst customs official on the planet, a nervous Brit and obviously a certifiable lunatic, who spent ten minutes literally screaming at me and my young family over some minor passport quibble.)

On this occasion, thanks to Crouch, I got off very nicely. I drove away with my rescuer, who identified himself as the Assistant British Adviser, or "dogsbody," as he later defined the role. He had been in Mukalla only a few months, having arrived just before the departure of the most famous British Resident Adviser of all, Colonel Hugh Boustead.

On the way to the Residency, I apologized profusely for causing all the trouble. I could just imagine what the experienced British officials, especially the obviously efficient Crouch, must think about such a gauche arrival. In an attempt to set things right I explained that this wasn't merely a pleasure trip; I was there to do research for a basic economic report on the Eastern Aden Protectorate. It would be circulated to the various American government branches and I wanted to be sure it was accurate. Crouch said he would be happy to help me and to introduce me around.

We stopped first at the British Residency compound. The centrepiece was a solid white colonial building, spacious and unfussy, complete with Union Jack and a toy cannon. The sentry, in a white garment, with red head-cloth and head-rope, and shouldering a .303 rifle, which looked too big for him, came to attention. He was a member of the Hadhrami Bedouin Legion, which, under British authority, policed the Protectorate. Although their garb seemed to vary somewhat depending on the availability of uniforms, these soldiers usually had a smartness about them that I had seen previously only in the Aden Armed Police.

As I got out of the Land Rover, Crouch pointed out a strange apparition of a building lying between the street and the glittering sea. This was the Sultan's palace and it had a distinctly Poe-esque or Lovecraftian look about it. It was surrounded by what appeared to be a double wall. Over the archway of the central gate stretched the bare branches of a huge dead tree, witch-like and ugly. Behind the gate and the courtyard adjoining, and across a stretch of bare sand, loomed the palace, a strange accretion of vari-coloured materials comprising low pointed towers, long balconies, and squat wings — a maddeningly incoherent piece of architecture.

Crouch took me in to meet the British Resident Adviser, Alastair McIntosh, an amazing character who might have inspired several Monty Python skits, as well as innumerable caricatures of soporific British officials in third-rate "end of empire" movies.

A rotund man, seemingly as broad as he was tall, with a round pink face, twinkly eyes, and a little moustache, he spoke in a high-pitched drawl that was often incomprehensible. Words now and then whistled out of his throat, but their meaning was usually hard to fathom. He was one of those people who in conversation don't actually seem to be paying attention to you. You got the distinct feeling that if you had suddenly disappeared before his eyes, Alastair would not have reacted at all. He would merely have stirred himself to a great physical effort, shrugged his shoulders, and waddled away. Like quite a few colonials, Alastair McIntosh drank constantly — reputedly a bottle of gin a day. He moved very slowly or not at all, and was renowned for napping on unlikely occasions. In Aden he had sometimes played the pipe organ at the garrison church, rarely matching the number performed by the choir, and no doubt falling asleep on the bench quite frequently.

In Mukalla, Alastair was surrounded by several assistants and adjuncts, some of whom were as eccentric as he was. Except for the likes of Crouch, it was a complete raree show and very amusing, but also somewhat puzzling, since the British were heading into the most difficult period of their rule and would have to evacuate South Arabia within the decade. On the other hand, you had to love a colonial service that could put up with characters as diverse as Alastair McIntosh and his predecessor Hugh Boustead.

Colonel Boustead, I soon learned, had already become a near-legendary figure. He had deserted from the British navy in the First World War, but subsequently joined the army and was awarded the Military Cross for gallantry. Before the medal could be awarded the King had to pardon him. An Olympic champion and a mountain climber, he had later fought with the White Russian army and had served in Sudan, both as district commissioner and as head of the Sudan Camel Corps. He had organized resistance against the Italian armies that overthrew the Ethiopian emperor Haile Selassie.

Anecdotes coalesce around such a man, but one that Mark Veevers-Carter told me bears repeating. It seems that on his departure from Mukalla, Boustead had arranged for gift watches to be distributed to all the important local shaikhs, and other dignitaries. At his farewell dinner, however, the colonel was confronted by one shaikh who had been overlooked, and who complained bitterly about not getting a watch. Whereupon Boustead reached into his jacket and detached his own watch, a family heirloom, which he presented to the man with his compliments. The shaikh, however, rejected the gift, insisting that he wanted a watch exactly like the others.

This is interesting in many respects, but in particular as a fairy tale of colonialism, with the neglected shaikh playing the part of the angry fairy, and Boustead in the role of the generous prince whose magnanimity goes right over the head of a mean-spirited guest. While uncomfortably aware that the moral of the story insidiously glorifies the rulers and demeans the ruled, I can only say that from my own experience of South Arabia the events may well have happened precisely as told.

EIGHTEEN

Mark and Wendy

Mark arrived at the Residency and greeted me with his usual heartiness. I was delighted to see him again. He apologized profusely for not having met me at Riyan, but seemed rather amused by my adventure at the customs post. It was the kind of absurdity he relished. When I explained why I hadn't wanted to open my bag, he winked and beamed.

He was a big man, strong, with just a suggestion of softness, despite his hulking shoulders. His gait was lumbering and easy and he wore a white cap, white T-shirt, and shorts. He looked a little bit like a sport fisherman, and even more like a pirate, complete with leer, and a restlessness that might be dangerous. We drove through Mukalla's streets and alleys, Mark's big cream and grey four-wheel-drive pickup hogging the road, his hand on the horn the whole time. Pedestrians scattered, camels snorted, and a few curses no doubt pursued us.

"How are things in bloody Aden?" Mark asked. I gave him a brief summary, whereupon he launched into a typically fierce attack on the colonial bureaucracy, which on some pressing matter had once again let him down. Expletives exploded, his black beard waggled, his white teeth flashed, and his eyes narrowed to slits.

I listened patiently, then explained about my report and my travel plans. Mark nodded and promised to take me fishing. Michael Crouch had already invited me to dinner and Alastair McIntosh had said he would set something up. My ride up to the Wadi Hadhramaut was being arranged.

We drove on, but did not have far to go, for at that point the Veevers-Carters had not yet moved into what Wendy called their "summer palace" on the shore. I found that there was a lot to see in Mukalla. All the way to the house I gaped at the throng in the streets, at the lime-white buildings, some with arches revealing fine courtyards, at rugged city walls and elegant-looking terraces high on the buildings, at craftsmen in doorways crouching over their work, at old men in skirts and white caps walking with canes or sipping coffee, at boys strolling hand in hand.

But the *Arabian Nights* aura was superficial. Blown-up photographs of Gamel Abdul Nasser decorated the walls of buildings and shops; Cairo

Radio blared away in the narrowest alley. Little boys (who would grow up to be terrorists and marauders, or possibly politicians in the liberated south) taunted the few strolling westerners with their inevitable "*Ayesh Nasser!*" ("Long live Nasser!")

In Mukalla one encountered a more interesting mixture of populations than in Aden, most of them from the four Eastern Protectorate states. Besides the local Qu'aiti people and visitors from the Kathiri State to the north, there were tribesmen from the interior of the (much wilder) Wahidi and (nearly anarchic) Mahra States, traders from up the coast in Oman, Somalis, Yemenis, and a handful of British and Europeans. The soldiers of the 1,200-strong Hadhrami Bedouin Legion, which was under British command, provided some law and order in the Eastern Protectorate. The HBL were a very colourful troop. Typical garb included an *amama*, or head-cloth, orange-red, almost saffron, with tiny yellow dots, an *aqal* or head rope, fronted by a metal clasp, a khaki jacket with an ammunition belt held up by crossed shoulder straps and worn over a bright red cummerbund, and a skirt and sandals. These uniforms, based on those of the Jordan Arab Legion, whose officers first trained the Hadhramis, were to become a familiar sight over the next several days.

The Veevers-Carter house was a rather anonymous square building on a crowded street at the edge of the city. Inside, it was dark and cool and the furnishings seemed rather improvised, but the books, clothing, sporting gear, linen, and some of the pictures suggested the sophistication of my hosts.

Wendy greeted us, looking suave and relaxed. I told of my encounter at the customs post and displayed my woefully mauled travelling bag, dispensing booze and chickens as I spoke. Her obvious gratitude allowed me to feel less guilty about putting them out. She showed me my room, a cavernous place sparsely furnished with a few tables, a couple of heavy lamps, rattan floor coverings, and rope-strand single beds covered with primitive futons. Books lined the alcoves of doors and windows and there were some framed literary and humorous sayings and photographs of local scenes. I was invited to nap — something I could never manage — and lay down for a while under the creaking ceiling fan.

After a decent interval I got up and took a stroll around the city. I ran into a British local, a tall, pale, silent, anorexic fellow, some kind of well-driller down from the Protectorate. We walked around together photographing everything in sight, and later parted, having hardly spoken two sentences to each other.

Mukalla harbour I found wonderfully picturesque, with fishing boats, dhows (some like pirate ships from a boy's dream), jetties piled with

Ta'iz gate.

Boys in Ta'iz.

MICHAEL STERNER

The Imam's Bodyguards.

Mukalla.

Harbour in Mukalla.

Sultan's Palace in Mukalla.

Wendy Veevers-Carter.

Guest room in
Veevers-Carter's
house in Mukalla.

Tom on roof of Veevers-Carter's house at Khalif.

Beach-seine fishing near Mukalla.

Silversmith and family in Mukalla.

Diana and Ethel Ruth Collett at Riyan.

Stopping on the Al-Kaff Road.

Tom and a young Hadhrami merchant.

Hadhrami Bedouin Legion soldier.

Boarding the Aden plane in the Hadhramaut.

A camel-powered well in Bayhan.

Salt trader and his camel in Bayhan.

Frontier outpost
in Bayhan.

A cemetery near the Bayhan frontier outpost.

Women at a well in Bayhan.

Departing from Aden, 1959 . With back to camera, Carmela Natale; from left around the airport table: Janet Stoltzfus, Evelyn Reed, Bill Deary, Tom, Ali Esmail, Marion Gay, Greg Gay, Bill Stoltzfus, Ali Muhammad.

coiled rope, ancient barrels, and drums, cargo bags strewn everywhere, primitive carts, ships in dry dock with masts tilting over the quayside, a rubble of half-repaired boats, and rows of warehouses with sagging balconies and awnings. My eye kept returning to the main harbour building, a long two-storey lime-white structure with a facade of beautiful rhythmic arches in a modified trefoil design. It was a busy place; men in caps and *futah* skirts wandered in and out of the archways like ghosts from a lost past. Behind lay the city and above it towered the citadel of the mountains, steep and forbidding. The shoreline curved away; bare rocks glittered with harsh light, but the sky's dazzling blue was softened by fleecy clouds.

I returned to the house just as my hosts were getting up from their siesta. Resident married couples in South Arabia, I learned, enjoyed this custom, a sensible one in a climate where the afternoon heat was brutal and all the stores and offices were shut up tight. Such siestas also offered a couple the possibility of sharing some afternoon intimacy without feeling as if they were playing at being decadent Romans.

Wendy appeared and gave the cook various orders about dinner. From time to time she went out to the kitchen to check on the preparations. Mark opened one of the bottles of bourbon and we had a drink or two. It struck me again what an interesting couple they were.

Wendy was a tall redhead with long thin arms, tapering shoulders, and a boyish slenderness. She had a striking look, one that by the 1980s would have been considered beautiful, although it was a bit avant-garde for the time. Her face was long and triangular, with high cheekbones, catlike eyes, and very full lips. She was soft-spoken and friendly, but reserved and careful.

Earlier I had read an article in the Aden English-language paper that referred to her as a "movie star," mainly because she had appeared on television in New York, but she assured me that rumours of her fame were greatly exaggerated. I knew that she was the daughter of Clarence Day, the hugely successful author of *Life With Father*, and assumed she was very rich, but not fully in control of her inheritance, since she was so careful with money, almost parsimonious. In fact we talked very little about her life with father (or mother), although she very kindly arranged for me to stay in Mrs. Day's 61st Street brownstone when I went back to New York later.

I have always had a curious reluctance to ask personal questions of anyone, no matter how well I know them — perhaps for that reason strangers often confide in me, and old friends surprise me with intimacies when I least expect it.

Mark and Wendy, however, were very discreet, and our talk was never confessional. What I learned about them came from others, and some of it was highly speculative. Mark, as many of us had noted, had the look of a buccaneer, and, indeed, the rumours suggested that he had formerly lived in the Caribbean, where he had been a member of a modern pirate gang that stole ships. According to the same (hopefully tall) tale, he had murdered a man and fled to central Africa, where Wendy turned up and immediately fell in love with him. When Wendy wrote back to "mamma" about her infatuation, Mrs. Day flew to Africa to meet her daughter's new love. As she put it to me later, "I walked into a dance hall where Wendy was surrounded by a crowd of men. I looked around and decided there was only one man in the room who was completely unsuitable for her. That turned out to be Mark." From that point on, Mark, who had pretty good survival instincts, must have decided to get them out of Mrs. Day's sphere of influence. And since her influence was pretty wide, places like Africa, Mukalla, and the Seychelles were nearly mandatory.

Not that Wendy was on bad terms with her mother. Mrs. Day kept in touch and even used her influence with magazines like *The New Yorker* to try to get some of her daughter's writing published. It must have been gratifying to her that Wendy later published some interesting books. Mark, of course, had to tread warily through the minefield created by his powerful mother-in-law. He did everything he could to legitimize himself, even claiming an Oxford University degree, although the word was that his Oxford studies consisted entirely of a few drawing lessons he had once taken in that city.

Like many, I was fascinated and thoroughly charmed by the Veevers-Carters. Despite the rumours, or probably because of them, they were very popular in Mukalla. Only the starchiest of the British disapproved.

When we sat down to dinner that evening I felt that I had entered some kind of fairy-tale country. Was I really in Mukalla with two such amazing people? The dinner quickly brought me back to earth. On my plate lay a portion of something dark, round, mushy, and rather tasteless. I had no idea what it was. Wendy saw my difficulty and explained, rather apologetically, that it was sheep's brains. I had been looking forward to some marvellous fresh fish, but, as my hostess pointed out, "We eat so much fish here we don't think of it as suitable for guests."

I managed to pick at the brains, wondering secretly if this was a regular culinary manoeuvre designed to discourage visitors, or some kind of rite of passage. If the latter, I must have passed, since my next meal with Mark and Wendy was some excellent fish and chips wrapped in newspaper.

I slept very well that night, and next morning, true to his word, Mark took me fishing.

It was a great experience, if not exactly what I expected. We drove out of town to the house at Khalif that the Veevers-Carters were later to occupy. On the way Mark picked up the first of his co-workers, an intelligent-looking young Arab in cut-off jeans and a powder-blue T-shirt, who served as foreman, translator, and, frequently, the target of the boss's wrath. We gathered up some large buckets and an immense tangle of netting and ropes, and shoved them in Mark's pick-up. Mark's two splendid Labradors jumped in, and we headed down the beach.

The city was quickly left behind and we were suddenly in the heart of a pristine natural world of exhilarating, almost perfect beauty. The beach curved away, seemingly forever, a wide stretch of sand, dazzling white except where the tide darkened it. Behind the beach was more sand, a low plain running back to the clear grey outlines of the distant rocky hills. The sky, lightly touched by some feathery cumulus, was a true embodiment of the Greek word "aether" — a blazing blue canopy, stretching over this vast, open, empty world.

As we drove along the sea margin, great flocks of gulls rose before us and settled behind, our passage a mere blip in their existence. Over the years I would see many great beaches, but none affected me like this. I felt as if I had been transported to a world out of time, to a place unpolluted by human need and striving. It was impossible to be there and not wish to dissolve one's hopelessly mundane body in that clear air, fine sand, warm sea.

Sometime later, to borrow a phrase from Thomas Hardy, "humanity obtruded upon the scene," although not, as the novelist had it, "hand in hand with trouble." We came upon a small group of locals, mostly of African origin, all in shorts, some with hats, most of them naked to the waist, who were milling about the shore and waiting for Mark's arrival. They must have been deposited there earlier that morning, and the sight of them did nothing to lessen the splendour of the beach, since they were, young and old, uniformly trim and compact, with gleaming dark skin, upright bodies, and strong faces.

The truck ground to a halt and Mark gave orders for the fishing gear to be hauled out and carried down the beach. Our fishing that morning was going to be by the beach-seine method, a very ancient one in which nets are dragged into the water, flung out in a half circle, and then pulled together, hopefully teeming with fish.

This seems like a fairly simple operation, but it does require coordination. It also requires good nets, strong ropes, and a willingness to walk pretty far out into the sea, which around Mukalla was infested with very nasty jelly-fish, as well as the ubiquitous sharks.

Mark' s mode of dealing with his workers was quite primitive. He cajoled, he screamed, he tore at his hair and beard — at times he even slapped and shoved, barking out commands in what was obviously a limited Arabic vocabulary that consisted of words like "jump!" "move!" "pull!" as well as various expletives. His patient assistant seemed to have to take the blame for any snags, but was adept at dodging the swipes of Mark's meaty hand.

Despite these tensions, a certain amount of male camaraderie, of matey warmth, crept in. The men swinging the nets, the splashing water, the screaming gulls, the ecstatic Labradors, the fish gleaming silver in the net — all these lifted me cleanly above my niggling disapproval. I put away my camera, grabbed hold of a rope, and pitched in.

Pretty soon we had a catch — not a big one, but sufficient to justify the excursion. As we drove back, leaving most the men to be picked up by others, Mark expounded on the potential riches of the sea around Mukalla. Mackerel, shark, tunny, and sardines swarmed along the coast, he assured me. What was needed was a freezing plant and a small fleet that could carry frozen fish to markets in East Africa. He was later to show me a pilot project, a fish meal plant close by the beach where we had fished. Mark stuck to his theme that most of his quite excellent ideas were being subverted by the colonial bureaucracy. Another perspective would be provided by Michael Crouch, who suggested that some of Her Majesty's property, including at least one small ship, was mysteriously disappearing under Mark's careless hand. Which no doubt served to enhance his local reputation as a modern pirate.

NINETEEN

Dinner at the Residency

That night Mark and I went over to the Residency for dinner. It was to be a male foursome and "informal," which was lucky, since I had not brought my "Red Sea kit," which included dark dress trousers, short-sleeved formal white shirt, black bow tie, cummerbund, and dark shoes. I made do instead with a white shirt, slacks, and my ordinary tramping shoes.

The interior of the place was like the setting of a Somerset Maugham story. Well-drilled, impersonal servants in white uniforms and red turbans appeared on cue. The cavernous rooms — "beastly hot" despite the twirling ceiling fans — seemed to resound with ancient half-forgotten voices. Here Colonel Boustead had recently bustled about, literally blowing a whistle to summon his subordinates; here Lowell Thomas, Freya Stark, and Wilfrid Thesiger — among a host of others of near-eastern fame — had visited. The portraits of King George VI and Queen Elizabeth, the worn carpets, the bulky ancient furniture, the guards in attendance, my sense of the Sultan's palace just opposite, the trucks, camels, and wayfarers passing outside, all these created an experience in which I felt like a privileged witness rather than a participant. Here was a world that was unique but evanescent; my role was merely to take note, to remember.

This happened often in Arabia. On one occasion in Aden I watched the Cameron Highlanders Regiment go through the ceremony of "Beating the Retreat." It took place in early evening, on the parade ground in front of the Crescent Hotel. In marched the soldiers. The shadows lengthened; sunset transformed the rocky hills and facades of the buildings into pure amber or gold; a small crowd of onlookers gathered beside the trees that surrounded the dusty open space. The kilted Scots began their drill, bagpipes poured forth their wailing song, the drums beat with relentless precision. The sounds echoed off the rocks and buildings and returned to us. With the others I stood mesmerized, sensing that time had stopped, that the river of the past had overflowed and somehow drowned the present; why else should we stand there in breathless awe and wish for that transcendent moment to last forever?

If there was a real sublimity in this kind of experience, the ridiculous was always close at hand. My dinner at the Residency veered quickly from Kipling and Maugham to Monty Python.

A servant led Mark and me into a reception room, where we found Alastair McIntosh, the Resident Adviser, with the fourth guest. Glass in hand, ensconced in an oversized chair, our host peered at us and, like Lewis Carroll's Tweedledum, appeared to say, "If you think we're alive you ought to speak."

We greeted him and I was introduced to Pat Booker, Assistant Adviser Coastal Areas. Booker, a clean-cut, sober Scotsman, was destined, as I was, to play straight man on this odd evening. I would see Booker later "on the trail," although not as promptly as I had hoped.

Drinks were served. Then more drinks. The conversation blossomed.

The Resident yawned, mumbling and whistling in my direction. "Here on business are you? Going to have a look around? Jolly good. Who's the consul now? Crawford is it? Eilts gone, I suppose. Don't play bridge, do you?"

"No sir, sorry."

"Too bad. Jolly good game. Passes the time. What about you, Veevers-Carter? Fishing all right? Lots of fish?"

"Well, today's catch wasn't much. It was just a demonstration. To show off our direction."

"It does pay to have a direction," put in Booker sarcastically.

"Quite."

"Did you ever find that missing cargo?" Booker wondered, still addressing the Fisheries Officer.

Mark looked a little grim. "Which missing cargo was that?"

"More than one, was there?"

"The bastards are always walking off with things," Mark insisted.

"Come, come, gentlemen, no shop talk. Another round of drinks, shall we?"

I swallowed my third or fourth gin and tonic. Alastair had his private bottle on the table beside him. It was emptying fast. The conversation turned to cricket, arcane stuff I could hardly follow, even though everyone's words were coming out more slowly. Then Booker, perhaps recalling the Resident's religious predilections, made some allusion to the Anglican service and the chanting of priests. From there we were led, by one of Mark's ingenious segues, to the cries of animals.

"It's clear that doves coo, but what do falcons do?" he challenged us.

"Scream?" I ventured.

"Sorry, no. What about you, sir? Care to guess?"

The Resident waved off the opportunity. He lifted his gin bottle and peered at it, as if unable to believe it was actually empty.

"Falcons chant," Booker countered.

A dangerous flash of buccaneer's teeth. "Thrushes?"

"Whistle." Booker was clearly well informed.

"Jolly good," said the Resident. "What about monkeys?"

"Chatter," claimed Mark.

"Gibber, surely." Booker was unrelenting.

"Damn it, man — they chatter!"

At this dangerous juncture, a turbaned servant appeared and informed the Resident, "Dinner, sahib!"

Each of us handled the business of finding our feet in a different way. Booker stood up quickly and stared resolutely at the door. Mark swung out of his chair and looked triumphantly around. I pushed myself up and hoped for the best.

The servant assisted the Resident. Alastair got to his feet and, looking like a very fat pink groundhog standing on its hind legs, blinked at us. He sniffed once or twice, his little moustache twitched, he muttered something like "Dinner, gentlemen," and shuffled off, leading the way to the dining room.

The table, elaborately set with silver and Residency china, and rather too large for four, sat in the middle of another cavernous room. The place had the feeling of some Edwardian men's club, where Bulldog Drummond might yawn and wish for an adventure. There were pieces of Malabar furniture, side tables, elaborate candelabra, and lamps that left much of the room in deep shadow, so as to give all our faces, I don't doubt, an air of foolish grotesquerie.

Another servant appeared with an elaborate prawn salad; wine was poured. The Resident raised his glass and nodded at the portrait of the reigning monarch. "To the Queen," he mumbled with close-mouthed reverence, and we echoed the sentiment.

As the wine flowed the conversation picked up again. Local problems did not seem earth-shaking. To judge by the Residency small talk, most of the Qu'aitis were unpredictable schoolboys, with a tendency to eccentric behaviour. They quarrelled among themselves, stole funds, refused to recognize what was good for them, made impossible demands, and artfully circumvented even the best of the British schemes to improve their everyday welfare. The Sultan was a good fellow, but always a bit exhausted — perhaps it was the harem duties; he had over a hundred wives. And although I would not be received at the palace, I was lucky. There was nothing to look forward to there but ridiculous pageants, flowery speeches, trays of fly-blown sweets, and warm bottles of Stim and ginger ale. It would be much more interesting upcountry.

Meanwhile the main course, roast chicken, was served. It was local chicken, and I could understand for the first time why the Veevers-Carters appreciated my frozen birds. We were having some difficulty finding any meat to cut when Mark boldly requested permission to take things in hand. The Resident nodded and we picked up our legs and wings and chewed away.

Were there many visitors to Mukalla? I asked.

Oh, yes, quite a few. Politicians, journalists, and travellers, and of course the military. Even an American Admiral, Commander of Middle Eastern Forces, had dropped in — in a very small flagship, some kind of seaplane tender in fact.

"Had to send a signal to find out who he was," the Resident observed. "Not like the old days. Flagships with rank pennants, all very clear." He favoured me with a glance and continued, "Foolproof system of identification. Vice Admirals, one-ball admirals, red, white, or blue. Rear Admirals, two-ball admirals, red, white, or blue. Jolly nice flags, too."

"One-ball admirals?' chortled Mark.

Booker cleared his throat. "Changed around 1864, didn't it?"

"No more balls?" Mark inquired, black eyebrows raised.

"Shouldn't think so." Alastair shook his head. "Damn shame, too."

The talk returned to cricket. After a bit of salad and several more glasses of wine, the Resident suggested, "Shall we, gentlemen?"

We staggered to our feet and headed back to the reception room, where we started in on the cognac and whiskey. The conversation sputtered and nearly died. I had trouble keeping the room in focus. Even so, Booker was saying something trenchant when we all noticed that the Resident had fallen asleep. His head slumped, his mouth and small moustache twitched; he swayed a little in his chair and began to snore. We looked at each other; our voices fell to whispers. No one quite knew what to do. When it was clear that he wouldn't soon wake up, Mark leaned over him and said very loudly, "Good night, sir!"

The Resident jumped a little and mumbled something that might have been a farewell. We tiptoed out of the room.

"It happens quite often," Booker said.

Mark drove through the sleeping town with manic skill. Wendy had long since retired. I refused a nightcap and collapsed on my hard-strung cot. After some tossing and turning I fell asleep.

When I awoke the next morning, with a colossal headache, Mark had already gone off somewhere. I had breakfast with Wendy and gave her my impressions of the previous evening.

"I hope you're keeping a diary," she said.

I consulted her on things to do. She mentioned silversmiths, sandal-makers, and the famous Mukalla honey. I wandered about the streets with my camera, swarmed over by boys begging baksheesh and chanting the praises of Nasser. At one point the lugubrious Derek, whom I had met the day before, turned up, and I failed to escape in time. We visited the silversmiths together. There was someone in Aden I wanted to buy a bracelet for.

That evening I had dinner with Michael Crouch. It was nothing like my Residency experience. If Alastair McIntosh was the Pole of Benign Torpor, Michael Crouch was the Pole of Well-Intentioned Hyperactivity. Intelligent, witty, and seemingly ambitious, he had great notions of what he wanted to do in South Arabia.

Over curry in his rather shabby bachelor quarters (Alastair was a bachelor too, but he was the Resident), Crouch described the ideal life (as he saw it) for a young British adviser in the Protectorate. To put it metaphorically, it was the pillar of fire by day and the pillar of cloud by night. He would travel about, he hoped, solving the problems of the tribes in the northern desert, resting in the shadow of a Land Rover at midday, sleeping by night in a special tent. He would learn better local Arabic and help in the transition from British rule to whatever was coming next.

All of this was presented in the typical low-key, self-deprecating, but completely confident style of a young man recently down from Cambridge and eager for unusual adventures. Of course Crouch could hardly have guessed how unusual some of those adventures would be. He was soon to be involved in armed skirmishes in the desert, he would be a witness to some of the worst violence perpetrated by National Liberation Front terrorism in Aden, including a bazooka attack on his own family-to-be, and he would participate (marginally) in some brutal interrogations perpetrated by the British. To cap it all, on a memorable day in 1967 he and the rest of the British advisers would be ordered to slip out of Mukalla by night, leaving in ruins the political and social structure they had hoped to build in the EAP.

In an autobiographical account published in 1993, Crouch would crit-icize many of the policies he had been compelled to administer; he would also depict quite a few of his colleagues in a less than favourable light. Even then, however, he would have little to say about the fundamental evils of colonialism: the suppression of freedom and the imposition of a sterile alien order; the racism, the exploitation, the dehumanization of both oppressed and oppressor; the denial of hope for the future. Despite the national rhetoric of good intentions and the political brilliance of many administrators, the British presence in South Arabia, as in Ireland, India, and elsewhere, was essentially an evil force.

That night in Mukalla, however, such thoughts were far away. We were simply two young men, near strangers, sitting face to face, sharing some wild thoughts and guesses about our personal futures. We had a few drinks, ate our curry, and smoked our pipes together. I was impressed by the bespectacled and thoroughly competent Crouch. If there was a suspicion — in terms of appearance and manner — that he was really Peter Sellers in the role of Michael Crouch, it was only because he was clearly a young man creating a fine and flexible persona, one that would allow him to hide his vulnerability — and some of his serious thoughts — behind an ironical exterior. He was thoroughly British in that respect, too.

TWENTY

Into the Hadhramaut, Almost

I woke up the next morning feeling deathly ill. Sweating and shivering by turns, I groaned and looked around my room. Was this really Mark and Wendy's house, or had I landed in some dreary existential film, with a script by Jean-Paul Sartre or Paul Bowles? Could I be suffering from three days of exposure to Mukalla's dust and smells, its hard-drinking inhabitants and chancy kitchens?

The Residence, Michael Crouch had belatedly explained, was known as "Dysentery Hall." The Veevers-Carters' dinner of baked brains hadn't been too inspiring either. Or maybe Crouch's own curry had nailed me. At any rate the dreadful chemical toilet in its cubbyhole down the hall became my dire cell and place of woe. In between trips, I tossed on my hard bed, moaned and complained, stared at the dingy walls, choked on the stifling air, watched the flies zoom around the lethargic ceiling fan.

Mark and Wendy appeared from time to time with homey nostrums or primitive pharmaceuticals: Jasmine tea, ginger ale, and some kind of African herb — although in my delirium I may have imagined the latter.

Mercifully, as the day waned I began to improve a little. I dropped off to sleep early and woke up next morning feeling frail but competent. That was just as well, since my ride up to the Hadhramaut was scheduled to leave at 3:30 that afternoon. I had a final nap, and before I knew it Wendy was shaking me awake.

"Your lorry is about due," she said. "Are you sure you're well enough to go?"

I wasn't, really, but there was no telling how long I might have to wait for another ride. I packed, expecting Booker and his small convoy any minute.

What arrived was something different, a single battered-looking Bedford lorry, piled high with gunny sacks and a few metal barrels, and manned by a driver and three chums, two of them carrying rifles. A belated phone call from Booker told me that his plans had changed and that he would meet me much later on the trail.

As I slung my bags up beside the gunny sacks, Wendy looked at me a little doubtfully.

"I don't think you have to worry," she said. "Booker is pretty reliable. But do get off at Riyan if you feel sick. The RAF can probably fly you up to the Wadi."

I climbed into the cab and leaned out the window. The truck rattled away. Wendy stood in the doorway and waved.

We drove through the gates of the city and headed up the dusty road toward Riyan. I was still a little shaky, but happy to be on the road.

By the 1950s the trip between the south Arabian coast and the interior of the Hadhramaut had become quite routine. The days of travel by camel or donkey, of chancy overnights in nearby, little-known corners of the Protectorate, were merely a memory. European residents, in fact, commonly urged their guests to do the run as an adventurous but relatively safe excursion.

Even so, my lorry ride to the interior occurred well before the era of Yemen travel clubs, tour operators, luxury hotels, and ubiquitous archaeologists and photographers. The EAP was relatively peaceful, but there weren't many Europeans around, and the facilities were limited. I had no idea who my companions were, where we would stop, or what they would be doing along the way. I wasn't sure whether the two men with rifles were guards or hitchhikers. I had no idea what was in the gunny sacks and barrels.

In the creaking, rattling truck we made slow progress. The distance between Mukalla and Riyan is only about twenty-one miles, yet it took a full hour to do the trip. We stopped briefly near the airfield where I had arrived a few days before. There was some confabulation among my fellow travellers, the two armed riders disappeared, and we picked up a soldier of the Hadhrami Bedouin Legion. He was a handsome, slender young man with skin the colour of light chocolate, a pointed beard, dark eyes, and an impressive Roman nose. His rifle was slung over his shoulder and a pack of Turkish cigarettes was stuck in his ammunition belt above his trailing red sash.

We pushed on, but we were only about a half-hour out of Riyan when the first breakdown occurred. The truck may have been overheating, and the mud guard had shaken loose. We made a brief stop and I wandered around taking photographs.

This was classic south Arabian desert country. Picture not sand dunes, but a flat rocky landscape, bleached out, dusty, almost featureless apart from many low, bleak escarpments. Apart from the main road, there were merely a few rutted tracks, which seemed to lead nowhere — except to an endless repetition of baked, parched rock. Here and there a mud hut stood beside a shabby oasis of two or three spindly palm trees, leafy green and implausible amid the rubble of the surrounding land. As I have already suggested, the desert is monotonous, unrelentingly harsh, and hypnotic. Sunlight beats down, dust swirls, every surface seems to boil with light. The hostility of this environment sharpens the attention of the traveller — but only to a certain point. The unremitting sameness of everything finally puts the senses on hold; actions become mechanical — one squints, wipes one's brow, or closes one's eyes on the burning fiery furnace.

I had taken Freya's Stark's remarkable book *The Southern Gates of Arabia* with me to Mukalla, and it was a humbling experience to read it not so very far from some of the trails that she followed. She had plodded out of Mukalla on a donkey, and on her long, slow journey northwest toward the Wadi Duan had come to know the Arabs who accompanied her — even joining them in a gentle mockery of the fastidious soldier dispatched to guard the party. She had shared meals with her companions — including one of rice and rotten shark meat — and one night joined them in watching for enemies lurking in the shadows beyond the light of the campfire. Her account is full of sharply appreciative sketches of individuals and is marked also by generalizations that could only come from an opinionated and experienced traveller. She values and dutifully records features of the landscape, the geology, the vegetation. She is informed about the ancient history of the region. Her account of the *djol*, the great plateau that lies between the sea and the inland cities, is poetic and evocative.

By comparison with all this, I could recognize myself as a hopeless duffer, a blinkered traveller, one shoved by events into a fascinating experience with almost none of the skills or experience necessary to do justice to it. I was also, alas, pressed for time: my consulate orders were somewhat confining, and I had already lost more than a day to illness. Instead of Stark's western route that led to the Wadi Duan and back toward Shibam, we were taking the more easterly track, the so-called Al-Kaff Road, which runs almost due north to Tarim and Seyun.

I was relieved when the men repaired our wretched vehicle and we rumbled along the road again, but at about 7:00 p.m. my companions decided to stop in a wadi. We pulled over and parked under a steep cliff, and they made it clear to me that they would wait here for Booker. It all seemed pretty vague. Darkness was setting in, and I must have looked a bit worried, because they made reassuring noises, laughed, and passed me their heavy goatskin bag full of water. Although I had no food, the water — bitter and lukewarm as it was — tasted fine. *Tamam*, I told them, and sat down by the cliff side.

The sun vanished; the landscape around me faded; it was suddenly cold. My hunger confirmed that I was recovering from my dysentery. The men had made a fire and sat around talking, smoking, and singing brief snatches of songs. They seemed to have forgotten about supper. Around 9:30 came a welcome sight: headlights on the road. Booker rolled up in a second truck. He apologized for not riding with me from Mukalla, but explained that he'd had a few things to attend to. A folding table and a cot were set up and we pitched the pup tents he had brought along. To my delight, preparations for supper began.

Booker and I sat down and had a couple of gin and oranges. Fish and chips followed. I winced as I remembered Freya Stark's condemnation of the practice of eating in segregation from one's Arab companions. Even so, this was the best food I'd had so far in the EAP.

After dinner we talked. Booker filled me in on the development of the coastal areas, his real specialty. There were a few sardonic asides at the expense of Mark Veevers-Carter. He explained something of EAP politics, of which I'd so far heard surprisingly little. By the time we headed for the tents a heavy dew was sifting down and the temperature had dropped remarkably. Before retiring I walked out in the desert and looked at the stars. The southern sky had for me such an unfamiliar beauty, its display was dazzling, overwhelming — and I never ceased to marvel at it. Much later, when I took up amateur astronomy, the influence of these desert nights was significant. I slipped into my tiny tent, shivered in my sleeping bag, tossed, turned, and woke to a cold dawn, with a soggy, dew-laden canvas brushing my face.

Breakfast was at 6:30. The flies had by this time found us out; they swarmed everywhere and the heat came up so fast it discouraged all appetite. I poked at some scrambled eggs, drank tea, and was happy when we pulled away from the campsite.

A short ride brought us to Ghail ba Wazir, with its tobacco plantations, one of the few organized co-operatives in the EAP. We stopped in a coconut grove deep in a valley near the Maa'di Pass. Fresh water ran there, palm trees blossomed. It was an idyllic place, despite the flies, the crude houses, and the obvious deprivations. Here the men bought coconuts and secured them inside the rim of the spare tire underneath the first truck. Three or four children — a little girl in an orange and black dress, another in white, a tiny boy in a khaki shirt but otherwise naked — came out to embrace their father, who was our driver. A burly, turbaned man with a gravel voice, he seemed very happy to see them.

The second lorry drove off to the east, but Booker, thank goodness, stayed with me.

The *djol* rose above us in near featureless majesty. Our truck groaned and rattled up a road that followed a series of ridges. There were many hairpin turns, not like the bends of a European road, but much more gradual. It was like climbing up a series of not-too-steep ramps. Even so, we were soon crawling up mesa-like ridges some thousands of feet above the surrounding land. Deep chasms hemmed us in, their gaping emptiness marking the rifts cut into the plateau by the wadis. We rode up the flanks of the ancient plateau, higher and higher, escaping from the implacable desert. The sky seemed enormous and very close.

Around ten o'clock we entered a wide valley, and were about to make a hairpin turn up the steep road to the overhanging ridge when the truck engine sputtered and gave out. The driver made a close inspection, and there was some discussion among the Arabs and with Booker. They decided it was carburetor trouble, but fixable. Since we would be there a while, I decided to hike up one of the adjoining ridges, both to get the feel of the land and to take some distanced photographs of the lorry.

After the morning's ride it was a pleasure to be on foot again. I scrambled up the slope, enjoying the air and the bright sky and not minding the slippery shale-like stuff underfoot. It was thrilling to imagine that, apart from the men who made the road, I might have been the first person to walk on this hillside for centuries, perhaps since the beginning of time.

As I climbed, the sun beat down and my pace slowed considerably. Somewhere near the top of the ridge I turned — and was surprised at how small and insignificant the lorry looked. From my vantage point I could see where the road climbed the opposite ridge. Beyond that appeared the very top of the plateau, riven here and there by deep chasms, its surface wrinkled, bare, and brown as deerskin. It was a good moment, made more piquant by the thought that if the truck should happen to pull away and leave me, I would surely be dead in a matter of hours.

I sat for a while, hatless, beginning to swelter in the heat; then, after taking a few pictures, I made my way carelessly down, slipping and sliding, coming dangerously close to falling on my face as, willy-nilly, I gathered speed, and ended my little excursion in a precipitous rush.

Booker smiled and handed me the goatskin bag of water. I drank heartily. The carburetor was soon fixed and we continued our journey, climbing steadily upward until there were no more ridges, nothing looming above us. We were wrapped in sky, light, and air; around us lay the plain, the *djol* itself, a bare scoured land, strewn with rock and marked by scrubby vegetation.

"The *djol*," writes Freya Stark, "has the fascination and terror of vastness, not only in space but in time. As one rises to its sunbathed level, the human world is lost; Nature alone is at work, carving geography in her millennial periods, her temporal abysses made visible in stone."

Stark here comes close to paraphrasing Thomas Hardy's description of Egdon Heath in *The Return of the Native*, and indeed the *djol* is a sublime landscape, one that overawes the human and evokes a Darwinian sense of slow transformation, of survival through simplification. Once upon a time it was a seabed; now, on this limestone plateau some seven thousand feet high, "it seems" — as Stark says — "absurd to reckon time in human years. The scrubby plants are scarce more momentary than men who pass in transitory generations."

We stopped. I was thrilled to get out and walk along beside the truck, to catch a glimpse of distant ranges and of the sea shining far to the south. I stooped and plucked a leaf of one of the round dark-green bushes called *deni*, the thoroughly drab but impressively resilient clothing of the plain. I carried it away with me and later placed it with some other Arabian mementos, including my diplomatic certification, or exequatur, signed by the Queen (or her signature machine). Much later my cache of treasures was stolen by some scurvy packer during one of my then frequent moves.

By early afternoon we had descended from the heights and entered the Wadi Disbah, a pleasant valley where we stopped for lunch and a break from the relentless heat. We soon picked up the Al-Kaff road, parts of which resembled traces of some ancient Roman construction. Booker explained that Hadhrami money over the years had contributed to the primitive paving: crude bricks had been laid along some of its length, a curious sight in that wilderness. Over 160 miles of this road were kept in good repair and improved, and tolls were levied to pay for the work.

Unfortunately, this semi-civilized touch did not prevent our much-tried Bedford truck from breaking down again. Repairs were again effected, and we began a long run through some bleak desert country. Many miles east and north of the Al-Kaff road lies the wildest part of the Eastern Protectorate. It is part of what the British called the "Northern Deserts Region," an awesomely bleak wilderness bordering on Saudi Arabia and the Dhofar region of Oman. On one of our stops Booker pointed out to me, far to the east, a high mountain citadel topped by some crude fortifications. Ancient ruins, he informed me, which he had long wanted to take a close look at. Later archaeological investigation probably identified this as one of the way stations or fortresses on the old frankincense route. The incense, which originated in the mountains of Oman, was carried by caravans all the way to the Red Sea and thence found its way into Europe. Out there in the eastern desert, Booker explained, lay the lost city of Ubar, mentioned in ancient texts and referred to by Bertram Thomas and other explorers of the Empty Quarter. Years later, the purported site of Ubar was to be located by satellite and radar investigation, but in the late 1950s all scientific exploration in the area was at a standstill.

In the afternoon we reached the fort of Rabat-Al-Maara, really just a small concrete blockhouse, guarded by HBL soldiers. Much later, at the border between the Qua'iti and Kathiri States, we halted at a customs post, a small whitewashed building beside a desolate escarpment. Soldiers in green headdress — Kathiri apparently — stood by or lounged in the shade. Our driver went through the ritual of identifying us and paying duties on the cargo, which I now learned consisted of fuel and engine oil, and bags of millet and tea.

In order to deliver some of our cargo we now veered east, and camped that night in a shallow depression in one of the most desolate and beautiful areas I had so far seen. It was a small piece of the desert of the imagination, a place piled high with windswept dunes, beyond which, in Shelley's phrase, "the lone and level sands stretched far away." As the day waned, sunlight softened the contours of the moulded sand and burnished the land to an amazing copper-gold. I felt half-swallowed by the shadows that my body cast.

As we were pitching the tents, an animal sprang from behind a nearby dune, paused for a few seconds to turn on us a glance of startled innocence, then bounded away. An outcry from the other Arabs alerted the soldier, who grabbed his rifle and ran between the dunes, shouting and firing wild shots into the encroaching dusk. But the animal was gone.

Was it an oryx, the near-legendary antelope of the Arabian desert, an animal that probably accounts for the image of the unicorn? I had caught a glimpse of a medium-sized animal with — I thought — two tapering horns. In the odd light and because of its hasty flight it was difficult to see whether the apparition had the white spotted coat of the oryx or was the more familiar, but by no means common, dun-coloured desert gazelle. The Arabs insisted that it was an oryx, and Booker, inside one of the tents, had missed the sighting. The soldier, after a short pursuit among the dunes, returned disappointed, but claimed that one of his shots had found its mark. I fervently hoped it wasn't so.

In my Aden office I had received more than one letter from American hunters who wished to organize elaborate expeditions to obtain an oryx trophy or two. Money was usually no object. Nor was money a problem for the wealthy Arabs from the Gulf States, who had nearly wiped out the whole Arabian oryx population. Curiously enough, it was Michael Crouch, the young man I had met in Mukalla, who was to play a key role in saving the Arabian oryx from extinction, when he served as deputy leader of an international expedition to capture and breed a few of the last remaining animals. Since most of them had retreated to the Rub Al Khali or inhabited the wilder parts of the northern deserts, far from our encampment, it seemed unlikely that we had actually spotted one. But "accidentals" are common in birdwatching, so I like to imagine that I had been granted a special vision on that memorable evening.

The next morning we dragged ourselves up at six o'clock. It had been a very cold night, and I froze through breakfast and until the sun began to warm things up a few hours later. We now had an easy run to Tarim, the most easterly of the three famous Wadi Hadhramaut cities. We were about to intersect one of the main routes of the ancient spice trade, and once again the landscape changed dramatically.

Driving through the great wadis was like no other Arabian travel I had experienced. Miles of smooth sand stretched away on all sides, making a vast level plain framed by steep-sided cliffs, dark ridges metamorphosing into buttes or mesas, their topmost peaks often crenellated like ancient battlements. In the heart of the plain one found a deep-cut rocky channel, which, in time of floods, would fill with water, but which for the most part remained empty, dry as a cauterized wound.

The ease with which one could drive the great wadis was surprising. One had the feeling of being in an almost artificial environment, of riding a toy truck on the smoothed-out floor of a child's sandbox. This pleasurable experience often led one to forget the crucial element of water. Why were the gouged-out channels of the riverbeds almost always dry?

During the 1940s the Hadhramaut had experienced a succession of great famines, and the British had attempted to stabilize water resources through "the pump scheme." They had introduced some seven hundred diesel pumps, and made plans for dams and other developments. The pumps and cisterns were designed to compensate for the often useless profligacy of such flash floods as did occur in that desiccated region. Much later, when I read Frank Herbert's *Dune*, the famous novel about tribes, empires, and the control of a precious spice trade in an imaginary future world, I was reminded of the Hadhramaut obsession with water. In conversation, the author confirmed to me that his inspiration had indeed partially come from the Arabian experience.

We drove on, and soon approached Tarim, Seyun, and Shibam, the three famous Hadhramaut cities, cultural artifacts of great significance, and fascinating destinations for all kinds of travellers. These once offered (in many respects) an archetypal image of fabulous Arabia, even though several other cities in the region — now decayed or lost in the sands — had in the past matched their splendour. The spectacular trio in fact lie along the east-west trade route that once made the region wealthy and carried its renown from China to Rome. Silk from China came this way, as did spices from India, and gold from Ethiopia. Myrrh was produced in what is now Oman and was used to make perfumes and cosmetics; frankincense, also produced in South Arabia, went to Egypt as an ingredient in the embalming process, and was used in religious rituals in Egypt and Rome. The figure of the Queen of Sheba dominates the Bayhan region to the west, which I was soon to visit, but in the Hadhramaut one thinks of the Magi, with their gifts of gold, frankincense, and myrrh. Much later one was to learn that the family of the bearer of quite a different "gift," Osama bin Laden, originated in the Hadhramaut.

As I rode toward the three cities I was not thinking of future terrorism, however. I was remembering the region's ancient glories and making notes on the Hadhrami diaspora, a phenomenon that began early in the nineteenth century and continues to this day. Significant numbers of local inhabitants have migrated to other Asian regions, India, Java, Singapore, East Africa, and Saudi Arabia in particular, where many of them have made great fortunes, parts of which they subsequently invested in their native Arabian region. At the time of my visit, these wealthy oligarchs dominated the economy and acted as a repressive force. Many were Sayyids (whose families, supposedly descended from Muhammad, had a special status), although their power was even then being challenged. Expatriate money also accounted for much of the unique material charm of the region, a charm that could not wholly conceal a great deal of underlying squalor.

Near Tarim, Pat Booker turned me over to Dick Gannon, a Britisher who was Assistant Adviser, Northeastern Deserts. Gannon greeted me with more curiosity than warmth. A stocky, broad-faced, rather portly man, probably in his thirties, he was dressed immaculately in a light blue suit, matching tie, and soft dark-blue shoes. He had a military air about him and, as I soon learned, was an ex-soldier and Arab Legion man known for his abrasive temper. (According to Michael Crouch's memoir, he was later to be sent home after he collapsed, sweating and raving, when his vehicle stuck in the sand and his escort — who disliked him — refused to help him extricate it.) The day I saw him he was very trig indeed, and seemed to look rather askance at my youth, tousled hair, and shabby clothes, and to resent my rather off-the-cuff manner. Perhaps he had already heard about the "incident" that had occurred on my arrival in Mukalla.

I made a quick evaluation of the situation and decided that there was no point in my staying over in the Hadhramaut for the two days left on my orders. I could not talk to the Arabs, I was still a bit shaky from my illness, and I was sartorially under-equipped for socializing with Gannon. All the information I needed from him I could get over a cup of tea. I asked if I could be given transport for a quick look at Tarim and Seyun and then brought back to the Aden Airways landing strip at Ghuraf to catch the Aden flight at 4:30. He agreed, and invited me to meet him there. We could have a talk, he suggested, and I could watch him review the HBL guard.

There followed a curious and tantalizing drive-by of Tarim and Seiyun, made more frustrating by the fact that my camera, with only a few shots left, jammed. My driver did his best to explain things to me, making use of vivid gestures and a few words of English. I was a bit dazed from my journey, the camp-outs, and the rapid changes of focus. Looking back, the experience seems like the enactment of an episode from Italo Calvino's haunting book *Invisible Cities*, for I followed no artificially imposed guidebook order — there were merely fleeting impressions and dreamlike juxtapositions. I saw the white dome of a mosque, a leaning tower with a cupola and railing, eyebrow arches over rows of windows, old city gates topped by flags, shadowy alleyways, beggars, camels, and donkeys, veiled women drawing water from wells. I saw Tarim, city of the Saiyyids, gleaming in the sunlight, and Seiyun, where the driver pointed at some lush gardens and a splendid house belonging to the Al-Kaff family. It was a square, white-columned building with a great porticoed entrance, alive with arches and recesses, its roof apartments half-hidden by incised pillars — an apparition recalling the megalomania and odd taste of some mogul from America's Gilded Age.

Sadly, although Shibam is only a few miles west, there was no time to go there, so we turned from Seiyun and returned to meet Dick Gannon at a small military post near the landing strip at Ghuraf.

There I watched him inspect the guard, and we had a brief conversation. Afterward, I accompanied him as he talked to some Hadhrami merchants and officials who were leaving on the Aden flight. I passed the time chatting with a young Hadhrami, and when I found that my temperamental camera had decided to work again I was able to record something of the strange beauty of that odd afternoon.

Our Aden Airways Dakota had landed right in the wadi. The vastness of the setting made it look like a toy airplane. The low-angled sunlight struck the tops of the ancient cliffs behind it and set them glowing in pink and gold splendour. In the foreground, some dozen Hadhrami travellers strode across the shadowy, dun-grey sand to board the flight, elegant in their turbans, western suit jackets, and long skirts.

I shook hands with Dick Gannon. Back in his office he would write a few puzzled comments about my fleeting visit and forward them to the British intelligence unit at Steamer Point. I had not of course discussed with him my reasons for cutting my trip short, but as soon as the plane touched down on the tarmac at Aden I began to regret my "sensible" decision. Perhaps I knew that it would be a long time before I would be able to return to the Hadhramaut.

TWENTY-ONE

The Unforgiven

A colony is a good place to learn about power politics. Halfway through my tour in Aden I was beginning to comprehend the complexity and fragility of the British system of rule. The old empire had been shattered by history; in South Arabia in the 1950s the British were groping for strategies that would sustain aspects of it, while appearing to give ground to Arab aspirations for self-rule. It was an impossible task: what resulted was a muddled policy based on outdated ideas, one that, given the contradictions within the Arab world itself, led quickly to chaos.

That kind of politics I was just beginning to understand. But there were other power structures, far closer to me than those, of which I was shockingly ignorant. I knew nothing, for example, of the subtleties and challenges of male-female relationships. I assumed that social problems and class conflicts could be sorted out by acts of spontaneous goodwill. And the notion of office politics had not even occurred to me.

During the 1950s the American Foreign Service was an organization in transition. The old service had been the preserve of the Eastern Establishment elite. An overwhelmingly WASP conscription filled the ranks with recruits who were mostly wealthy, Ivy League-educated, and male.

Foreign diplomats often assumed that this was still the case. The French Consul in Aden, Jean Portal, became a friend of mine; we played tennis and ate quite a few meals together. One day, delicately probing, he remarked, "In France, diplomatic personnel are drawn from the older established families. It's true in the States too, is it not?"

"Nope," I said, and looked him in the eye. I didn't explain further and he didn't ask.

In fact I was from an odd and rather indefinable Irish-Scottish subculture in New York. My sole contact with the Ivy League, apart from some graduate work at Columbia, had been as a valet in the Harvard, Yale, and Princeton clubs in New York City. I owed most of my education and my arts expertise, which impressed some people, to my reading, my visits to the museums and galleries of the metropolitan area, and the performances I devoured at the New York City Opera and Ballet, the Philharmonic, and the Met. From childhood, I went to the alternative cinema houses that once proliferated in the city, haunted the second-hand bookstores, both uptown and downtown, and bought my clothes at well-known establishments such as Bloomingdale's and Abercrombie and Fitch. My grandmother, also born in New York City, had an apartment in the east seventies, and I later rented one near York Avenue and the Queensboro Bridge, so that even when our family moved north to the suburbs of Westchester I had easy access to the city. In nearby White Plains I attended a newly created but well-funded Catholic high school where I had Alan Alda and John Gregory Dunne as classmates. Cash-strapped and working class or not, I wasn't exactly a kid from the boonies.

Much later, in an obituary notice that reviewed Bill Crawford's career, he was described both as the product of an educated elite background and as a new officer who was part of the post-Second World War democratization of the foreign service. This seeming contradiction was the result of the obituary writer's attempt to have it both ways. In fact, Crawford was the son of a very successful and well-off academic. As a boy he attended the best American and foreign preparatory schools and — as noted — he later attended Harvard. His recruitment in Washington therefore hardly signalled a social revolution. That only came about in the late 1950s, when young working-class men like myself were encouraged to seek careers in diplomacy.

I owed my acceptance into the foreign service to the fact that I had sailed through all the examinations and interviews, but more potently to the fact that the State Department was just then making a determined effort to achieve some diversity, accepting new recruits from all over the country and from all walks of life. There was a catch, of course. One of the problems of growing up outside of a power structure you later enter is that you haven't learned the rules at an early age. The courses we took at the Foreign Service Institute could hardly compensate for not being to the manner born. Some of us new recruits were bound to bear the brunt of class resentments, especially when we ran into problems. I don't want to overstate the case: we didn't have to be accompanied to our offices by the National Guard. Yet many of us had to watch our backs at evaluation time.

If the pre-Second World War foreign service was a closed shop socially, the "new" foreign service was still dominated by those from "correct backgrounds." It was also rife with male chauvinism, which —

although this is not so surprising given that it was the 1950s — could take odd forms.

The wives of officers, for example, were not allowed to have their own careers, but were stringently rated on their power to function as "representatives of their husbands — and America." Which meant they had to know how to entertain, to dress appropriately, and — except when mouthing witty nothings — to keep their mouths shut. One woman friend of mine, a talented visual artist, gave up her role (and her foreign service husband) shortly after her partner was told by a rating officer that her art was "too advanced" to bring credit on America abroad.

The foreign service rating system, in theory, seemed to guarantee a certain amount of fairness. After six months, supervising officers were required to write "Efficiency Reports" on personnel working with them. These reports were reviewed by at least one other officer, and then discussed with the subject. If one had a problem, one could, in theory, appeal the rating.

When my evaluation time came up in Aden, Bill Crawford decided that Michael Sterner was not senior enough to review his report (this despite the fact that Sterner had been in charge of the consulate for about four months while Crawford was in Yemen). I did not realize then that I might have questioned Crawford's decision on that point; I was a novice at the rating game. When he called me in to discuss my efficiency, Crawford was matter-of-fact, if a little brisk, in his manner. He had seen a few rough edges in my performance, but he was not going to be as stringent about those as he might have been — he didn't want to ruin my career on this first rating. If my report writing continued to improve; if I could be more cheerful about my "representational duties"; if I could relate more enthusiastically to the local community — in short, if I made a 180-degree revolution in my attitude and efficiency, things might still work out for me. Crawford explained that he was leaving room for this transformation by giving me the formal rating of "performance clearly meets essential requirements."

While I objected to the implications of a few of his remarks, I was rather happy with the interview, and went away feeling that on the whole I had come through very well. It had not occurred to me to ask to see the actual document penned by Crawford.

My illusion of well-being was rudely shattered some weeks later. One day the mail pouch brought a letter from the State Department. I read it with amazement and outrage. It purported to sum up some of the "deficiencies" noted in Crawford's efficiency report — an astonishing array, ranging from defects of character to near-criminal offences.

It seems that my service in Aden had not been quite so satisfactory as Crawford had indicated in our interview. On the contrary, I was personally flawed — "introverted," "irresponsible," "impatient," and "immature." Wondering if the alliteration was compulsory, I was almost glad to read that I was also "painfully shy and diffident," that I had "few acquaintances outside of the consulate staff," and that I had had "several experiences [obviously bad] with the local traffic police." Even my supposed virtues and achievements had been painfully won; for example, I had "originally made numerous mistakes in my drafting," but had managed to overcome this "as a result of greater care and experience."

The State Department's letter, signed by the chief of the Performance Evaluation Branch, offered me much wise, almost fatherly advice on how to do better, suggesting that I "accept the criticisms in a constructive manner by undertaking at once all possible steps to improve [my] usefulness to the post and to the Service." It was important that I change my ways so that I should not "bring discredit" on the country I represented. The writer then referred me to my chief, who would surely offer me "sympathetic assistance and guidance in overcoming [my] present problems."

I sat dazed for a while after reading all this. The stiletto had clearly been applied by a master. When I recovered myself, I went to see Crawford (who had been sent a copy of the Department's letter) and protested the outrage. Although he didn't quite manage to suppress his smirk, Bill was almost sympathetic. He explained patiently that he had my best interests at heart, that while he wished he could have written otherwise, he had his responsibilities. I left the office in a fury, enraged most of all by the gap between our interview and the language of the letter. Actually, I didn't know the half of it. Much later, when I returned to Washington, I read Crawford's actual report, and found that the Department had everywhere softened his language and omitted some of his most blatant lies. The written report was so thoroughly negative that I was amazed that I had not been recalled by the Department when they received it.

The impact of such an experience on my idealistic and enthusiastic young self can be imagined. Why did I not appeal the rating? Why did I not try to extend my stay in Aden and wait for the arrival of the foreign service inspectors? These officers visited posts approximately every two years and did their own ratings; they would soon note my competence and set things right.

For one thing I was nearly in a state of shock and had really no idea of what to do. Secondly, when I finally considered what an appeal would entail — letters, documents, testimonials, perhaps even a return to the States — I began to back off. Such complexities dismayed me; and what would the result be, even if I were vindicated? I did not want to win love by litigation; I wanted to be judged competent — as I deserved to be — on the basis on my everyday performance.

At the time I could not account for Bill Crawford's hostility. Michael Sterner, who, in a letter written some time later, testified to my competence, put it down to a "personality conflict." Crawford was "over-zealous in the demands he made on his junior officers," Sterner wrote. He also noted that "Mr. Henighan had his own way of doing things, and he refused to be intimidated into doing them otherwise simply because his way did not conform to the foreign service norm." (I took that as a compliment.)

Despite all of this, and even in the face of his conniving, Crawford and I had remained on speaking terms, and it seemed to me that on almost every occasion I had jumped to his tune smartly enough to justify something better. It was only afterward that it became clear to me that what he resented was the fact that I refused to be impressed either by his background or by his own mastery of the foreign service career game. He also probably sensed that I was simply not taken in by his facade of giving all for the cause: I found he lacked a sense of perspective, not to mention humour and self-irony. There was also something distinctly robotic about his devotion to duty, while on both the personal and intellectual levels he was quite unforthcoming (we never once had a serious conversation about anything).

Although the early warnings I got about Crawford from Esmail and Bruce Condé came, so to speak, from left field, they proved quite relevant. Later, when Bill and Ginger departed from Aden, I was given the task of buying their farewell present. I took this job seriously and searched high and low for something suitable, getting in touch with several of their friends, who, I thought, might like to help me find a special Aden-related gift. I was surprised at the indifference these ostensible friends displayed in connection with the Crawfords' departure. Nobody wanted to help; nobody seemed to care that our consul and his mate were leaving the colonial scene.

Both Bill Crawford and Michael Sterner were products of the eastern establishment tradition. Their backgrounds were roughly equivalent, and, as I've noted, both had attended Harvard. This ensured that Crawford would be more tolerant of Sterner and his initial lack of focus than he was of a young officer who, like myself, had no such roots. Crawford's attitude was reflected through Cathy O'Hara — in those days girl Fridays learned to harmonize with their bosses. While emotionally Cathy depended on me, she refused to acknowledge that I might be capable of having a career equivalent to that of Crawford or Sterner. Crawford's attitude was also revealed in his treatment of Carmela Natale. As an Italian woman from Boston she was readily classifiable, and Crawford treated her with a condescending geniality to which, good-naturedly, she took no offence.

The consulate was thus a microcosm of the American class and career system, with establishment power at the centre and others forced to make obeisance to their "superiors" or else pay the price. Michael Sterner's consistent open-mindedness and goodwill turned what was for me an impossible situation into something much more palatable, but no one was in a position to expose "the boss," even when he concocted reports that were untrue and intentionally detrimental to a young officer who had initially admired him. And however much the consul's dislike can be attributed to some ultimately unfathomable "clash of personalities," there was a strong tinge of elitism at the heart of it. After all, how could he be expected to acknowledge a young man who challenged him unexpectedly often, who refused to wear the stars and stripes on his sleeve, and who had only a mythical sense of what it must be like to have one's fare paid all the way to Harvard Yard?

Just before Bill Crawford left Aden, another of my efficiency reports became due. I breathed a sigh of relief when he turned the task over to Bill Wolle, who had arrived at the consulate some months earlier, and had the rank of consul. I remember sitting with Wolle as he explained to me that he had written a very favourable report and recommended me for promotion. Then, after a pause, he added — and his manner conveyed both understanding and almost a shy reticence — that Bill Crawford, after reading his comments, had decided to exercise his privilege of review. Crawford, Wolle noted, had dissented strongly from his rating and suggested that the deficiencies he had noted earlier had by no means been overcome.

I was not really surprised, though I was amazed that the man should devote some of his final busy days at the consulate to such a task. I nodded my understanding, shook hands with Wolle, thanked him, and went back to the business of searching for a farewell present for good old Bill and Ginger.

TWENTY-TWO

Love in the Tropics

The irony of my Aden situation did not escape me. In the sphere of action, in which it seemed clear to me (and to many others) that I had succeeded quite well, the official rating system had deemed me a failure. In that other, inner sphere, where I struggled to achieve romance and real connection, and where I considered myself a definite flop, I suddenly succeeded. I woke up one day knowing that I had found my Joycean beach muse, my confidante and soulmate. It was — as the British say — really quite provoking.

My romance with Diana C. was a strange one, both conventional and in some respects *outré*. What else could it be in Aden? Nineteen-fifties North American dating mores had nothing to do with it; my experience was right out of a nineteenth-century novel, Jane Austen perhaps, with a soupçon of Stendhal and a large dollop of Victorian "respectability." Between us all was discreet and tentative, and even though she lived and worked as an au pair close by in Khormaksar, we spent relatively little unfettered time together.

Diana felt a great responsibility to her cousin David, his wife, and their children, Ian and Joanna, and sometimes when we met, these young charges of hers were in the foreground. Our dates consisted of walks on Khormaksar Beach, drives to Little Aden to visit the gardens, or socializing with her cousin's set. We played table tennis in Crater, climbed the rocks at Marshag, and roamed around the souk. There were the usual misunderstandings, sulks, and reconciliations, but no violent passion. At first, as in a Jane Austen novel, most of the wooing was done verbally and within a certain established decorum. She was only seventeen and, unlike many American girls of her age and younger, no Lolita.

Such a relationship, however, seemed to me a wonderful gift, a sojourn of bliss amid the jaded goings-on of the Colony. I had found a charming companion, a spirited and boyish chum, and she was a revelation to me: Miss J. Hunter Dunne from the well-known John Betjeman poem, or Valentine Wannop from Ford Madox Ford's Parade's End.

Perhaps it would have done me good to take the plunge into wild sexual passion, as I was soon tempted to do and later did. There was a Mrs. Wilkins, a charming older lady who hovered occasionally on the scene, very friendly and possibly available, while a tempting French beauty named Colette would soon appear. Either of those would have been a very different show — and arguably more appropriate. My karma, however, decreed otherwise. Even then, I was hardly ever one to throw caution to the winds.

Not that there were no Byronic episodes. As we moved toward greater intimacy, the leash — held fairly tightly by her cousin, although with some confusion and not much effectiveness — loosened. There were drinks in my flat and a crossing of ever more boundaries. Soon I proposed a little adventure: a hike up Gold Mohur Valley, a climb down to the rocky shore, and some very private sea bathing.

At Gold Mohur beach, the rocky cliffs rise inland some 1,650 feet and more above the bathing enclosure. The high promontory called the Elephant's Back, on which the Aden lighthouse sits, juts out seaward, dividing Gold Mohur Bay from the rougher, wilder Conquest Bay beyond. As you sat on Gold Mohur beach facing the sea, the Elephant's Back towered above you on the left, and the Gold Mohur Valley stretched away behind you, a bleak and uninviting wasteland.

We decided to walk up Gold Mohur Valley, climb the rocks beyond the Elephant's Back, and circle down onto Conquest Bay. It was a great place to get away from the crowd and our outing was sure to be intriguing.

On the day of our excursion we left fairly early. It was winter in Aden and seemed almost cool. We were without hats and wore very little clothing; we carried one small canteen of water. At first the going was easy. We scrambled up the rocky hillsides, making jokes and having a good time. Noon came along and the temperature rose.

I have since learned a great deal about the perils of heatstroke and dehydration, but in Aden I was blasé and consumed by the bravado (or stupidity) of youth. The air temperature that day was some 95 degrees Fahrenheit — not very hot by Aden standards, but we were climbing on rocks that reflected heat, and there was no shade whatsoever. Because we had some water we felt safe, but we didn't know that when you are very active in such heat your body loses more water than you can consume. We also made the mistake of trying to save the small quantity we had, even though we soon began to feel very thirsty. And, foolishly, we kept on walking.

We climbed several hundred feet, crossed a spur of the cliffside, then cut down into Conquest Bay. We soon finished off the canteen, but at least we had reached a position above the rocky shoreline. It was not what we expected. Just below us, waves crashed on the cliffs; there were few footholds and the undertow appeared fearsome. We could see the sandy beach on Conquest Bay but, given our increasing exhaustion and thirst, a climb down and back was unthinkable. The lack of shade had begun to punish us and, desperate for relief, we wriggled down to a ledge just over the seething water and tried to splash ourselves cool. This worked well for a while, but at one point, reaching down, Diana slipped and plunged into the maelstrom. As she fell, I made a grab and caught hold of her arm. I managed to anchor myself; if I had gone over it would have been serious. Only an exceptional swimmer could have made it through the heavy swells and reached the beach. Not to mention the possibility of sharks.

There was a terrible moment when, just able to cling together, we gazed at each other in full recognition of the danger. Then I braced myself and pulled her up, while she squirmed and twisted and somehow threw her body onto the saving ledge.

We sat there gasping, out of breath, rendered almost inert by the sudden realization that we had barely escaped a catastrophe. The sea no longer looked so inviting. We collected ourselves at last and made our way back up the cliff. Sheer determination carried us to the floor of Gold Mohur Valley, but we were dizzy and near-comatose from exhaustion. I have never been so thirsty. The relentless brightness and the heat had become hateful.

I still remember the feel of the gravel underfoot, the shade of the scrawny trees in the Gold Mohur parking lot. We staggered to the club bar and I had an ice-cold Coca-Cola. No drink has ever tasted better.

This experience, for all its foolishness, was a turning point. It bonded us and gave us a sense that our fates were twined together. It represented the outer, unconscious, sun-dazed pole of our developing relationship. There was also a night side, an entry into secret knowledge and an initiation. Oddly enough, this also took place at Gold Mohur Beach.

One steaming night when Diana had gotten off rather late and nothing else offered, we decided to go for a swim. Khormaksar beach was close by but dangerous at night because of the risk of sharks. It was also far too public.

I remembered that Gold Mohur virtually shut down after dark; there would be a watchman, but he would hardly bother us. With any luck we could have a safe swim and some time together; we could also escape the oppressive heat.

With a sense of excitement, we drove the familiar route to the beach (even now, I could drive it in my sleep). We descended from the crags, a hot rush of air in our faces, and raced along the shore, enjoying the smell of fish, the sting of sand, the feel of our own bodies bumping together in the semi-darkness.

We arrived at the Gold Mohur parking lot. I had never seen the club so deserted. A watchman appeared and, satisfied that we were harmless, muttered a greeting and went back to his dimmed lantern and his sleep. We walked down to the water and entered a magical world. Above stretched the faintly glowing, overarching sky; around us rose shadowy cliffs, while beacons twinkled here and there on land, and the sea was alive with light like an alchemist's brew.

We strolled along the beach, hypnotized by the night, the silence, and the shimmering light in the water. That light was not a reflection of the sky, but something else, like nothing we had ever seen before. The heat, the season, the changing tides, had washed in swarms of micro-organisms, and their light pulsed in the water like a thousand tiny candles.

It was very hot. We stripped and plunged in, dived and swam around. The febrile light ran over our skin. It was wonderful.

We clung together and made love in the shimmering water. We frolicked naked on the beach, where we had taken possession of the night and of each other.

Only later did I connect this with a scene from one of my favourite movies — viewed as a child and many times as an adult — the absurdly-titled but elegant *I Walked with a Zombie*. In the film, Frances Dee stands on the deck of a ship in a never-never land version of the Caribbean, entranced by the beauty of the night and the glowing light of the water. But a cynical Tom Conway reminds her, "That water — it takes its glow from millions of tiny dead bodies; it's the glitter of putrescence. There is no beauty here — merely death and decay."

A one-sided view, as the film reveals, the view of a wounded man who requires redemption, and a judgment partially contradicted by the beauty of the scene itself. Yet also an appropriate sentiment for the dwellers in a colonized world, for a society based on slavery and injustice, as Aden itself was based on oppression and injustice.

Our private night at Gold Mohur was sheer pleasure and magical light, harmonious oneness with nature and each other. It proved a rare moment, an idyllic interlude in lives fraught with contradictions, a gleam of poetry in a world permeated by death and decay.

Our escapades together, my half-naive connection with Diana, soon led to a tightening of the social nets around us. When we decided to become engaged — I'm almost tempted to say "plighted our troth" — the mills of the gods started grinding.

David C. summoned me one day. We sat in his study and drank cognac together; then he asked me what my intentions were in relation to his cousin.

It was one of those moments when everything seems unreal. I might have made a joke, except that David was a formidable man, not large, but imposing and confident — highly intelligent, precise, and articulate. A stocky redhead and quite literally a highbrow, he was certainly capable of telling anyone off, if he thought it necessary.

I mumbled something about our deepening affections and our hope, in due course, that we might marry.

He went on at length about our youth, our differing backgrounds, his cousin's inexperience, and explained that he had an enormous responsibility to Diana's mother (whose husband had died some years before), a responsibility that he intended to fulfill to the best of his ability. He hoped I understood the situation. (I did.)

He then shifted ground to the practical.

"You realize that you will have to undertake to provide for Diana in the manner to which she is accustomed?"

I examined my conscience and concluded that I never intended otherwise. It occurred to me, too, although I didn't say it, that she wasn't exactly living in royal style.

The interview soon drew to a close. David extended his hand. He was satisfied with me. However, there was one more thing. He had suggested to Diana's mother that she come out and meet me. She was an avid traveller and would enjoy the trip. It was essential that she get to know me before anything definite could be arranged. He was sure she and I would get along splendidly.

Not long afterward, Mrs. C. did indeed arrive. I was eager to get the ordeal over with, but it was deemed preferable that she "settle in" before I actually met her. I suppose that this time was spent sorting things out between her and Diana. In due course, however, we did meet. It was the beginning of a long and uneasy relationship.

There was something really admirable about Ethel Ruth. She was very grounded in this world and far from undefined or malleable; in fact, she had the vivid reality and enduring strength of a literary type. She belonged to a definite category, not obviously that of the Dickensian dowager, or the Jane Austen wit. No; she rather resembled one of H.G. Wells's indomitable shopkeepers, but with some of the social pride and sense of status of E.M. Forster's stringent middle-class females (not the soulful ones).

Ethel Ruth had been born in Bromley, Kent, where her father was twice mayor. She had married into a solid upper middle-class English family like her own, and had opened a drapery shop in Bishop's Stortford, in Hertfordshire. There she lived in a house called The Granary, which had few conveniences but much charm. Ethel Ruth herself had many conveniences, and perhaps somewhat less charm. I always imagined her carrying an umbrella, but I don't suppose she brought one to Aden.

She was thin as a rail, with lively eyes, a definite nose, and a very prim mouth, which could either twist into a smile or press tight in disapproval. I experienced quite a bit of the latter, since we disagreed on almost everything, but I liked her smile.

She arrived, I believe, with strong suspicions about me, and hoped to expose me as a shifty Jane Austen villain, a Wickham or a Willoughby, someone who had swept her daughter off her feet, probably with ulterior motives. I certainly couldn't pass for Mr. Knightley, but I had no ulterior motives. I just wanted to be happy.

I entertained Mrs. C. as best I could, but as I've explained, the Colony was rather claustrophobic, even for those on short stays. Ethel Ruth was on quite a leisurely stay, and some kind of escape seemed called for. I don't know who suggested Mukalla, but it was an amazing choice: the prospect of seeing Diana's mother and Mark Veevers-Carter together was mind-boggling.

Mark and Wendy responded to my request for lodging for all three of us with amazing speed and generosity. I put together an extra large load of chickens, lima beans, cognac, etc., and made a note at all costs to avoid the customs post.

By this time the Veevers-Carters had moved to their "country place" at Khalif, on the outskirts of Mukalla, where the fish-processing (such as it was) went on. Their house, set on a rocky promontory, looked rather like a small graceless castle or a seedy California high school with pretensions. It was a white boxy structure with two floors and a large roof terrace, enclosed by a balustrade with ornate pointed pillars. The place was roomy and sunny, and although the smell of fish permeated everything, you could swim off the dock close by. While not exactly a desirable residence, the house had chutzpah and we all appreciated it, not least Mrs. C., who was a great sport about these things.

The Veevers-Carters were wonderful hosts; if they gritted their teeth it didn't show, and I suspect they genuinely enjoyed the odd experience of entertaining me and my potential fiancée and mother-in-law. Certainly, the parallel to their own situation must have struck them. Did they see me as a Mark-like interloper actually *getting on* with his future mother-in-law, or did they look deeper and notice a few cracks in our polite facade? Later, Wendy arranged for Diana and me to stay in her mother's New York brownstone, which, I suspect, was a rather rare privilege. She also found us a small Malabar chest, which we bought and carried away as a treasure from Aden.

Just after we arrived, Mark showed us routinely around the house. At one door he dramatically paused, like some Bluebeard half-anxious to boast about his latest crime. He pushed into the room and flicked on a light. In the centre of a very large space enclosed by bare white walls was a magnificent toilet, sans flush, but wonderfully encased and mounted, and set so far above the floor that it was reached by a small flight of steps.

"The throne room," Mark announced. He had designed and constructed this wonder himself.

The next several days were spent in taking Mrs. C. to every conceivable site of interest in and around Mukalla. Mark provided a Land Rover, and my two passengers, lightly dressed, one wearing a blue polka-dot kerchief and the other a yellow, enjoyed the rides. We visited the harbour and the forts, parked and walked around the town, drove some way along the coast road, and explored the beach. The Veevers-Carters gave a dinner and we met some of the Mukalla residents. Mrs. C. had the right connections and could fit in very well, even with those who were suspicious of Mark and Wendy.

By the end of the week, however, Mark was getting slightly restive under the conditions of our visit. Quite possibly the strain of always being on his best behaviour finally got to him. He was also obviously trying to figure out exactly why I had gotten involved with a seventeen-year-old girl to the extent that her rather formidable mother was brought all the way to Arabia to check me out.

At one point, unable to contain himself any longer, he took me aside after dinner. Speaking man to man, he probed me a little, without asking any improper questions, about my real interest in Diana. Beneath his casual discourse I sensed the implicit question, *What in hell are you getting yourself into this for?* When he very nearly put that exact question, I had to make an answer.

The answer I gave Mark surprises me even now. Perhaps I was playing a game with him, as I have often played with those who tried to probe me. Perhaps I didn't know what I was saying, or possibly, at the critical moment, I was inspired by the devil to tell the truth.

I looked Mark in the eye, cleared my throat, and replied in a whisper, "She's got money!"

It was not what he expected. He gaped at me; his jaw dropped and his mouth hung open. Then came a flash of white teeth and a smile of recognition.

"I see ... I see."

I sensed his respect for me shoot up to the stratosphere, which, under the circumstances, I had no reason to be proud of.

Another side of Mark soon revealed itself. One morning he discovered that his Arab assistants had been guilty of some trivial lapse in preparing the fishing rig. Mrs. C., Diana, and I were standing beside the Land Rover, about to go for a drive, when Mark burst from the garage-shed that formed part of the house, a rather alarming figure, obviously in a towering rage. Brandishing a small whip, he began to scream at his assistants, an older man and a boy, who were unlucky enough to be standing close by. Not satisfied with this verbal abuse, he laid into them, whipping them across the head and shoulders until they fled and disappeared in the direction of the nearest house.

Having exhausted some of his fury, Mark suddenly became aware of our presence. He wiped his brow and approached us with a sickly smile. "Only way to treat 'em," he muttered. "Horsewhip the bastards, that's what I say. That's all they understand. Horsewhip the bastards!"

None of us made any comment. We climbed into the Land Rover, glad that we were soon to be leaving Mukalla.

Mrs. C.'s visit to South Arabia came to an end. Not everything had gone smoothly, but nothing had been bad enough to cause her to try to change her daughter's mind. Plans were soon being made for the wedding, set to take place in England at the end of my tour of duty.

While the British were mostly indifferent to this surprising romance, the Americans picked up on it remarkably. They seemed quite charmed by the notion of my finding a bride in Aden. Several times I recounted to an eager audience some of the more poetic details of the wooing. When, after Diana's departure, I threatened to become distracted by other women, I was properly chided by one or two consulate wives. Later, a home movie of the wedding was sent to Arabia to be shown in the consulate, and one of the women wrote me that there was "hardly a dry eye among the audience."

It was a strange turn of events for one who had been finding himself more and more alienated from the life of the British in the Colony. Of course I was, in most respects, and remained for several years, an avid anglophile. I loved English literature, Blake and Shelley, Dickens, E.M. Forster, and H.G. Wells. I loved English music, Byrd, Vaughan Williams, and Britten, the drawings of Blake and the landscapes of Constable. When I was in East Anglia I sought out the little country grave of Edward Fitzgerald of *Rubaiyat* fame, climbing fences and crossing fields to reach it, and sat entranced beneath the rose tree from Persia that decorates the place. I empathized with the British thriller writer Geoffrey Household's description of his favourite pastime, "doing mostly nothing in a field." It was an English field he meant, and after Arabia — and before the automobile and unrestrained Thatcherism quite ruined it — England was one of the most perfect places in which to commune with a benign and human-scaled nature.

The strange turn that led to my connection with England and my new affiliation with a host of (mostly indifferent) middle-class English relatives puzzled me. When I landed in England to get married, a Rolls-Royce picked me up at the airport. After my marriage I was duly inscribed in *Burke's Peerage*. This was pretty good work for a poor boy from New York, who saw himself as brimming with idealism. Maybe there was more of Wickham or Willoughby in me than I had suspected.

TWENTY-THREE

Independence Day

During my second year in Aden, many things changed. Bill Crawford and Michael Sterner departed and left me as the longest-serving officer at the post; Cathy O'Hara, too, went on her way, and new personnel arrived. On the political front, the situation was rapidly deteriorating. The bombings had started, noted British correspondents were flying in to cover the worsening situation, and even *Newsweek* ran a piece with the banner "Trouble in Aden."

My own troubles in Aden, however, were just ending. Bill Crawford's replacement was a nonpareil named William Alfred Stoltzfus, a brilliant Arabist and diplomat who was also kindly, considerate, and appreciative of the efforts of all his staff.

When he arrived in Aden Bill Stoltzfus was in his early thirties. Slow of manner, thoughtful, and soft-spoken, he was a medium-tall, well-built man with a strong, handsome, hawk-like face. Stoltzfus never wore sunglasses, and I have a vivid memory of him standing in bright desert sunlight, eyes shielded or half-shut, taking note of things near and far, while patiently informing me about some interesting aspect of Islamic culture.

Before the Stoltzfus family transferred from Jidda, Cathy O'Hara opined that while the man himself was all right, his wife was reputed to be a dreadful neurotic, so we should prepare ourselves for the worst.

I don't know whether this information came via Ginger Crawford or from some other source, but in the event Janet Stoltzfus turned out to be the perfect counterpart to her husband: warm, considerate, unflappable — a charming woman, dark-haired and attractive, who, despite the worst of Aden's weather, always looked stylish. Very soon she had the whole consulate staff feeling like a happily bonded family.

Some months before Bill and Janet arrived, yet another Bill — William D. Wolle — had been assigned to Aden as a second consul. A fair-minded man, Wolle — as I have explained — had supported my promotion despite Crawford's niggling objections. Wolle was very tall, a veritable beanpole, with dark eyes and carefully trimmed dark hair. He was slow-moving, soft-spoken, and quietly intelligent, all in all a colleague to treasure. By comparison, his Norwegian wife, Mimmi, was impulsive, outspoken, and fiery, a very handsome woman and a delightfully independent one. Kind and considerate, she was also wonderfully unpredictable. Once, when she got fed up with her husband's being constantly away in Yemen, she took off her wedding ring and cruised the Crescent Bar, "just to see what was going on."

And on one lonely October night, which also happened to be my birthday, I was sitting in my Khormaksar apartment, hardly thinking about the occasion, when there came a brisk knock on my door. I opened it and there stood Mimmi, with a birthday cake she had specially baked for me. I was thrilled, but so dumbfounded I almost forgot to invite her in.

Working with and for Stoltzfus and Wolle was a delight. By the time they arrived, I had so many friends and contacts in the Colony that problems were usually solved by a single visit or phone call. When I had trouble locating someone I needed or was afraid I would be shunted off, I used a method that is probably standard for journalists, but that I figured out for myself. I would simply call the highest-ranking person in the office in question (it was once an Air-Vice Marshal), and even though I was usually passed along, I could then approach the next person and inform him (it was always a him) that I had just spoken to his chief. Going down the ladder like this achieved much better results than going up.

My most interesting assignment during this time, one that I will describe in the next chapter, was my visit to Bayhan in the Western Aden Protectorate to report on the famine there.

Before I left on that trip, however, I had to organize the 1959 Fourth of July celebrations at the consulate. It was a job I relished. The previous year's festivities had seemed to me terribly dull, and Bill Stoltzfus readily gave me licence to improve things.

I ordered the usual food and champagne, but decided on a few unique touches. I had found an old transcription machine in the consulate storeroom and some oversized discs, including recordings by Kate Smith of "God, Bless America," and "The Star Spangled Banner." I acquired a loudspeaker from somewhere and had it hooked up to the player. This machinery was placed on the consulate balcony.

I then contacted the British Army and requested four or five men who could handle a flare gun in Wyatt Earp style. Grateful to the volunteers who turned up, I had a couple of bottles of champagne opened for them, to give them something to sip on while they waited. Unfortunately, I made the mistake of having the champagne delivered by Babouri, the consulate driver (he was generally known as "Babouri," local Arabic for "driver," so he was obviously the genuine article). He was not a man to pass up an opportunity; without informing anyone, he proceeded to help himself liberally to the champagne, concealing a few bottles in his truck for future delectation.

The reception began at sunset, and it was a big one. The Governor and Lady Luce attended, plus all the important politicos and an array of military brass, not to mention virtually every social hanger-on in the colony. Two U.S. military ships were in port, and Admiral O'Flaherty, Commander of Middle East Forces, and many of his officers also appeared.

Everything went beautifully. Why not? I had worked for seventeen straight hours to set things up. "Tom, I've never seen anyone like you in the foreign service for getting things done," Bill Stoltzfus told me. "Without Tom there would have been no Fourth of July," added Bill Wolle. I was in ecstasy. All of Railroad Bill Crawford's niggling "evaluations" dissolved in a moment.

What a scene! The shabby curved street in front of the consulate was crammed with cars. Lanterns, bunting, and balloons decorated the grounds. Tables were spread with good things to eat and drink. And at the appropriate moment Bill Stoltzfus led the assembly in raising a glass to the United States of America.

I gave the signal and my troops did not fail me. "The Star-Spangled Banner" blared from the balcony. Another signal and the British soldiers, encouraged by the champagne, stood up on the roof platform and fired flare after flare into the night sky. The rockets' red glare had hardly begun to illuminate the harbour, however, when several nervous British guests made a break for their cars. Some may have thought it was a terrorist attack; others were possibly upset by the debris showering down on their Jaguars.

Nonetheless, Kate's rendition was a big hit. Recovering from their initial surprise, the notables clapped and shouted "Hear! Hear!" and the party regained its equilibrium.

Despite a few rocky moments, Part One of my Big Production went off splendidly.

I had also, alas, planned a Part Two. Since a couple of American warships were in Aden harbour, I was keen to do something special for the ordinary sailors, who, because of the ironbound distinctions of rank, could not be invited to the consulate reception. My idea was to give the boys a cookout and beer party on one of the Colony's splendidly deserted beaches, and some days before I had sent invitations to every local organization that might be presumed to supply suitable female personnel for the occasion. I arranged for a couple of barrels of beer and piles of hot dogs, and ordered a truck to pick up the visiting sailors at the Prince of Wales pier. From there they would be carried to the beach at Gold Mohur Bay, between Ras Boradli and the Elephant's Trunk Rock, my carefully chosen paradise, which — although normally dark as a coalpit and quite forlorn on moonless nights — was to be lighted and rendered suitably romantic for this occasion.

The disaster that ensued was monumental.

Aden, as I have several times indicated, was notably lacking in "suitable" female companions (that is, unattached "white" women), and on this occasion my invitation attracted not one single outside guest. Worse still, the person assigned to light up the beach and drive the sailors there was none other than Babouri, who was even then lying in a heap near the consulate steps, more than a few rockets flaring in his champagne-dazzled brain.

Unfortunately, someone managed to rouse him, and, dutiful as he was, he hastened — more or less — to the Prince of Wales Pier to pick up the first detachment of waiting sailors. Those unfortunates found themselves packed tightly in the van of a small military truck, driven at breakneck speed by a drunk along Aden's most treacherous corniche road, and deposited on a dark, steaming cauldron of a beach, with only two barrels of warm beer and a few dozen uncooked hot dogs to console them.

Who knows what horrors they imagined on the way there? On one of his runs to the beach Babouri thumped the truck so hard against the overhanging rocks that its frame was bent; yet, to his credit, and as if to guarantee the disaster, he made every trip successfully, losing not a single sailor on the way.

By the time I got there, a hundred or so American sailors were roaming the dark beach, screaming curses at the officers who had engineered this brutal training exercise and disguised it as a party. The beer barrels had been forced open, their completely inadequate contents had been gulped down, and a near riot was in progress. Some sailors clambered up the rocks, desperate to escape the place; others — those who had not heard about Aden's vicious sharks — threatened to swim back to their ships.

I immediately put in a call for help and managed to reach Ali Ahmad, who soon brought over some pressure lamps, a cook stove, and a fresh supply of beer. To my astonishment (and eternal gratitude) Janet Stoltzfus and Mimmi Wolle also volunteered to come along and help.

Although the arrival of the women was in most ways a great blessing, it also gave me a few uneasy moments, since the sailors greeted them as if they were — at the very least — ministering angels who had just fallen out of the sky. Fortunately, Janet and Mimmi were quite able to take care of themselves. They calmed things down sufficiently to enable us to radio the ships for help. The sailors were removed by a landing craft before they could wreak on us the vengeance they so understandably longed for.

Later, Admiral O'Flaherty sent a message of thanks by way of Bill Wolle, who recounted it to me, almost with a straight face. The admiral avowed that the reception was marvellous and that my efforts to entertain the boys were also greatly appreciated, then added, "Perhaps next time, though, you might consider having a baseball game."

During the next few days my Aden contacts were put to good use. The truck that Babouri had mangled belonged not to us but to the Yemen mission of Chuck Ferguson, and ever since Bill Crawford's break with the man he called "Chucky-Wucky" there was no love lost between the two posts. We had to return the vehicle in good condition or suffer some embarrassment.

I called around and was told that only the Royal Air Force might have the facilities to do the job. To my joy, when I contacted them and explained things they agreed. Even better, they refused to send a bill. "Just consider it a little return for past favours," they told me.

In due course Babouri, whom I had ritually cursed and consigned to the lower regions for his part in the "Dark Beach" fiasco, headed back to Ta'iz with Ferguson's truck.

Oddly enough, although I was preparing for a visit to Bayhan in the Protectorate I too had to go unexpectedly to Ta'iz. The purpose of my trip was both mundane and highly unusual. One day a woman had appeared in the consulate waiting room, a tiny figure, dressed as a Yemeni, in flowered chiffon, her head covered, her face half-hidden by a gauzy veil. Ali Esmail came back and announced, with his usual formality and a flash of that familiar razor-sharp smile, that this was a case I should look at. That was uncommon enough — Esmail seldom bothered me with details; mostly I just signed the papers.

"She speaks English, sir; she's from Chicago," he explained.

"From Chicago?"

It was hard to believe. True, the woman was pale, but she was obviously sick, her face spotted and unhealthy, her eyes dulled and vacant. She spoke English, but with great difficulty. An Arab woman spirited from a Yemen mountain village to Chicago she might have been; but a Chicago woman in Arabia?

Yet she was that, exactly. Poor, and somewhat slow of mind, she was an American who had connected with a Ta'iz man somewhere in the slum margins of Chicago. When he brought her to Yemen, she had borne children, suffered intermittently from fever and hunger, and practically lost her life and her language. The dream world she inhabited I never penetrated, but one thing was clear, she wanted to go home. It was not that easy, however. I would have to visit her in Ta'iz to check things out; after that, I could decide whether to renew her passport.

To my delight, Esmail was allowed to accompany me. A crewcut CIA communications man whose services were needed in Yemen came along as well. Janet and Bill Stolzfus and their children were also in or near Ta'iz, and I looked forward to spending a few days with them there.

We had already motored some way past Lahej when we had an interesting encounter. I myself was driving our Willys Jeep, and turned to say a word to our CIA passenger. The instant I looked away I heard something click on the windshield. It was not a hard sound, like a pebble, but subtly different. I turned and saw what looked like small pink darts striking everywhere around us. The windshield was hit again, several times, Esmail cried out in Arabic, and I pulled the jeep to a stop in the rutted track.

Esmail and I got out. We crossed the dirt track into the nearby field, my Somali friend striding eagerly ahead of me. A lanky figure in a white shirt and khaki trousers, he stooped suddenly, caught one of the pink flying things, and held it up for me.

"Locusts," he announced.

I felt a thrill of joy. The locusts came on in a crazy but relentless pattern, thousands of them, silent as windblown pink petals scattered and guided by some invisible force on that breathless, windless day.

In such a barren wilderness I could not think of them as a plague, although Biblical images rose to my mind. They were more like a manifestation, a reminder of the wanton power of nature, its crazy patternings, which could deliver a storm of hungry insects to such a stony and resistant place, whose poor scrub bush they seemed uninterested in devouring.

Some subtle shift in their original environment had brought them from a solitary to a gregarious phase, and now they tumbled in masses across our path, heading somewhere, toward Lahej's cultivated fields perhaps, to announce themselves. Yet to Esmail and me, urbanized fellows both, they were a wonderful distraction. Transformed into kids, we beat the scrub to stir them up, tossed them in the air, made them jump, trampled them into the ground as we sprang about, laughing, half-dancing amid the swarm.

But the heat soon wore us down. We rejoined our CIA friend. He had not bothered to get out of the jeep — although our antics had at least made him smile.

A little later we made another stop, to stretch our legs and enjoy the pleasant hill scenery. After some minutes, the roar of a motor on the road behind us caught our attention. We waited, and a Land Rover appeared. It looked like a typical British staff car, except that it bore the hammer and sickle on a plate beside the licence. The three passengers eyed us; we eyed them. I felt like an earthman watching the arrival of an alien being. Did they feel the same? I could hardly have guessed that just a few years later, after I had departed, the British would have evacuated South Arabia, and dusty, familiar Khormaksar, my temporary residence, would be the home territory of innumerable Russian "advisers."

"Last time I came up it was the Chinese," said our CIA friend. "They're all over the place."

I remembered Mr. Joshi's comparison of the Arabs to locusts. Now we were the locusts, East and West rivals swarming into Yemen for our own strategic purposes.

In the few short months since my last visit, Ta'iz had undergone a dramatic — and visible — transformation. It no longer felt remote, full of exotic possibility. Dragged into the world of East-West conflict, its tensions were almost palpable, and a sense of chaos and cross-purposes hung over the place. The everyday absurdities remained, but they were of a different and darker character. I had a pleasant few days with Janet and Bill Stoltzfus, and from them, too, got a sense that the situation in Yemen was fluid and uncertain. The game was afoot, but the antagonists were sometimes obscure and the objectives vague, not only to a young vice consul, but also to those diplomats who had much more inside information than I did.

In view of this atmosphere, I was not surprised to be taken by Esmail through the city streets at night — almost surreptitiously — to an upstairs apartment, where a small group of relatives waited with the Chicago woman.

Grim-faced and suspicious, the Arabs seemed to expect that I would confront them with some outrageous demand. Perhaps they felt guilty about the woman or, more likely, Esmail had already dunned them for a commission and turned them sullen. At any rate, after some exhausting negotiations we hauled out the consular seal and issued the passport. We also set a date for the woman's flight to the States, which they agreed to book. Esmail would stay in Ta'iz for a few days to make sure things went as planned.

Since I had to return at once, I drove Janet Stoltzfus and her two sons back to the Colony. Bill had to go off to Sana'a and she had decided not to stay in Ta'iz.

I well remember that drive. I was in high spirits and Janet seemed to have no qualms about speed. We flew along, *allegro con brio*. Even when one of her boys got carsick she assured me that they were all enjoying the ride. She was a very special woman.

Just before we left, however, Esmail had approached me with some surprising news. It concerned Babouri, our eponymous driver, who, it seems, had learned of my arrival in Yemen. He had been relieved to come to Ta'iz, just to get away from my scornful eye. Now here I was again. Obviously I had come up country to capture him, to arrest him or make him pay for his theft and the damage to the truck.

Esmail warned me that he had heard, in the souk, as it were, that Babouri had recently acquired an automatic pistol and was stopping frequently for target practice along the length and breadth of the Yemen mountain roads. He had determined to sell his life very dearly.

When he saw that this news had sunk in, Esmail bent over me and said with his sardonic smile, "Perhaps it's time to return, sir. To beat a timely and strategic retreat? Unless by chance you are interested in a shoot-out?"

I told him I was leaving that morning.

Of course I didn't really think Babouri would try to kill me. He was a calculating and ingenious fellow and not at all an irrational one. Besides, I was a young man; I had no real fear of death. I had my illusions to protect me.

At the same time I no longer felt so isolated, so detached from public events. Although my sense of adventure hadn't left me, I was beginning to realize that overseas service was not designed merely to fulfill my personal life-quest. In truth I was beginning to sense that I was a representative, a minor delegate, of the colonial-imperialist powers that moved and shaped world events, and whose mastery, apart from their own squabbles and rivalries, was — as we all thought — quite secure. Threats of troubles ahead, the visible signs of the Cold War, could not shake my confidence in our ultimate success. I had no idea then that history would obliterate so much that I was experiencing on those bright, romantic Yemen mornings. Everything would change; realities that seemed self-sufficient and indestructible would disappear. Drifting away, I would enter other lives and scenes; sometimes — in a more subtle way than Bruce Condé — I would appear to be caught between worlds, to carry a passport to an undiscovered, unreal country, unable to put my feet on any solid ground. The ecstasy would become harder and harder to recapture. Except in memory and nostalgia, little of those first naive days would remain. It would take me a long time to come to terms with that vivid past.

TWENTY-FOUR

The Emir's Coca-Cola

For years after I left South Arabia I experienced involuntary flashes of memory, instant recollections of some moment I had experienced there. Most commonly I would see a landscape — the bend in a great curving wadi, distant mountain ramparts, a hillside terrace. More rarely, I would glimpse a face or a gesture, or recollect a landscape with figures.

I might be crossing a street in New York City, or trudging along some avenue in Ottawa or Toronto; I might be raking leaves, sitting on my porch, or driving my car, when, without warning, I would lapse out of present reality, then just as suddenly return, puzzled as to what might have induced this odd and fleeting involvement with the past.

Psychologists can explain such things, but my personal reference point for such experiences is a notion of the poet William Wordsworth, who wrote about the power of recollection and its key role in activating the transfiguring imagination. Wordsworth cherished what he called the "inward eye," and referred to the efficacy of "spots of time," recollected experiences that are capable of renewing our everyday lives. Such experiences — as Wordsworth understood them — confirm the power of the mind, stimulated in the past by an encounter with some significant reality, to draw upon and extend some inner meaning in the present.

My fleeting memories of South Arabia were, I think, more than mere jolts of nostalgia. I have many memories garnered from travel, and can recall many more at will, but none have ever thrust themselves on me so persistently as the Arabian ones. True, those Arabian visions occur no longer, yet when they came they stirred me to write both poetry and prose in an attempt to recapture my brief Arabian sojourn. This book is merely the final and most comprehensive of my attempts to embody a past that has thrust itself on me in a poetic but fragmentary form for many decades.

I visited Bayhan in 1959, to report on a serious famine that then gripped the area. In spite of my mission, I landed there thinking that I had at last found the Arabia of my dreams. Within a few days I saw camel caravans laden with salt appear as if by magic from the enveloping desert. Tribesmen on horseback galloped out of the dawn, firing rifles and singing to themselves from sheer exuberance in a ferocious manner that bore no relation to the many Hollywood caricatures of such occasions. I even got a glimpse of a few traces of the near-mythical world of Sheba.

The British had insinuated themselves into most of South Arabia before the Second World War, and over many decades had continued the job of "pacifying" the region. Bayhan, which eventually became part of the Western Aden Protectorate, for a long time remained rather untamed and chaotic. In the late 1940s Nigel Groom became the resident political officer, and began the near-impossible job of dealing with feuding tribes and introducing western notions of social order — and consistent British influence — to the region. The ruling family, headed by Sharif Hussain bin Ahmad al Habili, was related to the Hashimite Grand Sharifs of Mecca, who had established their power in the region in the middle of the nineteenth century. The Emirate became part of the Federation of Arab Emirates of the South in 1959 and of the Federation of South Arabia in 1962. Sharif Hussain (actually regent for his son, Amir Saleh bin Hussain) became the Minister of the Interior in the Federation. Although lionized in Wendell Phillips's account, Hussain was a complex and difficult man, and reputedly an ambitious one, until his bubble burst with the dissolution of his dynasty by the People's Republic of South Yemen in 1967.

These striking events, however, fade into insignificance when one contemplates the depth of historical experience that saturates the region. No mere slave of his political work, Nigel Groom had taken note of the fascinating pre-Islamic ruins in Bayhan, and it was his reports on the subject that led to the somewhat ill-fated Wendell Phillips expedition. The Phillips dig, abortive though it was, began to reveal something of the early civilizations of the south, and subsequent work has only deepened and broadened perspectives. The evolution of language and language scripts, the securing of water resources, the opening up of the incense trade routes, the exchange of technologies and religious ideas, the development of enduring governments and administrative practices, the creation of significant art — South Arabia's past has been shown to be immensely rich and productive, one of the most interesting in the Near East.

By at least the end of the second millennium B.C.E., Ma'rib (situated between present-day Bayhan and what was in 1959 the disputed Yemen border) had established itself as the capital of the Sabean Kingdom. It flourished at a key point in the lucrative caravan trade that brought the precious frankincense to the Mediterranean. The Queen of Sheba's legendary visit to King Solomon in the tenth century B.C.E. suggests the extension of the influence of the Sabeans northward. Their hegemony also stretched eastward, encompassing the Qatabanian and Hadhramaut kingdoms. In the second half of the sixth century B.C.E. the great Ma'rib Dam was built. A group known as the Mineans succeeded in rivalling Saba, as did the former vassal state of Qataban. For centuries thereafter three or four kingdoms fought for dominance; finally the Minean power waned, and in 24 B.C.E. a Roman army penetrated to the very gates of Ma'rib, only to be turned back by hunger and disease.

During the next centuries the Himyars, peoples from the southern Arabian coast, began to extend their influence inland and much trade shifted from the old land routes. By the late third century C.E., King Sammar Yuharis of the Sabean-Himyaric Empire had conquered the whole region and claimed the title, "King of All the Arabs." Later, Jewish and Christian missionaries arrived to turn the kingdom toward monotheism. Under the rule of Abukarid Asad in the early fifth century the empire reached the apex of its power. In the fourth and fifth centuries the Ma'rib dam was breached, but repaired. When a Sabean-Himyarite king of Jewish faith attacked and persecuted the Himyarite Christians in 517, however, the Christian Abyssinians invaded South Arabia and established a kingdom there, one that in 597 fell under Persian dominance. In the seventh century the final destruction of the Ma'rib dam took place, an event so catastrophic that the 34th surah of the *Quran* refers to it. With the arrival of Islam in the seventh century, however, a new and more profound unity was established not only in the south, but in the whole Arabian peninsula. The religion of Muhammad brought Arabia into the mainstream of world history as none of the ancient kingdoms had.

When I visited Bayhan, there were few remains of the grandeur implied by such a history, yet what I saw opened up my mind in ways that hardly ever occurred in Aden, while stocking my imagination with images I could never forget.

Climbing off my Aden Airways Dakota in the great wadi I noticed a huge cargo plane being carefully unloaded nearby and inquired about it. I was told that the oversized crates being borne away on the backs of the airport workers consisted of the Emir's "privately doctored Coca-Cola." "Doctored how?" I asked. My informant, a British pilot, shrugged his shoulders. "Who knows? With extra sugar, Scotch, Spanish fly? Anyway, it's special."

This was an odd beginning to a trip whose purpose was to report on a famine.

I did not meet any of Bayhan's ruling clan, for the very good reason that the British somehow neglected to arrange such a meeting. At various points they made elaborate apologies for their oversight, but their explanations sounded a little hollow. Had they been informed I was likely to write a kind of exposé, or was I just too junior an officer to warrant an introduction? I did see a great deal during my several days' visit, however, so any hobnobbing with the rulers would probably have been superfluous.

Landing in Wadi Bayhan I was assaulted by a ferocious dry, oven-like heat, something that may seem too obvious to remark on — yet Aden and Mukalla were almost always drenched in humidity, and Yemen was often cool. In Bayhan I felt as if I were encountering the true desert climate for the first time.

At the same time this great valley, walled in by — and here and there interrupted by — bare, iron-hard mountains that glittered in the sunlight, produced no sense of claustrophobia. From the first it seemed to me a passageway, a grand causeway to the very heart of Arabia, and, indeed, when we drove north to look at Hajar bin Humeid and travelled a little beyond Nuqub and the ruins of Timna, we got a glimpse of the great sandy wasteland beyond. This was the Ramlat as-Sab'atayn, a true desert such as I had hardly seen, a bleak and bare landscape that embodied for me the very essence of geographical mystery. Now it is freely travelled by tourists, locust hunters, archaeologists, and photographers, but like all places in South Arabia it remains vulnerable to violence. In those days we had not yet been acclimatized to such vistas by the grand perspectives of films such as *Lawrence of Arabia* and *The Sheltering Sky*, and right there, climbing out of a Land Rover, I got my first uninhibited view of the daunting power of nature in her brightest, most unrelenting aspect.

My lodging in Bayhan was with a Scot named Eric Patterson, a rangy, good-looking, congenial young man who served as an agricultural adviser. He occupied a brown two-storey barracks-like building, rigorously faced with white beams of stone or wood, so that it resembled a compulsive child's drawing. Adjacent to it — wonder of wonders! — stood a small swimming pool, then almost unheard of in South Arabia. A British medical unit was working in the area, and a few doctors and nurses came over and frolicked in the pool. Patterson and I stayed up late, drank whiskey, traded wry comments on our love experiences, and discovered a common enthusiasm for Duke Ellington. Patterson told a sad story of having a romance with an "unsuitable" (that is, working-class) girl, broken up by the intervention of his mother. "You might sleep with her kind, but you don't marry them," Mum had told him. I was struck by the puritanism and snobbery this implied, yet ten years later, when I and a young woman friend tried to find a rental lodging for a few months in the north of England, we were turned away so many times that the real estate agent acting for us begged my friend (and future wife) to wear a wedding ring and "just pretend."

Lying in a small bed squeezed in a cubbyhole of the building and reading myself to sleep with one of Patterson's books on sexual technique, acutely aware of the oppressive heat and of the great valley outside with its ancient ruins and present poverty, I had one of my first genuine experiences of the "absurd," a state of mind in which meaning and being part company, one that my university students of the 1960s understood only too well.

The delightful extravagance of the swimming pool was the first in a linked chain of associations to the key fact of water. The Phillips expedition had discovered elaborate irrigation channels — canals, stone watergates, and cisterns — stretching from the village of Bayhan-al-Qasab to a point five miles north of Hajar bin Humeid, and had concluded that at the height of Qatabanian civilization the whole wadi had been a garden of plenty. The Ma'rib dam had only been the largest and most spectacular example of the control of water resources by the ancient Arabian civilizations. Modern Bayhan, for various reasons, was not able to access and control enough of this precious resource, and, despite the existence of a few wealthy families and a tenacious population, the Bayhanis suffered greatly from this failure.

During the next few days, some of my most instructive moments were spent beside wells that revealed different aspects of life in the Wadi Bayhan.

In one place I sat in a hut beside a small patch of irrigated field and waited for women to come out and fetch water from an old-fashioned bucket well. They arrived, three of them, unveiled but wrapped in black, looking like wraiths in the sunlight, but chattering to each other in their high-pitched singing voices. They leaned over the low rectangular concrete, placing their goatskin bags and pans on the ledge. Framed by the doorway with scant green fields and a few distant scattered houses behind them, these dark-clad figures shed their local reference and took on the character of something timeless. For centuries women had fetched water from such wells, and as they worked, had talked about their personal joys and sorrows, about village life. What I saw was a token of something static and burdensome, yet beautiful in its enactment, one of the deep roots of our whole civilization.

I waited, a voyeur in the darkness of the shed; the sunlight made slanted patterns on the heavy wooden door. Finally, with their bags and pans dripping a little water, the women moved away, their voices still sounding in the morning's silence. I came out of the shed, walked around the building, and climbed into my Land Rover.

Farther up the valley, in a palm grove, a tiny oasis, I visited another well. No fine rectangular concrete structure here, but crude stones around a sizable hole in the ground. No women coming to fetch, either, but an old camel man driving two of the recalcitrant beasts back and forth, endlessly, hour after hour. Crude rope lines were attached to the camel's humps, and these, wound around pulleys, drew up bags of water from the well. When the camels had pulled the ropes to their farthest extension, the lifted bags struck a log and tipped out water, which ran down between a crude line of stones and irrigated a nearby field.

Here again was something ancient and primitive. Yet the Qatabanians, who might once have fetched water in a similar fashion, had achieved much greater technical mastery. Not content with being condemned to marginalized living by their daunting environment, they had acquired skills so as to make the valley bloom. Now Bayhan was almost back at the beginning; the wheel had just been invented. There is no straight line in history.

Eric Patterson drove to me a third well, one powered by a gasoline engine. No chattering women's voices here, no creaking ropes and snorting camels, but rather the clatter of machinery, an insistent chugging and sputtering that might have been the station identification for some well-intentioned but Sisyphean enterprise. This well, surrounded by a low concrete wall and topped by a crude wooden scaffolding, was the ugliest of the three. Whatever ropes had once been attached to the scaffolding had been removed, and this gave the construction a gaunt and haunted look. No camels were in sight and no women, but some dozen men and boys stood about, shouting, chiding, urging each other on, though nothing in fact was being done.

A long metal pipe projected from the well; it was held up by a crude stilt, and looked out of place amid the stone and wood, yet it was the object of everyone's attention, the centre of all the excitement. When water poured out of the pipe, spilling over the sides of wooden buckets held by the boys, a clamour arose. Patterson, who lounged nearby, an idle bystander, was suddenly the sorcerer, and the Arab gang excited apprentices. This was progress. Would the Qatabanians have thought it a miracle? Perhaps; but they would certainly not have seen it as a thing of beauty.

We drove over to the palace near Nuqub, where by now the Emir was doubtlessly enjoying his doctored Coca-Cola. Cutting across a broad swath of the wadi we had a marvellous postcard view of the valley. About fifty yards ahead, a black-clad shepherd drove his flock of black goats across the yellow-pink sand. Behind him, a long strip of irrigated green field ran like a ribbon, and a hundred yards or so beyond that, fronted by bald sandy patches, rose the Emir's palace. In the far distance, to the left, a small village nestled against the bare hills. More buildings, discreetly apart from the palace, ran off to the right.

The pink and white palace, sleek-lined, with symmetrical towers and domes, a porticoed entrance, and carefully spaced windows, rose high above the earthen walls that enclosed the grounds. Unlike the Sultan's Palace in Mukalla, there was not the slightest touch of the Gothic about the place.

Beside the gate we ran into one of the British officials, who apologized for not arranging that I should meet the Emir. Perhaps I would like to run over to the Wadi Mablaqa? There was some actual fighting going on there. (That was nothing new, as I learned in due course.) We were very close to the disputed border with Yemen; it would be interesting to get a glimpse of an actual skirmish, and besides, the wadi lay directly along one of the ancient spice routes.

A long bumpy ride in the blazing sun took us to a small fort in the heart of the wadi. It was a crude structure near a large bend in the dry riverbed that ran through the desolate, mountain-rimmed valley. A few houses sat on the dusty plain beside it.

Climbing up on the ramparts, standing with a couple of tribal fighters behind a rough parapet complete with apertures for shooting from cover, I was confronted by a scene out of a low-budget *Beau Geste* remake. The little fort was nearly deserted, but the sounds of small-arms fire echoed from up the valley. A patrol was out on a scouting mission, I was told — it was a quiet day in the Wadi Mablaqa. I looked up and saw a flag flying from a short pole, a dark green and blue ensign decorated with a white star and a white scimitar, framed by two white horizontal lines. The flag, representing, as I was told, the Bayhan emirate, was attractive, but there was an air of make-believe about the scene; a ten-year-old would have been thrilled but not at all frightened. Deadly days there had been, however, and much worse, I was sure, were to come. I had indeed been deposited here during a very quiet time.

Such wry reflections ceased as I leaned across the parapet and looked down at the rough ground between the fort and the wadi. A small cemetery occupied this spot, and there, set between two sturdy, scrawny olive-like trees, were some fifty or sixty simple headstones. Closer to the wadi stood a more imposing memorial, a sepulchre of milk-white stone, large in comparison with the others, yet not so large as many western memorials to the very rich.

These dead, unknown to me, in such an obscure place, amid grand and desolate scenery, suggested at once the barely visible imprint of human life and history on relentless nature. I was awestruck; the place seemed both wonderful and terrifying, and I wanted to go down and sit for a while amid the gravestones. But with gunshots up the valley, adequate cover for snipers close by, and a sad record of wanton killings among the tribes, I was advised not to move forward from where I was. I lingered on the parapet a while, and then it was time to leave, but this cemetery took its place among those "spots of time" bequeathed to me by Arabia.

The next few days were spent among the ordinary people of Bayhan. What I saw was discouraging, although the local crisis did not have the all-encompassing, catastrophic impact of the African famines that the world was to see somewhat later, mostly on television. Border skirmishes are one thing, total war is another. The Bayhanis had not been displaced and forced into refugee camps; relief agencies, although inadequate in numbers, lent some assistance. There were, as I have noted, some medical personnel, and minimal facilities. Yet I saw emaciated, starving children and adults forced to a marginal existence with no hope of betterment, a colonized society in which those who were willing to serve the system and capable of doing so would survive best, while the others would have to depend on good luck, charity, or a miracle.

In the Colony the British had introduced many material improvements; in Abyan there was the irrigation scheme that changed the landscape and improved production. But in Bayhan, as in Mukalla and the other areas of their huge "protected" territory, their main concern seemed to have been to make the old tribal system work for their political purposes. The emphasis was not on human betterment, but on keeping order, introducing coherent administrative structures, and ensuring "public safety," that is, effective control by Her Majesty's forces and those who co-operated with them.

The worst aspect of all this was the static quality of British rule. A hideous kind of entropy stifled everything. The various notions of tribal federation hardly affected the ordinary Arabs of the Protectorates. For them, there seemed to be no path at all to real change. The hopelessness that resulted goes far to explain the hatred that confronted the colonizers when the situation finally got out of control. Many ordinary people in the western industrial countries have found it difficult to account for the violent outbreaks that sometimes occur when a group has endured an extended, enforced powerlessness. They would understand such violence if they experienced the conditions that generate it. Repression has its price. When you have nothing to lose, you may stop at nothing.

I visited hovels where emaciated children lay on filthy bedding, too weak to brush the flies from their faces. I saw women racked with disease and unable to feed their babies. Tuberculosis, cataracts, yaws plagued the settlements. Food and medicine were in short supply. Camel urine still served as the main disinfectant.

I made my notes and wrote my (rather scathing) report for the State Department. Then, only a month after visiting Bayhan, I headed off to England, ready, in good conscience, not only to continue my foreign service career, but to take part in the safe and comfortable middle-class life of my relations by marriage. I visited the local pub, enjoyed the cricket matches, and roamed the back lanes of Hertfordshire, where I was soon to be married.

My marriage, my love of English literature and the English landscape, my own shallow roots in "America" allowed me to settle comfortably, if temporarily, into a false persona. My first public lecture, in Hamburg, was on Aden. After that I rarely spoke about the place, or if I did it was to dwell on adventure and comedy, or to evoke the local colour. My Arabian experiences became something remote, a vivid dream tinged by romance and nostalgia. I hardly paid attention to the political developments in South Arabia; I shunned the terror and violence that changed things there forever. I myself had been temporarily colonized, but in most respects I was enjoying it. Only later did I begin to grasp a little of the historical reality. Only much later did I begin to understand the danger for America as the United States followed the British into the morass of Middle Eastern colonial and post-colonial politics.

TWENTY-FIVE

The End of Something

It was nearly time for me to leave the Colony. Things were still rather quiet, although a few terrorist bombs had exploded in restaurants and bars, and I had to write reassuringly to my family. I continued to find such incidents rather exciting. I had no idea of the horrors soon to come.

In the months ahead no one would sit complacently at the Crescent Bar, the Gold Mohur Bathing Club, the Union Khormaksar Club, or the Rex Restaurant. No one would talk reassuringly about the wise provisions of the British administration. Soon government advisories would be posted. They warned foreigners not to leave their servants at home alone in their houses or flats, for now it was recognized: the enemy was within and would strike without compunction. Whatever good the British had done seemed to be forgotten; every blow at them revenged an ancient evil. They were murdered just to persuade them to go away.

Although I anticipated little of this terror, some experiences of my final months in Aden — as I now realize — foreshadowed such events. After the first bombings, late in 1957, the Colony enjoyed a period of relative stability, one that lasted until well after my departure in 1959. When Diana C. left to arrange for our wedding in England, I felt sad, but at the same time liberated. Cathy O'Hara was no longer around to draw me into her frivolities, but I was more than ready to initiate my own.

My replacement, a New Yorker named Bill Deary, whom I knew from the Foreign Service Institute, arrived quite a few weeks early. About the same time, a young woman named Colette joined the French Consulate as an au pair. Blonde and beautiful, with a great deal of French chic and charm, she made an immediate hit in the Colony, and in particular with Deary and me. The three of us went through several weeks of madcap adventures in true F. Scott Fitzgerald style, with crazy parties and some wild drives around the Aden hills — a few in the consulate's official sedan — until the sad day arrived when I had to confess that in fact I was departing Aden very soon to get married.

Such escapades did nothing to undermine my increasing zest for my official work. I knew the Colony well, was on great terms with everyone in the consulate, and, with Crawford out of the way, I could perform my consular and other duties without looking over my shoulder. At one point Bill Deary and I drove out to Abyan, in the Protectorate, about thirty miles east of Aden. It is a fascinating region, divided by two great watercourses descending from the mountains, although these are often dry and thus useless for irrigation. The *Pax Britannica* that established a truce among perpetually feuding sultanates, however, had enabled the area to be developed for agriculture. The British had targeted fifty thousand acres for development, and in nearly half of these irrigation projects had been constructed, although problems had arisen, because the improved flow of water had also increased the salinity of the soil.

Certainly this massive project gave incentives to local landowners and provided work for many otherwise unemployed tribesmen, but it also worked somewhat to the British advantage, since the resulting cotton crops were specially designated for purchasers in Lancashire.

Deary and I toured Abyan — a vast plain of cultivated land, green fields framed by distant mountains, a few scattered villages, roads running up mesa-like rises or winding among canals. Staring at the sluice gates and walking beside the irrigation channels, we recalled the Middle East's ancient quest for water; we imagined the roar as it coursed from the mountains, an exciting and terrifying sound, and recalled the timeless flood stories and the powerful gods of water, such as the Babylonian Enlil. We remembered the blue bracelet of Ishtar, and the rainbow of Jehovah, which promised, after the deluge, that no similar catastrophe would ever be visited upon the people.

Men and women make pacts with the gods they discover in nature, but history seems relentless. We were told about the ancient past of Abyan. We already knew of the great Himyaritic civilization, originating in the south, that was to rival Qataban and Saba. The Greek *Periplus*, a kind of mariner's manual probably written in the first century C.E., describes the lively sea trade along the Arabian coast, just south of where we stood. In the next century, the Alexandrian geographer Claudius Ptolemy published a description of the same Arabian coastline, together with a crude map. These texts pointed to shifting patterns of trade, and to the eventual closing out of the old spice routes.

Much farther north, archaeologists were soon to discover many pieces of red-painted Persian pottery, also dating from Roman times. The tenth-century Arab historian Al-Hamdami in *The Antiquities of South Arabia* discusses the Abyan area in some detail and mentions some towns connected with the incense trade. Under our feet were bits of blue and white Chinese pottery, which had found their way in medieval times to these great Islamic civilizations of the south. The Chinese knew South Arabia as "the land of milk perfume." Abyan was only "isolated" and "backward" according to the western imperialist or Eurocentric conception of time and space.

Colonialism wipes out memory, but with the end of British rule, a mere eyeblink of history later, Yemen in general and Abyan in particular were to become the centre of covert international power struggles. They would also draw the attention of those seeking the roots of the terror that reached the shores of America itself on September 11, 2001. To many ordinary Americans, understandably fearful and shocked, that attack was without precedent. Yet the precedents were many, and several of them were connected with Yemen and Abyan.

On December 29, 1992, a bomb exploded at the Gold Mohur Hotel. The target was America, or more specifically its military — often posted there en route to Somalia. Why this attack? In general, because after the withdrawal of the Soviets from Afghanistan, Britain and the United States became the most obvious enemies of Arab nationalism. Since it was clear that the United States was determined to move into the "power vacuum" left by the British and the Soviets in East Africa and Arabia, the attacks were inevitable.

Who were the attackers? The background is Byzantine in its complexity. To fight the Soviets in Afghanistan, the CIA and the British Secret Intelligence Service (MI6) had trained mercenaries who became known as Jaish-e-Muhammad (Muhammad's Army), or the Islamic Jihad (seemingly unconnected with the al-Jihad of Palestine). Some members of this group originated in Communist South Yemen, but as a result of the Afghan experience returned home as converts to Islamic fundamentalism. In 1994, when South Yemen, which had become unified with the north in 1990, again sought to break away, the Afghan militants fought alongside the North Yemen army. One of their main leaders, Tariq-al-Fadhli, who claimed to have inherited the old Abyan sultanate, made direct alliances with the ruling North Yemen party. (Other fundamentalist converts, adhering to a radical mujahideen tradition, have declared opposition both to the current Yemen government and to the Saudis.)

After its victory the northern government refused to give real power to its mercenary allies, who set up an independent military training camp in Abyan. The emerging group, the Aden-Abyan Islamic Army, included — besides the fundamentalists — some disaffected Yemeni liberals and democrats from the "occupied" south, deposed tribal rulers, and old Protectorate families, a situation that practically assured the group's fractionalization, but not necessarily its impotence.

In fact, the core of this force — brought into existence by struggles within militant Arab nationalism, kept alive by the continuing discord between Islam and the First World countries, later refocused to exploit Cold War rivalries so as to receive training from American and British covert agencies — was the group that bombed the Gold Mohur Hotel in 1992.

On December 28, 1998, some members of this group, led by Zein-al-Abideen Abu Bakr al-Mehdar, known as Abu Hassan, who had met Osama bin Laden in Afghanistan during the Soviet war, kidnapped sixteen westerners in Yemen. Three British tourists and one Australian died when their rescue was botched by Yemen government forces. Abu Hassan was later executed by the Yemen government, which claimed to have wiped out the terrorists. (It had long denied the existence of any such force as the Aden-Abyan Islamic Army, no doubt seeking to protect its erstwhile allies in the war against the South Yemen Marxists).

On October 12, 2000, a small boat carrying powerful explosives struck the *U.S.S. Cole* in Aden harbour. Seventeen American service personnel were killed and thirty-nine injured. The "Islamic Deterrence Force" and the group "Muhammad's Army" that afterward claimed responsibility were also believed to be connected with the Aden-Abyan Islamic Army. The next day, October 6, a bomb was thrown at the British Embassy in Sana'a, the Yemen capital, by members of the same group.

Some personnel of the Aden-Abyan Islamic Army had been recruited in London by a radical Mullah, Abu Hamza al-Masri, and were British nationals. In 1998 and 1999, the Yemen government had arrested some of these terrorists, who had already targeted other "western" sites in Yemen for attack.

The bombing of the *U.S.S. Cole* delivered an initial shock to the American psyche, but in view of the American policy of moving into the power vacuum left by the British departure from South Arabia, such incidents were almost inevitable.

In October 2002, the Aden-Abyan Islamic Army claimed responsibility for the attack on the French supertanker *Limburg*. They had apparently mistaken it for an American vessel, but they justified the attack on the grounds that "the unbelievers' nation is one," and stated that the tanker was in any case supplying the u.s. Navy, which was preparing to strike "the brothers in Iraq."

On December 30, 2002, three American Baptist missionaries were murdered by an Al Qaeda-inspired gunman at their hospital in Jibla, a town 120 miles south of Yemen's capital, San'a. This killing caused *The New York Times* to reflect on the extensive network of terrorists believed to be still active in Yemen, despite its government's declared support of American policy.

In the light of all this, the Abyan terrorist connection can be seen as a portent of things to come in Yemen. Abyan, long before British rule, had been connected with a larger international world. Now, in the aftermath of colonialism, that region — indeed, all of Yemen — has become part of a complex network of alliances, conspiracies, and rivalries that includes not only Southern Arabia and Saudi Arabia, but Afghanistan, Somalia, and Pakistan. In these areas, the United States, Britain, France, Russia, and other great powers are now playing a very complex and dangerous game. Their policies depend for their success, in some cases, on co-operation with dubious local regimes, and are aimed at supporting transnational "police" actions, while protecting mega-economic interests that have little to do with grassroots democracy. Such efforts extend the dubious notion of power-bloc interventionism that over the years has subverted the ideals of peaceful resolution implicit in the United Nations charter, and ignore the more humane outreaches advocated by leading scholars, thinkers, and enlightened politicians around the world.

On the macro-scale of nations the present political crisis has too often been simplistically presented as a struggle between "democracy" and "terrorism," despite the fact that it involves a far from idealistic economic and political policy on the part of the West, internecine rivalries within Islam, various national states in conflict with transnational political and religious interests, the existence of Israel vis-à-vis the Palestinians, and other factors. Those who think that such a Gordian knot can be severed by a single violent stroke are naive.

After I returned to the Colony from Abyan, little suspecting the future connection of that notably cultivated region with violence and terror, an incident occurred that changed some of my perspectives on my Aden experience. Trivial in itself, this encounter forced me to confront on the personal level important issues of suspicion, failed communication, and violence.

Before Diana C. departed, she and I had gone for a drive to Little Aden, Crater, and various spots around the inner harbour. We ended up beside the docks in Ma'alla, taking photographs of the ships and the jetties. At one point we sat at the end of a pier, chatting and staring down into the water. Often murky and dark, on that day it was clear, really vivid with sunlight. Two manta rays swam there, feeding and possibly enjoying the temperature.

Manta rays, whatever their true nature, have, to the casual eye, an alien and sinister look. Their dark triangular shape seems to embody a fearful symmetry that makes one wonder, fancifully, if these sea-dwellers have evolved in order to give human beings design ideas for weapons of terror. If sharks are the aquatic equivalent of the poet William Blake's cosmically frightening tiger, manta rays — at least in appearance — would do quite as well.

For a good fifteen minutes Diana and I sat and watched the huge rays patrol the sunlit waters around the jetty. Rooted to the spot by the awe we both felt in their presence, we did not speak, and became oblivious to everything around us.

It was all the more shocking to be startled out of our contemplation by a sudden, shouted challenge. We jumped up and saw two Arabs — Adeni men, short in stature, wiry, and looking a bit dishevelled in their rather shabby *futahs* and caps — charging down the jetty in our direction. The men screamed, pointed at us, and indicated in no uncertain terms that we should get out of there pronto. This notion was underlined by some fist-shaking and near jostling that seemed both ridiculous and threatening.

For a few minutes I attempted to deflect this assault, falling back on some primitive Arabic phrases, smiling and raising my hands in gestures that were intended to show that we had meant no harm, and that they — whatever their problem — were being just a shade overzealous.

This, however, only enraged them further. Diana suggested that we would be wiser to depart rather than try to extend this unpromising dialogue any further. Luckily, my car was parked close by and we reached it easily.

I started the engine and prepared to drive away. Our persecutors, however, did not desist. They stormed up to where we were parked, leaned on the door next to my seat, and slapped at the car reprovingly.

I had had enough. I set my foot above the accelerator, rolled down the window, and, mustering my resources, spat quite energetically in the face of the nearest Arab. Then I gunned the car off the jetty, wheeled around on the road, and sped off. The scene behind us was anything but pretty. The Arabs pursued with the energy of outrage; they seemed to have picked up sticks or small clubs on the run, and if they had caught us things would not have gone well.

Diana and I had little to say to each other about this incident. The jetty was not a restricted space; the Arabs did not appear to be watchmen. We could not imagine what had set the two of them so ferociously against us. Did they mistake us for someone else? Perhaps they had been chewing *qat*, and were among the few in whom it inspired extreme aggressiveness?

I cursed my lack of Arabic, but the situation seemed odd indeed, and perhaps speech would not have helped: I might have told them what I thought of their intrusion. Yet the sudden outbreak of irrationality — on my part as well as theirs — depressed us both.

This incident, like my vision of the naked young man on the beach in Khormaksar, evoked complex thoughts. Unlike George Orwell, who confessed, in his essay "Shooting an Elephant," to an almost visceral dislike of the Burmese he was stationed among, I did not find local faces and manners upsetting. I liked the Arabs. As to the colonial fact, my attitude, I imagined, was objective. I was very conscious of *not* being one of the colonizers and I felt quite capable of making judgments about the British in Aden. A naive and all-too-typical American, I had accepted too many assumptions about the power of goodwill, the effectiveness of "freedom" and "democracy." Surely, if some changes could be made, if independence for South Arabia could be expedited, everything would be all right. The Arab nationalists would achieve their goals, the British would happily depart.

This simplistic view of things was confirmed by my own anglophile enthusiasms. I was about to make my first trip to England, to marry into an English family.

On the beach at Khormaksar, however, and now on the jetty in Ma'alla, a much darker world revealed itself. It was a place that my youthful idealism and energy could hardly penetrate.

My encounter with the two Arabs was a small reminder of the human impulse to violence, one that would soon take over the whole colony. Much later, I understood. The brutality of the French and Russian revolutions, the terrible acts of many soldiers during the Second World War, ethnic cleansing, and the horrors of genocide, all these, alas, seem to derive directly from human nature. They seem in truth almost inevitable in a world where law breaks down or where nations or groups plunge into armed conflict. Underlying British rule, and accompanying its imperial opportunism, was the patriarchal sense that they as rulers knew what was best for the ruled. But behind the benevolent mask of this authority many Arabs recognized the old father tyrant, eager to crush the dependent soul.

It is easy to ascribe a violent revolution to political connivance and the will of conspirators. But when the violence gets out of hand, when it becomes wanton pleasure in killing for the sake of killing (as it did in Aden), then another explanation seems called for. Although one may be tempted to invoke ideological or sociological causes, I believe there is a deeper compulsion: in such cases some dark backward of human nature is being touched, some power of blackness that reason and love cannot constrain. No one is exempt from this power: the menace I had projected on the manta rays was my own.

A few weeks later I sat in the familiar down-at-heel waiting room in the Aden airport, drinking a last beer with some friends and colleagues and waiting for my flight to Ethiopia.

Bill and Janet Stoltzfus were there, and Bill Deary. Esmail and Ali Muhammad had come along to see me off, and so had Evelyn, Cathy's replacement. Carmela Natale, and Greg and Marion Gay, a couple of newcomers who were taking over for the Rodmans, were also at the table.

As the conversation ran through the usual well-intentioned banalities of an official parting, I sat observing myself and my own departure, not sad to be leaving Aden, but wondering what the future held for me beyond the rituals of return to America and the new adventure of a marriage in a country I had never visited, into a family with which I had nothing at all in common. Although the last several months in the Colony had gone well for me, and I knew I had done some good work, I was not altogether happy about my time in Aden. There had been too many hesitations, too many issues unresolved, too many shadows in the sunlight. As I shook hands all round, waved, and climbed into the plane, I suddenly remembered a line from one of my favourite poets of those self-conscious younger days, Ranier Maria Rilke, who wrote, "We live like that, forever taking leave."

Then, as we gained altitude and I got my final glimpse of the Colony from the air, I remembered my arrival.

Flying in two years before, a little bleary-eyed and already dyspeptic from an early breakfast in Khartoum, I had talked to another passenger, an Australian businessman who had come that way many times. He had stopped once or twice in the Colony, but only overnight. I explained that I was going to stay much longer; I was going to live and work there for two full years. He nodded thoughtfully, but had no comment.

As we circled, preparing to land, we had a wonderful view of everything, of the bleak rocks and Shamsan, of the great harbour and the ships, of Steamer Point and the causeway, of sandy Khormaksar and roads running past the low buildings that clung everywhere to the shoreline. The Australian pointed out a few of these landmarks, still rather meaningless to me, and wished me well.

"To be honest, I don't envy you," he confided. "It's a pretty dreary place. I wouldn't live here for anything. Hot as blazes, and dull, I think. Nothing ever happens."

Disappointing words to a young man beginning his first overseas adventure. I needn't have worried, though; Aden proved to be a transforming experience. Despite the climate and the abiding claustrophobia, despite the dreariness of most of its man-made things and the tedium of many nights, quite a few things happened. I learned something about other countries and races, and about colonialism, its distortions and failures. I encountered personal injustice, and found out that success in any career I chose in life would not be a gift from on high. I met fascinating people, and visited unforgettable places. And rarest of all, haltingly, and without really trying, I learned one or two things about myself.

TWENTY-SIX

Afterword

On December 7, 1967, the United States gave diplomatic recognition to the People's Republic of South Yemen. Relations were broken off by the PRSY on October 24, 1969, ostensibly in protest against some aspects of American policy in Israel, but more likely — according to analyst Fred Halliday — in order for South Yemen to align itself with the other radical Arab States, all of which had severed diplomatic relations with Washington during the 1967 Arab-Israeli war. To the United States, of course, the PRSY was a threat to its neighbours, especially to the American "facade" state of Saudi Arabia, but also to Oman, and to the Yemen Arab Republic to the north.

The PRSY, which became the People's Democratic Republic of South Yemen (PDRY) in 1970, was also, from the beginning, and long before the *Cole* incident and the Twin Towers catastrophe, known as a training ground for terrorists. CIA subversion in the PDRY — sometimes with British assistance — continued through the 1970s and early 1980s, but South Yemen was not targeted for "liberation" in the manner of Nicaragua, nor branded as a launching pad for terrorism to the same extent as Libya, and the United States remained quite aloof from the South Yemen civil war of 1986. It did, however, criticize the Soviets for alleged intervention in the crisis, a typical case of America condemning its Cold War opponent for practices that successive American governments had espoused without self-recrimination all over the globe.

For the people of South Yemen the post-colonial period offered little respite. It was marked by violent internal struggle that resulted in continuing political instability, by structural economic changes that did not result in significant economic benefits, and by endless plots and counterplots vis-à-vis the Yemen Arab Republic to the north. The unified Yemen state that emerged from the 1994 civil war, and survives today, is no longer rabidly Marxist, and Soviet power had waned some years before. After the September 11 attack in New York and the American invasion of Afghanistan, the Yemen government seemed eager to maintain good relations with the United States, and, by co-operating — or appearing to co-operate — in the suppression and tracking down of terrorists, to avoid a more direct American intervention. The fact that such an intervention was even considered possible would have seemed shocking to me in 1959. Yet America's Afghanistan campaign, which appeared justified to most observers, was followed by the 2003 invasion and occupation of Iraq, a much more precipitous adventure, while various elements in the George W. Bush administration advocated the forceful overthrow of other "hostile" or unstable governments in the Middle East.

The very dangerous and morally dubious Iraq occupation is not unrelated to the deep roots of American foreign policy, for these lie tangled in a mythology of national innocence, combined with the older notion of "manifest destiny," a sinister but limited concept, which seems almost modest in the light of the Bush administration's megalomania, and its new notion of America's "world destiny." Such grandiose posturing could only derive from a self-absorbed contemplation of national achievements uncorrected by historical insight and irony.

I understand the allure of this dangerous mythology because I myself grew up with many illusions about my country, all grounded in the belief that the United States is historically privileged, a "moral" nation and a beacon of "freedom and democracy" in world history. Although I had read Thoreau, de Tocqueville, and other eloquent critics of American society and values, and devoured all the socially aware and protest journalism I could get my hands on, I saw few imperfections in the American system. While intermittently cognizant of some of our national failures and of the perpetration of certain kinds of social injustices in our country, I had nonetheless acquired quite a few over-simple notions — for example, that free enterprise, however flawed, can be corrected so as to serve the public good, that anyone can achieve high office in America, that the press is objective and tells the truth, and that (except for the slave owners in the old south) America had treated its minorities well. I also firmly believed that we had dissociated ourselves from the older European imperialisms, with their brutalities and their determination to achieve homeland prosperity however much misery this might cause in the colonies that succumbed to their power.

Politically, I was a convinced liberal; as a child I'd heard glowing reports of the social and political transformations of Roosevelt's New Deal. I believed strongly in civil rights, freedom of speech, and progress through education and democracy. If everything wasn't quite right in America and the world, our democracy could surely make things right in the long run.

My views began to change, however, after I read a remarkable book, *The Irony of American History*, by Reinhold Niebuhr, published in 1952, a book that — had we but known it — sounded a brave and prophetic warning of unfortunate things to come. Niebuhr's arguments are far too subtle and complex to do justice to here, but their main thrust is easily stated. At the height of the Cold War, Niebuhr, a celebrated and influential Protestant theologian, deconstructed the American myth of innocence while at the same time casting a discerning eye on our professed national idealism. He pointed to the dangers of inordinate American power and suggested that, as an antidote, the United States pay more heed to its allies and friends. He pleaded for respect for both "the self and the other," asked for national patience in the face of historical provocations, and warned about the American penchant for self-inflation, including presidential proclamations that "have congratulated God on the virtues and ideals of the American people, which have so well merited the blessings of prosperity we enjoy" (45). He also expressed doubts about the health of American mass culture and questioned the country's over-reliance on technological excellence as a measure of national success.

Such a book was a revelation, but only the first of many. Painfully, I began to discern flaws in America's self-assured perfectionism: a failure of social conscience and compassion within, a ruthlessness and narrow opportunism in its dealings with the world. There was nothing to be proud of, I decided, in what American policy had accomplished in Iran, Lebanon, Nicaragua, Panama, Chile, Grenada, or even Afghanistan. America's renunciation of treaties controlling nuclear weapons, its vote against the protocol designed to enforce the Biological Weapons Convention, its refusal to support either the UN Convention on the Rights of the Child or the Ottawa treaty banning land mines seemed not only wrong, but incompatible with the values that created the country. American attempts to help solve the tragic conflict between Israelis and Palestinians — an issue to which the United States should be devoting all of its skills and energies — have been pathetically inadequate and inconsistent, no doubt because successive governments have lacked the courage to stand up to the combined pressure of the domestic Israel lobby and the pro-Israel notions of the American fundamentalists. The United States record on protection of the environment has been poor, and on issues of world poverty it does relatively little, providing comfort mostly to the economic interests that would rather not see the problem solved. American support of tyrants such as the Shah of Iran, Mobutu in the Congo, Pinochet in Chile, Suharto in Indonesia, Marcos in the Philippines, Taylor in Liberia, and, initially, Saddam Hussein in Iraq, among many others, makes absurd the pronouncement of George W. Bush that the United States will be instrumental in achieving "freedom's triumph over all its age-old foes."

As a young man I was also a great reader of the Swiss historian Jacob Burckhardt, and in his letters had found a reference to the *terribles simplificateurs* that he feared would dominate the coming centuries. The phrase, which might be best translated as "the frightening simplifiers," I had confidently applied to Hitler and Stalin. Only later did it become clear that it could equally well apply to Nixon, Reagan, the senior Bush, Lyndon Johnson, and Bill Clinton — but surely most appropriately of all to the religiously minded and seemingly well-intentioned George W. Bush.

All of this had close relevance to my experience in Aden. For a century and more, the British ruled in the Middle East through the so-called "Arab facade," the establishment of regimes that would serve imperial power in exchange for United Kingdom backing. The peoples of the region, who were inclined to make radical pleas for freedom and equality and to demand a more than marginal economic existence, could not be allowed to upset the power structure that would keep western economic investments and oil supplies safe.

The United States has now been playing the political game in the Middle East for decades, but its foreign policy has been wildly inconsistent. It has supported dictators like the Shah of Iran, the former and present military rulers of Pakistan, Zia ul-Haq and Pervez Musharraf, and even Saddam Hussein during his war with Iran, but has done nothing substantial to connect with the ordinary people in the Islamic states of the region. While it helped end the unnecessary and shameful Sinai-Suez War of 1956, it invaded Lebanon for no very good reason in 1958. It has since launched attacks on Libya and the Sudan and bombed and invaded Iraq. Recently, the government of George W. Bush has urged the Palestinians to democratize, yet the United States continues to ignore the lack of democracy in Egypt and Saudi Arabia, even standing by while the latter nation blatantly finances terrorism.

Far from transcending the old British imperialism, the United States seems to be in the process of replacing the British as the number one arbiter of Middle Eastern destiny. Unfortunately, this has meant that as a colonial power in Iraq and elsewhere it has suffered a defeat not altogether different from what the British suffered in Aden. Several months after the Iraq war was declared "won," and even after the capture of Saddam, there was no real security in Baghdad. Iraqi confidence in the occupation was minimal, and armed opposition quickly began to manifest itself. Insurgents appeared and opted for a strategy that involved not only striking at the Americans but intimidating the ordinary Iraqi citizen. A new ruling council, subject to the occupiers and dependent upon them for support, recapitulated the unfortunate structure of the "puppet" regimes of the past. At home, the governments of Bush and Blair in particular were faced with embarrassing questions about the intelligence information used to justify the invasion in the first place. The United Nations was for too long largely excluded from the process of coalition rule, and the symbolic transfer of power to a new Iraqi government in 2005 promises to lead only to further internal conflict and disruption, or else to the emergence of a new "strong man," one who will make a mockery of the United States claim to have brought "freedom" to Iraq.

Almost everywhere in the Middle East the United States is as unpopular as the British once were, and with good reason. Americans parade their ideals, as the British once did, while at the same time flaunting their power and acting largely out of a narrowly defined self-interest. Even now, rather than simply projecting "evil" on those who are hostile to the American way of life and to United States policy, American's efforts should be directed toward solving some of the economic and social problems that underlie the present tensions. That is the way to defeat Islamic extremism, which portrays the United States as a self-aggrandizing materialistic monolith, innately hostile to Muslim religion and culture. If the United States does not find new and co-operative solutions, if it relies on military power and economic threat alone, it will endanger its own values and face decades of internal and external problems that a more consistent policy, anchored in a vision of true democracy and a sense of planetary responsibility, might have solved.

Future historians may well ascribe the beginning of America's decline as a world power to its failure to lead the way to further planetary transformation at a time when global leadership is so badly needed, and tribalism and fanaticism have tempted so many groups and nations to embrace the dark backward of human violence, mindlessness, and xenophobia. The traditional American ideals of "freedom," "justice," "democracy," and "liberty" seem increasingly hollow and inadequate. Reinhold Niebuhr suggested in 1952 that startling gaps exist between the exalted notions that are claimed to shape United States foreign policy and the often evil results that ensue from the implementation of such policy. Perhaps it is time to expose the "hidden variables" buried in such virtuous poses, and to be more alert to the potentially negative consequences of American idealism.

We need to be more cynical about the motives of those who cloak themselves in virtue, but we also need a deeper and more ironical awareness of the complexity of virtue itself. For, as human experience and the more sophisticated forms of psychological analysis both inform us, a one-sided, unthinking, and less-than-selfless pursuit of "virtue" is likely to lead to an unconscious identification with its very opposite.

The vast numbers of people who have taken to the streets to protest the one-sidedness of World Trade Organization and World Bank policies, and to condemn the Iraqi war, constitute an advance guard of the disappointed. With the end of the Cold War, they and others like them expected an era of planetary responsibility and a new internationalism based on co-operative action for economic, social, and cultural improvement. Instead, the United States, which has more potential than any other country for initiating creative change, has fallen into economic instability and unbalance, and veered toward a ruthless and one-sided foreign interventionism.

As if the Bush doctrine of pre-emptive strikes were not bad enough, the assassination of individuals deemed to be "terrorists" in other countries has also been sanctioned. In October 2002 a Yemen revolutionary, Qaed Salim Sinan-al-Harethi, was targeted and killed by a CIA-inspired missile attack, one that also killed an American citizen. This kind of deliberately engineered assassination by a great power, although advocated in at least one classic treatise on society, Thomas More's *Utopia*, smacks of a truly Roman fear and arrogance.

In the microcosm of Aden, British imperial rule collapsed in violence when it came face to face with the extremism it had unwittingly nurtured. Today, the arrogant reach of United States policy — severed from, or perverting, the values of American national beginnings — seems destined to stir up powerful resistance all over the world, and especially in Islam, where religious fundamentalism and political opportunism work hand in glove. Unless a humane centre can be found, one that displaces both the arrogant assumptions of the advocates of the United States imperium and the fanaticism of the Islamic terrorists, the future for all of us will be bleak indeed. *Solitudinem faciunt, pacem appellant.*

British South Arabia, 1957-58

Compiled and drawn by United kingdom Directorate of Overseas Surveys, used by permission

South Arabian Chronology

9000 B.P.

Neolithic cultures in south Arabia. Hunting-gathering and animal husbandry by 5000 B.C.E.00000 and settled agriculture by 3000 B.C.E.

Twelfth century B.C.E.

The ancient "spice kingdoms," Ma'in, Saba (Sheba), Qataban, and Hadhramaut flourish and vie with one another for power. Elaborate irrigation and complex civilization. Queen of Sheba's legendary visit to King Solomon.

After 600 B.C.E.

Building of the great Ma'rib dam by the Sabeans.

30 B.C.E.

Rome controls Egypt; increase of trade in Red Sea.

24 B.C.E.

A Roman army reaches Ma'rib but withdraws.

100–200 C.E.

A coastal people, the Himyars, extend their influence northward and westward. Decline of the old kingdoms accelerates when sea journeys using the monsoon winds replace land routes. Rise of Christianity causes decline in demand for incense associated with old pagan rites.

Before 300 C.E.

King Samma Yuharis of the Sabean-Himyaric empire conquers the whole region and claims the title, "King of all the Arabs."

After 300

Jewish and Christian missionaries arrive and introduce monotheism, converting some Himyaric monarchs to Judaism.

After 400

Apex of Sabean-Himyaric power under Abukarid Asad.

Fourth–fifth centuries

Ma'rib dam breached, but repaired.

525 C.E.

Abyssinian Christians conquer south Arabia.

Seventh century

Persian control established. Final destruction of the Ma'rib dam. Islam comes to south Arabia. North Yemen comes under control of the Zaydi (Shi'i) sect, who establish the Imamate.

Twelfth–thirteenth centuries

Power in Yemen held by Egyptian Sunni caliphs.

1513–1516

Portuguese attacks on Aden.

1520

Yemen becomes part of the Ottoman Empire. Intermittent control of tribal areas by local forces and the Imamate.

1800

Puritanical Wahabi sect spreads through south Arabia and disrupts control of Ottomans. Egyptian forces of the Ottoman Empire drive out Wahabis.

Nineteenth century

American merchant ships, mostly from New England, become serious rivals of the British East India trading company in the area.

1839

British occupy Aden. Colony becomes part of the Bombay district.

1840

Ottoman Turks take over direct control in north Yemen.

1869

Suez Canal opens and increases importance of Aden.

1886

British begin to make treaty arrangements with tribal leaders in the south.

1918

End of Ottoman power in south Arabia. Imamate regains power.

1934

(North) Yemen sovereignty recognized by Britain.

1937

British set up formal protectorate structure. Aden ceases to be part of British India.

1945

Yemen joins Arab League.

1947

Yemen joins United Nations.

1954

Completion of Aden oil refinery.

1956

President Nasser nationalizes the Suez Canal. France and Britain attack Egypt. Canal is reopened in 1957.

1959

Federation of Arab Emirates sponsored by British.

1962

Revolution in northern Yemen kingdom. Imamate ends and Yemen Arab Republic is proclaimed.

1963

Aden Colony becomes part of new Federation. Founding of National Liberation Front of Occupied South Yemen (NLF), the revolutionary group that would ruthlessly press for control and independence via terrorist tactics. Resistance begins at once in the Radfan area of the Western Protectorate.

1964–1967

Terrorist campaign by NLF and others results in nearly four thousand deaths in the Colony and Protectorates.

1967

Egypt's defeat in the Sinai Peninsula war drives Arab nationalist parties throughout the Middle East to the left.

1967

British withdraw from Aden and Protectorates. NLF defeats and exterminates its rivals. British hand over government to NLF. People's Republic of South Yemen, which includes most of the old British territories, comes into existence.

1968

Leftist elements purged by new government of President Kahtan al Sha'bi.

1969

President al Sha'bi ousted by left. Salim Rubiyya Ali becomes president. Diplomatic ties with U.S. severed. Nationalization of property. Saudi-backed Royalists defeated in North Yemen.

1970

Proclamation of Peoples Democratic Republic of Yemen (PDRY). Yemeni Socialist Party becomes the only legal party.

1972

War between PDRY and the Yemen Republic. U.S. establishes full diplomatic relations with the Yemen Republic.

1974

Military regime of Colonel Ibrahim al-Hamdi assumes power in the Yemen Republic and attempts some rapprochement with the south.

1977

PDRY sends troops to fight with Ethiopia in Ethiopia-Somali war. Al-Hamdi assassinated in Yemen Republic, probably by pro-Saudi faction, upset by his policy of accommodation with the south.

1978

Al-Hamdi's successor in the Yemen Republic is killed by a bomb purported to come from President Salim Rubay Ali of South Yemen. Brief civil war in South Yemen. President Salim of PDRY assassinated by pro-Moscow faction. Arab states break with PDRY. Guerrilla war promoted in north by PDRY. U.S. seeks to establish diplomatic relations with PDRY.

1979

Second PDRY-Yemen Republic war. PDRY signs twenty-year treaty of peace and friendship with the Soviet Union. U.S. moves naval units into the Arabian Sea, and supplies some arms to the Yemen Republic via Saudi Arabia. Negotiations to merge the two Yemens.

1980s

Many Marxist Yemenis volunteer for the anti-Soviet Afghan war and become converts to Islamic fundamentalism.

1980

Ali Nasir Muhammad becomes President of PDRY.

1982

Guerrilla war in Yemen Republic ended. Unity talks between north and south.

1986

Bloody and destructive civil war in Aden ends Ali Nasir presidency.

1990

Unification of the two Yemens proclaimed and ratified. Ali Abdullah Saleh becomes president.

1991

The newly unified Republic of Yemen supports Iraq in the Gulf War.

1992

Bombing in Aden's Gold Mohur Hotel targets American troops heading for Somalia.

1994–1995

South Yemen again declares its independence. Third war between north and south won by the north, once again diminishing the role of extreme Marxist elements in the south.

1998

Sixteen western tourists kidnapped by terrorists. Four die during rescue attempt by Yemen government.

1990s–2002

Thousands of Yemenis trained in Afghanistan terrorist camps; 53 are incarcerated in Guantanamo Naval Station in Cuba after the conflict in Afghanistan. President Saleh co-operates with the United States in the pursuit of terrorist suspects.

2000

U.S.S. Cole is attacked in Aden harbour. Seventeen American service personnel killed and 39 injured.

2002

French tanker *Limburg* attacked near Aden. CIA assassinates a suspected Al Qaeda member in Yemen. Three American Baptist missionaries are murdered in Jibla, a town some 120 miles south of Yemen's capital.

2003

One American and one Canadian oil field worker are murdered in Yemen. U.S. invades Iraq. Thousands of Yemenis protest; some demonstrators are killed. Widespread fear and unrest across the country.

2004

Yemen offers peacekeeping troops to post-occupation Iraq. Offer is rejected by the new Iraqi government.

Bibliography

Note

This bibliography is intended for the general reader and lists chiefly those works that I turned to most in my own reading and research. In the past few decades, quite a few academic articles have been published on the British occupation and on subsequent Yemen politics and history. There are many books on Yemen geography and natural history, on its social structure, and on its art and architecture; there are also several new guidebooks. Numerous papers on the pre-history and archaeology of South Arabia have been published in recent years by French, German, British, American, Russian, and Canadian scholars. Much more extensive excavations — chiefly American and Canadian — are underway or in the planning stage.

Albright, Frank P. "The Excavation of the Temple of the Moon at Mârib (Yemen)." *Bulletin of the American Schools of Oriental Research* 128 (December 1952), 25–38.
> One of the scholarly papers that resulted from the Phillips expedition (see below).

Burckhardt, Jacob. *The Letters of Jacob Burckhardt*, edited Alexander Dru. London: Routledge and Kegan Paul, 1955.

Burrows, R.D. *The Yemen Arab Republic: The Politics of Development 1962–1986.* Boulder, Colorado: Westview Press, 1987.
> One of a useful series from this press on South Arabia after the British occupation (see also Wenner and Stookey).

Burton, Richard. *First Footsteps in East Africa; or, An Exploration of Harar.* London: Longman, Brown, Green and Longmans, 1836.
> The account of Richard Burton, the inimitable Victorian traveller, who didn't think much of Aden, where he recovered from a spear wound acquired in East Africa and began to plan his version of the *Arabian Nights*.

Crouch, Michael. *An Element of Luck: To South Arabia and Beyond.* London: The Radcliffe Press, 1993.
> Quirky, witty, occasionally bitter autobiographical account by a British official whose service covered several regions and most of the crisis period.

Doe, Brian. *Southern Arabia.* New York: McGraw-Hill, 1971.
> An archaeological guide to southern Arabia, nicely illustrated. A basic reference, although recent work has added much information.

Dresch, Paul. *A History of Modern Yemen*. Cambridge: Cambridge University Press, 2001.
An excellent summary, with special focus on the post-1950s political and economic development in greater Yemen.

Eilts, Hermann. "Along the Storied Incense Roads of Aden." *The National Geographic Magazine* 111, 2 (February 1957), 230–254.
Eilts, a former U.S. consul in Aden and an Arabic scholar, writes here for a popular audience.

Foster, Donald. *Landscape with Arabs: Travels in Aden and South Arabia*. Brighton: Clifton, 1969.

Goitein, S.B., editor. *The Land of Sheba: Tales of the Jews of Yemen*. New York: Schocken Books, 1947.

Groom, Nigel. *Sheba Revealed: A Posting to Bayhan in the Yemen*. London: Centre for Arab Studies, 2002.

Halliday, Fred. *Revolution and Foreign Policy: The Case of South Yemen, 1967–1987*.
Sympathetic and scholarly account of the first twenty years of the independent South Arabian state.

Hansen, Eric. *Motoring with Mohammed: Journeys to Yemen and the Red Sea*. New York: Vintage, 1992.
A lively personal narrative, especially good on the author's encounters with many ordinary-extraordinary Yemenis.

Harper, Stephen. *Last Sunset*. London: Collins, 1978.
Vivid journalistic account of the last days of Aden as a British colony.

Hébert, Jacques. *Yemen: Invitation to a Voyage in Arabia Felix*. Montreal: Heritage, 1989.
A Canadian politician's impressions.

Henighan, Tom. *A Basic Economic Report on the Eastern Aden Protectorate*. Washington: Department of Commerce, World Trade Information Service, 1958.

—- (with Michael Sterner). *Basic Data on the Economy of Aden Colony*. Washington: Department of Commerce, World Trade Information Service, 1958.

—. "Arabian Adventures in the Land of Sheba." In *Literary Trips: Following in the Footsteps of Fame*, edited by Victoria Brooks and Michael Carroll. Vancouver: Greatest Escapes, 2001.

Ingrams, Doreen. *A Time in Arabia*. London: Murray, 1970.
Personal recollections by a well-known British resident, wife of one of the historically important British advisers.

King, Gillian. *Imperial Outpost–Aden: Its Place in British Strategic Policy*. London: Oxford University Press, 1964.
A brief account closely analyzing and dismissing the claim by the British that they required Aden for strategic purposes.

Kostiner, Joseph. *The Struggle for South Arabia*. London: Croom Helm, 1984.
Detailed study of how the various Arab insurgency groups wrested Aden from
the British.

Little, Tom. *South Arabia: Arena of Conflict*. London: Pall Mall Press, 1968.
Good account of the general background and chief events of the British loss of
Aden.

Lunt, James. *The Barren Rocks of Aden*. London: Herbert Jenkins, 1966.
A down-to-earth soldier's memoir, with some blunt comments and unabashed
anecdotes.

Mackintosh-Smith, Tim. *Yemen: Travels in Dictionary Land*. London: John
Murray, 1997. Probably the best recent travel account, by a distinguished
travel writer who lives in Yemen.

de Maigret, Alessandro. *Arabia Felix: An Exploration of the Archaeological History of
Yemen*. London: Stacey International, 2002.
A basic survey of archaeological sites and findings, mainly in northern Yemen.

Maréchaux, Pascal. *Arabia Felix: Images of Yemen and Its People*. London: Thames
and Hudson, 1980.

Niebuhr, Reinhold. *The Irony of American History*. London: Nisbet, 1952.

Oxford Regional Economic Atlas: The Middle East and North Africa. London:
Oxford University Press, 1960.
Superseded, but usefully reveals the focus of the time and provides statistics
for that era.

Paget, Julian. *Last Post: Aden, 1964–67*. London: Faber and Faber, 1969.
A crisp, detailed account of military events and the British fight against terrorism in Aden and the Protectorate.

Phillips, Wendell. *Qataban and Sheba*. New York: Harcourt, Brace, 1955.
A fascinating account of the ill-fated Phillips expedition by its irrepressible
leader.

Prokosch, Frederic. *Nine Days to Mukalla*. New York: Viking, 1953.
Fiction. Not quite a camp classic, but at the very least, camp.

Reilly, Sir Bernard. *Aden and the Yemen*. London: Constable, 1959.
A former governor's view of the Colony at a critical moment in its history.
Revealingly, it embodies most of the typical British illusions about what
should and might happen in the development of Aden.

Scott, Hugh. *In the High Yemen*. London: John Murray, 1942.
An account of Yemen published at a time when the country was still relatively
unknown to western readers.

Sicherman, Harvey. *Aden and British Strategy*. Philadelphia: Foreign Policy
Research Institute, 1972.
A brief American monograph on the British loss of Aden, clear and helpful.

Stark, Freya. *The Southern Gates of Arabia*. London: John Murray, 1936.
A classic work on the region. Learned and evocative.

—-. *Letters.* Edited by Lucy Moorehead. London: Compton Russell, 1975.
More personally revealing than her "official" narrative accounts.

Stookey, Robert W. *South Yemen: A Marxist Republic in Arabia.* Boulder,
Colorado: Westview Press, 1982.
A sweeping and Marxist-tinged but well-detailed account of the transformation of South Arabia. Surveys its past history and its years as a modern independent state.

Trevaskis, Sir Kennedy. *Shades of Amber.* London: Hutchinson, 1968.
Narrative and analysis of the period of insurgency by one who was a key
British player in the events of the time.

Waterfield, Gordon. *Sultans of Aden.* London: John Murray, 1968.
Detailed, fascinating account of nineteenth-century British dealings with
Aden, centred on Commander Haines and his rise and fall.

Waugh, Evelyn. *When the Going Was Good.* London: Duckworth, 1946.
Contains a hilarious account of Waugh's 1932 visit to Aden.

Wenner, Manfred W. *The Yemen Arab Republic: Development and Change in an
Ancient Land.* Boulder, Colorado: Westview Press, 1991.

Guidebooks

Bradley, Chris. *Discovery Guide to Yemen.* London: Immel, 1995.
Hamalainen, Pertti. *Yemen.* Hawthorn, Australia: Lonely Planet, 1996.

Films/Videos

Arabian Nights (Fiore delle mille e una notte). Franco-Italian production, Pier Paolo
Pasolini, director and, with Dacia Maraini, co-writer. 1974.
A rambling, unfocused version of the *Arabian Nights.* Visually and dramatically less than captivating. Some value this as a post-modern deconstruction of
the classic tales and for its unabashed homoerotic emphasis.

Web Sites

Yemen Gateway. http://regional.searchbeat.com/yemen.htm.
A useful entry point to many sources of information on Yemen.

Yemen Explorer Tours. www.al-bab.com/yet/.
Provides very good general travel information and useful links, including one
with the British-Yemeni Society, which, among other activities, publishes very
useful material on Yemen.

25TH
ANNIVERSARY
EDITION

1979   25 YEARS   2004

PENUMBRA
PRESS